SCRAMBLE

MEMORIES OF THE RAF
IN THE SECOND WORLD WAR

SCRAMBLE

MEMORIES OF THE RAF
IN THE SECOND WORLD WAR

MARTIN W. BOWMAN

TEMPUS

First published 2006

Tempus Publishing Limited
The Mill, Brimscombe Port,
Stroud, Gloucestershire, GL5 2QG
www.tempus-publishing.com

British Library Cataloguing in Publication Data.
A catalogue record for this book is available from the British Library.

ISBN 0 7524 3762 7

Typesetting and origination by Tempus Publishing Limited
Printed in Great Britain

CONTENTS

ONE
THE THIN BLUE LINE

They told me when they cut the ready wheat,
The hares are suddenly homeless and afraid,
And aimlessly circle the stubble with scared feet,
Finding no place in sunlight or shade.

It's morning, and the Hampdens have returned.
The crews are home, have stretched and laughed and gone,
Whence the planes came and the Chance-light burned
The sun has ridden the sky and made the dawn.

He walks distraught, circling the landing-ground,
Waiting the last one home that won't come back,
And like those hares, he wanders round and round,
Lost and desolate on the close-cropped track.

'Missing', Herbert Corby

In September 1939 RAF Bomber Command had fewer than 400 operational bombers, including tiny obsolescent Handley Page Hampdens and Fairey Battles. It fell to the twin-engined Vickers-Armstrongs Wellingtons and Armstrong Whitworth Whitleys to carry the brunt of the offensive to Germany for the first two years of the war.

On Monday 28 August 1939, having been advised to report to the Recruiting Depot at Bradford, Yorkshire, I caught the train from my home in Hawes at the head of Wensleydale and set off on the first leg of a journey that would last six years and five months. I was nineteen. During the summer of 1939 I had been accepted as a wireless operator. AC2 Moore's feelings were a mixture of excitement and apprehension and I certainly had no

Blenheim gunner. (IWM)

Blenheim landing. (IWM)

idea that within twelve months I would be flying over Western Europe as a member of the crew of a Bristol Blenheim. I was at Padgate, a training establishment on the outskirts of Warrington, when on Sunday morning, 3 September, the radio in my hut was switched on and instead of the normal programmes, serious music was being played. It was then solemnly announced that the nation was to be addressed by the Prime Minister, Neville Chamberlain. His address began: 'This morning the British Ambassador to Berlin handed the German Government a final note saying that unless we hear from them by 11 o'clock that they were prepared, at once, to withdraw their troops from Poland, a state of war would exist between us. I have to tell you that no such undertaking had been received and that, consequently, this country is at war with Germany…'

The remainder of his speech was drowned by cheers and excited conversation for, it must be remembered, we were all youngsters who were actually excited at the prospect of being at war with our old enemy. Considering that the last war, the war to end all wars, had ended only 20 years earlier with an appalling loss of life, we should have had a clearer idea of the reality of war. I suppose those who were actually involved were reluctant to talk of their experiences and our attitude had been influenced by books recording the heroics.

AC2 (later Sergeant) Jim 'Dinty' Moore

Wimpys. (IWM)

Wellington crew ready for an op. (IWM)

Who'll fly a Wimpy, who'll fly a Wimpy,
Who'll fly a Wimpy over Germany?
I, said the Pilot, I, said the Pilot
I'll fly a Hercules mark Three.

There was obviously something wrong the way this war was being fought and as far as we were concerned, we were being used in a role for which we had never been trained... In 1939 the officially accepted theory was that fighters had such a small speed advantage over the 'modern' bomber that any attack must become a stern chase. It was also accepted that fighters attacking a section of three bombers flying in 'Vic' would attack in 'Vic' formation...

Sergeant Frank Petts, Wellington pilot, 9 Squadron, September 1939

Next morning we marched to our classroom where we were met by a rather scruffy looking Warrant Officer with a DFM. This fellow set the ball rolling by remarking that he understood we were troublemakers and we might as well know from the beginning where we stood with him. He added that gunners were known as the 'shit' of the air force and had a flying life expectancy of one hour. He added sourly: 'Most of you will be hosed out of your turrets before you're much older'.

They Hosed Them Out, *John Beede*

From my mother's sleep I fell into the State,
And I hunched in its belly till my wet fur froze.
Six miles from earth, loosed from its dream of life,
I woke to black flak and the nightmare fighters.
When I died they washed me out with a hose.

Randall Jarrell

Above: *Hampden passing a loco steaming through the English countryside. (BAe)*

Clockwise from far left, opposite:

'German night-fighters could be directed towards us, with their radar and that was the most likely position from where they would attack us.' (Via Mick Jennings)

One morning a Wellington returned with a dead rear gunner. He had taken an explosive cannon shell in his chest and the waist up had been literally blown to pieces.' (IWM)

Who'll fly a Wimpy over Germany?/I, said the Pilot, I, said the Pilot/I'll fly a Hercules mark Three.' (IWM)

[The Aeroplane

" Remember, the 500 pounder goes on No. 212a Kolnstrasse; avoid at all costs the Swiss Consulate at No. 216."

From a safety point of view, the front turret was preferable to the rear, which could be an exhausting trek to reach in our flight gear. The rear gunner was protected by two slabs of armour plate which could be joined together to protect the rear gunner's chest. However, in the front turret I could only rely on armour plate behind the pilots to stop bullets hitting me from the rear.' (Malcolm Freegard Collection)

'We soon found out that the "Wimpy" was a super aircraft for all crewmembers, certainly more comfortable than the Blenheim.' (Via Mike Bailey)

One morning a Wellington returned with a dead rear gunner. He had taken an explosive cannon shell in his chest and the waist up had been literally blown to pieces. When this became known the plane exercised a morbid fascination for crew, particularly the gunners, and most made their way over to view the grisly scene. When Kiwi and I got there, the erks were trying to remove the evidence of this fellow's passing with scrubbing brushes and hose. This, I think, is how the story about hosing gunners out of their turrets originated. It was the only way to remove the blood and guts splattered in the confined space.

They Hosed Them Out, *John Beede*

> The night when you went in low, the moon was grey,
> Like an old nun's face a–dying,
> And the wind was high and shrilling
> Calling for day,
> Moaning for day, because the night was evil
> And intent for killing.

And the sea beneath was seamed and wrinkled
Like a coffin's leaden lining,
And no star twinkled.
And the land beneath lay like a leprous flower,
Floating on the stagnant waters,
And it was death's hour.
Oh! the night when you went in low, no thing seemed living
But your own heart beats and your engine's throbbing.
Only the little fiend-thoughts alive,
Preening and prancing and mobbing
At the gates of your reason.
And the thing that you fought was over-thinking,
Beyond all Fear, who had had his season,
The night when you went in low...

'To Derek', Flight Lieutenant Anthony Richardson RAFVR

Plans were laid for the first RAF raid of the war to take place during the afternoon of 4 September 1939. While fifteen unescorted Blenheims took off for a strike on the *Admiral von Scheer* at Wilhelmshaven, eight Wellingtons of 9 Squadron and six Wellingtons of 149 Squadron, also without escort, flew on over the North Sea towards Brunsbüttel. Their targets were the battleships *Scharnhorst* and *Gneisenau*, which had earlier been spotted by a Blenheim reconnaissance aircraft from RAF Wyton. Two Wellingtons and five Blenheims failed to return. Worse was to follow.

It is now by no means certain that enemy fighters did in fact succeed in shooting down any of the Wellingtons... the failure of the enemy must be ascribed to good formation flying. The maintenance of tight, unshaken formations in the face of the most powerful ironsides. Had it not been for that good leadership, losses from enemy aircraft might have been heavy.

Air Commodore Norman Bottomley, Senior Air Staff Officer at Bomber Command HQ, commenting on the loss of six out of twelve Wellingtons of 99 Squadron, 14 December 1939. Following the heavy losses in daylight, Bomber Command Wellingtons, Hampdens and Whitleys switched to night attacks, just as the Luftwaffe had done. Bomber Command became largely a night-bombing force but losses continued to rise

15

A[n] RAF pilot who had been dropping leaflets over Germany returned to his headquarters four hours after he was due. His CO asked him why.

'Well, sir,' he answered, 'all was so quiet that I went down and shoved 'em under the doors.'

Peterborough in the Daily Telegraph

Our friend is the night
It hinders their sight
Though their guns still fire
We never shall tire
In our search for military might.
We have all felt fear
When the guns come near
But we'll not blame you.
Our aim will be true
From the aircraft we hold so dear.

For years we've been told
Of heroes of old
We now feel proud too
To join in your 'few'
Of brothers who dared to be bold.
It's comfort to know
You support us so
On missions each night
It helps us make light
Of worries we feel such don't show.

We feel a strong bond
And feel very fond
Of air crew past by
Who've all lov'd to fly
Through the clouds, blue skies and beyond.

To those who have fell
We still toll the bell
And those that now fall
We will miss them all
And meet in heaven not hell.

'Our Friend is the Night', Jasper Miles

On 29 September 1939 144 Squadron was ordered to make an armed reconnaissance of the Heligoland Bight in an effort to discover the movements of certain large ships believed to be breaking out into the North Sea. Two formations of six and five Hampdens set out. The first found a flotilla of destroyers in the Bight and attacked from a height only a few feet from sea level in the face of a curtain of light anti-aircraft shellfire. One Hampden was hit but got home safely; the remainder of this formation dropped their bombs without scoring a hit and then left the scene. The second group of Hampdens arrived some minutes later to meet both ship and fighter opposition:

'If you can't take a joke you shouldn't have joined!' (RAF)

the enemy had been well and truly alerted. Not one Hampden returned from this engagement and the Germans claimed to have shot them all down. Later from German sources it was established they had fallen to fighter attack. The latter point is significant, but at the time it was assumed the ship defences were responsible for the losses. Once again the chief lesson learned was that low-level attacks were hazardous in the extreme and the possibility of a hit with a bomb, dropped at speed on the approach, was chancy.

John Searby, who, at the outbreak of war, was flying Blenheims with 108 Squadron. Then, after a spell in Canada and on Ferry Command, he became a flight commander in 106 Squadron when Guy Gibson was in command. This was followed by command of 83 Squadron at Wyton

There was a lad in the year ahead of me at school who joined the RAF early in the war and told us how wonderful it was – flying seemed heroic to schoolboys like me and it was what we all wanted to do. The following year he was dead. But when I volunteered for aircrew in 1941, all I felt was excitement. As far as I was concerned, it was a big adventure. Training took six months and during that time the axe fell – they decided there were too many pilots and we were offered training as navigators or bomb aimers. I was nineteen and desperate to get into action, so I chose the bomb aimer course because it was the shortest. Looking back, I didn't think about what being a bomber really meant.

John Aldridge

TWO
THEIR FINEST HOUR

The English have lost the war, but they haven't yet noticed it; one must give them time, but they will soon come around to accepting it.
  Adolf Hitler, on the fall of France, 17 June 1940

Even though large tracts of Europe and many old and famous States have fallen or may fall into the grip of the Gestapo and all the odious apparatus of Nazi rule, we shall not flag or fail. We shall go on to the end, we shall fight in France, we shall fight on the seas and oceans, we shall fight with growing confidence and growing strength in the air, we shall defend our island, whatever the cost may be, we shall fight on the beaches, we shall fight on the landing grounds, we shall fight in the fields and in the streets, we shall fight in the hills; we shall never surrender...
  Winston Churchill, a speech to the House of Commons, 4 June 1940

> Touch me gently, wake me softly
> Let me start to sing,
> Free to use my strength and power
> Throbbing on the wing.
>
> Let me roar my throaty war-song
> As we start to rise,
> Challenging the unseen dangers
> Lurking in the skies.
>
> Keep me happy as we settle
> Steadily to fly
> Purring like a drowsy kitten
> Loudly in the sky.

Let me never fail my masters
In the searchlight's glare;
Let me keep them safely airborne
In my loyal care.

Let me help them do their duty
On their awesome flight,
Let me bring them through the hazards
Of the savage night.

Winging through the cloudy darkness
I will sing my song,
Reaching lip to dawn's pale sunlight
Though the night was long.

Let me sing of men returning
Safely homeward bound,
Then my thrusting heart shall sing
In glorious joyful sound.

'Song Of The Merlin', Audrey Grealy

SINGLE-ENGINE FIGHTER STATISTICS, BATTLE OF BRITAIN 1940

LUFTWAFFE

Date	Strength	Serviceable
1 July	893	725
1 August	860	N/A
1 September	680	438
1 October	700	275
1 December	680	N/A

RAF

Date	Strength	Serviceable
6 July	871	644
3 August	1,061	708
7 September	1,161	746
28 September	1,048	732

LUFTWAFFE BOMBER/FIGHTER STRENGTH 1940

Month	Strength
March	3,692
June	3,327
September	3,015
December	3,050

FIGHTER PRODUCTION 1940

Month	German	British
May		325
June	164	446
July	220	496
August	173	476
September	218	467
October	144	469
Total	1,870	4,283

What General Weygand called the Battle of France is over. I expect that the Battle of Britain is about to begin. Upon this battle depends our own British life and the long continuity of our institutions and our Empire. The whole fury and might of the enemy must very soon be turned on us. Hitler knows that he will have to break us in this island or lose the war. If we can stand up to him, all Europe may be free and the life of the world may move forward into broad, sunlit uplands. But if we fail, then the whole world, including the United States, including all that we have known and cared for, will sink into the abyss of a new dark age made more sinister and perhaps more protracted, by the lights of perverted science. Let us therefore brace ourselves to our duties and so bear ourselves that, if the British Empire and its Commonwealth last for a thousand years, men will still say: 'This was their finest hour'.

Winston Churchill, a speech delivered first to the House of Commons and then broadcast, 18 June 1940

Above left: *'We shall go on to the end, we shall fight in France, we shall fight on the seas and oceans, we shall fight with growing confidence and growing strength in the air, we shall defend our island, whatever the cost may be, we shall fight on the beaches, we shall fight on the landing grounds, we shall fight in the fields and in the streets, we shall fight in the hills; we shall never surrender...' (Ralph Hull)*

Above right: *'We watched in awe one day in August when nine Dornier 17s swept in to bomb the airfield at Biggin Hill. They were intercepted by two Hurricane squadrons and a great fight ensued. Two of the Dorniers were downed and the rest were driven off.' (Ralph Hull)*

'A Hurricane swoops and fires its guns,/A short sharp burst of chattering sound,/The sickening dive and the screaming power/As a Messerschmitt spirals to the ground,/The sky a melee of wings and guns/As the aircraft weave in the furious fray,/And the pilot's thought when the fight is done —/How many friends has he lost today?' (Ralph Hull)

Within viewing distance of the action in the skies over Biggin Hill we watched encounters between German and British planes.' (Ralph Hull)

I was visiting a big aircraft factory the other day and I was talking to a crowd of workers. I was not quite sure how they were reacting to my remarks, so I turned to a little old man who looked particularly 'surly' and said to him: 'How long do you think you can stick this war?' Without hesitation the chap said: 'One week longer than the bloody Germans.'
'Father of the RAF', Lord Trenchard, June 1940

Except for the darkness at night, Halton was just like any other boarding school in peacetime. Everyone went home for Christmas to show off their uniforms and new found skills. Then back to normal routine until Easter. Then home again. In August 1940 there was a sudden panic and all apprentices over the age of eighteen were issued with Ross Rifles (Canadian 303s with ring sights). The object of the weaponry was to defend the airfield when Off Duty. Instead of the hard beds in the Barracks Blocks we were housed in tents on the edge of the airfield. I noticed that just over the hedge the local farmer had cut his field of oats, so half a dozen sheaves were borrowed to make a comfortable bed. Armed apprentices were called Parashots and we were excused much of the drill and physical training and even the Church Parade when it was our turn to guard. While this was going on the rest of the RAF were fighting The Battle of Britain. For some unknown reason Halton, which was only 40 miles from London, was never attacked. Training carried on as usual. Once the Battle of Britain was over and Hitler had moved against Russia the airfield guard was stood down.
Bernard James 'Jim' Sprackling, Halton engine apprentice 1939–41

We waited for the bombers at around 3,000m [10,000ft] and then accompanied them in the direction of England. My Staffel was positioned to the left rear of the bombers. Oberleutnant Henrici, my Rottenführer, flew at the rear of our Staffel and we were thus at the cad of the entire formation. As we crossed the English coast, Henrici and I saw about four or five Hurricanes approaching us. We left the formation and attacked the British aircraft. During the battle, I found myself behind a Hurricane and opened fire. At that same moment, I was hit in the back, at the level of my shoulder harness. I must have lost consciousness immediately. When I came to, my hands were covered in oil, and I thought only of bailing out. I found the emergency release for the canopy, unfastened my parachute harness from the seat, and shot from the aircraft. Shortly thereafter, I again passed out. I don't know for how long; I came to my senses only long enough to pull the parachute handle. I can recall nothing of striking the ground, being discovered, or being transported to the hospital. I next regained consciousness in a hospital near Dover, following an operation…
Feldwebel Gerhard Kemen, JG 26, shot down on 14 August 1940 by Pilot Officer R.F. Smythe of 32 Squadron, who was immediately shot down by a Messerschmitt. Smythe force-landed at Hawkinge without injury but his Hurricane was scrapped. Kemen was transported to a Canadian POW camp in 1941, was repatriated with several other wounded pilots in 1943, and returned to active duty in time for the final battles for the Reich – this time as ground staff

At 1300 we took off from Caffiers. Our mission was to escort a bomber formation in an attack on Kenley, an airfield near London. Flying at about 6,000m [19,500ft] altitude, we reached the target without being attacked and were only then engaged by British fighters, which were primarily interested in the bombers and Bf 110s. I was still right beside the bombers when a Spitfire immediately beneath me attacked a circling Bf 110 from behind. It was simple for me to get behind the attacker by a short manoeuvre. We then had a Bf 110, a Spitfire, and a Bf 109 (myself), flying in a row. While the rear gunner fired at the Spitfire and the Spitfire in turn attempted to silence the rear gunner, I found it easy to put a long burst into the Spitfire, which immediately smoked and broke away in a split-S. I had approached

'On September 7 hundreds of bombers targeted the London docks, setting them ablaze, lighting the way for more destruction throughout the night. We lay listening to wave after wave of bombers passing overhead.' (Ralph Hull)

very near the 110, whose gunner was firing continuously, and turned away to keep from ramming it. At this moment I felt a blow beside my left foot in the cockpit, and my engine quickly came to a stop. Good Lord! – the Bf 110 gunner, seeing me pointed at him (like the Spitfire), had taken me to be another enemy, and had hit my aircraft.

Streaming a white cloud of fuel, I feathered my prop and glided unmolested in the direction of the French coast, hoping that I might reach the water of the Channel and eventually be fished out by a German rescue aircraft. The sun shone brightly; the seconds seemed like hours. Around me, the bitter combats continued to rage. Damaged German bombers, British and German fighters fell away, smoking, burning, or breaking up. Parachutes opened or failed to open – it was a gruesome but also an exciting spectacle. I had never before been able to observe such an air battle. My glide took me ever nearer the ground; I would never be able to reach the water of the Channel. I glanced at my watch; it was about 1400. I was aware that this was the end of my fighting career and tears streamed down my face. I finally crashed my loyal Bf 109 (into many pieces) near Rye, south of Folkestone, and woke up later in the hospital, suffering from back and head injuries.

About a week later, I was taken by subway to the interrogation camp in London. The caption to a photograph an English photojournalist took of me and my guards stated that I had quite a sense of humour for a German. I had cheerfully told the ticket taker that I did not need a ticket, as I had a season pass – a season that stretched into six years of imprisonment as a guest of the British King.

Oberleutnant Jupp Buerschgens, a ten-victory 'experte' of 7th Staffel, JG26, shot down flying a Geschwader escort to the London area in the Battle of Britain, 1 September 1940

NATIONALITIES OF PILOTS AND AIRCREW WHO FLEW OPERATIONALLY UNDER FIGHTER COMMAND CONTROL IN THE BATTLE OF BRITAIN, 10 JULY–31 OCTOBER 1940 (NOS KILLED IN PARENTHESIS)

RAF (British)	2,365 (397)
Fleet Air Arm	56 (9)
Australia	21 (14)
New Zealand	103 (14)
Canada	90 (20)
South Africa	21 (9)
Southern Rhodesia	2 (0)
Jamaica	1 (0)
Ireland	9 (0)
USA	7 (1)
Poland	141 (29)
Czechoslovakia	86 (8)
Belgium	29 (6)
Free French	13 (0)
Palestine	1 (0)
Total	2,945 (507)
Wounded	500

LOSSES, JULY–NOVEMBER 1940

RAF pilots	975 killed
	443 wounded
RAF aircraft	925 destroyed
	343 damaged
Luftwaffe aircraft	1,537 destroyed

TOP-SCORING PILOTS, RAF FIGHTER COMMAND, JULY-NOVEMBER 1940

Name	Nationality	Squadron	Aircraft	Total	Remarks
Lock, Pilot Officer E.S.	British	41	Spitfire	22 + 1 shared	WIA 7.11.40
Lacey, Sergeant J.H. 'Ginger'	British	501	Hurricane	18	
McKellar, Flight Lieutenant A.A.	British	605	Hurricane	18 + 1 shared	KIA 1.11.40
Frantisek, Sergeant J.	Czech	303	Hurricane	17	KIA 8.10.40
Carbury, Pilot Officer B.J.G.	New Zealand	603	Spitfire	15 + 1 shared	
Doe, Pilot Officer R.F.T.	British	234/238	Spitfire/Hurricane	15	
Urbanowicz, Squadron Leader W.	Polish	303	Hurricane	15	
Hughes, Flight Lieutenant P.C.	Australian	234	Spitfire	14 + 3 shared	KIA 7.9.40
Gray, Pilot Officer C.F.	New Zealand	54	Spitfire	14 + 2 shared	
Crossley, Squadron Leader N.M.	British	32	Hurricane	13 + 2 shared	

'Red 1 (Squadron Leader D.R.S. Bader) on sighting e/a opened full throttle and boost, and climbed and turned left to cut off enemy and arrived with Red 2 (Sub-Lieutenant R. J. Cork) only, on the beam slightly in front. Squadron Leader Bader gave a very short beam burst at about 100 yards at e/a, which were then flying section of three line astern

Above left and right: 'Don't just yell ring like 'ell!' (Author)

in a large rectangle. Then accompanied by Red 2 gave short bursts at the middle of e/a of back section. The e/a started smoking preparatory catching fire. Squadron Leader Bader did not notice result, which was later confirmed by Pilot Officer Turner as diving down in flames from the back of the bomber formation. At the time of Squadron Leader Bader's attack on the Me 110 a yellow-nosed Me 109 was noticed reflected in his mirror and he turned to avoid the e/a. Big bang was heard by him in the cockpit of his Hurricane. An explosive bullet came through the right-hand side of fuselage touching map case knocking the corner off the undercarriage selector quadrant and finished up against the petrol priming pump. Squadron Leader Bader executed a steep diving turn and found a lone Me 110 below him, which he attacked from straight astern and above him and saw e/a go into a steepish straight dive finishing up in flames in a field just north of railway line turning approximately east. (west of Wickford due north of Thameshaven).

Red 2 sighted e/a to east and above. He climbed to meet e/a and carried out a beam attack of the leading section of bombers, firing at a Do 215 on the tail end of the formation. Port engine burst into flames after two short bursts and crashed vertically. Red 2 was then attacked by e/a from rear and hit a starboard mainplane. He broke away downwards and backwards nearly colliding head on with an Me 110. Red 2 gave short burst before pulling away and saw front cabin of 110 break up and machine go into vertical dive. Two of the crew bailed out. Whilst Red 2 was following e/a down, e/a was stalling and diving. An Me 109 attacked Red 2 from the rear, one shot from the e/a going through the side of Red 2's hood, hitting bottom of reflector sight and bullet proof windscreen. Red 2 received a number of glass splinters in his eyes so broke away downwards with half roll and lost sight of e/a.

242 Squadron combat report, 7 September 1940. The Bf 110 destroyed by the famous legless fighter ace, Squadron Leader Douglas Bader, and Sub/Lieutenant Cork, crashed at Downham Hall, near Wickford. Both crew members, Leutnant Hans Dietrich Abert and Unteroffizier Hans Scharf, were killed. Bader was shot down and taken POW on 9 August 1941. He had scored twenty, with an additional four shared victories

Above: *Father of the RAF, Lord Trenchard. (USAF)*

Left: *Some of the WAAF have got a special permit/And show themselves uncommonly well-dressed…*
(Author)

Above: 'What do they know of the waiting hours…' (Author)

Right: 'While the rear gunner fired at the Spitfire and the Spitfire in turn attempted to silence the rear gunner, I found it easy to put a long burst into the Spitfire, and which immediately smoked and broke away in a split-S.' (Ralph Hull)

Clare and I were not the only ones who came back home from being evacuated. Children from South and East London returned in their thousands. Their parents, contrary to what the planners of the mass evacuation had supposed, had not been happy at parting from their children. When no air raids had taken place as predicted, the children came back. The East End of London, stretching along the Thames for 6 miles and inland for a depth of 3 miles was one of the worst slum areas in the western world. Between the wars various schemes had been undertaken to improve things, but the root cause – poverty – had not been addressed. So no headway was made. However, the 'phoney war' was now over and the Blitz was about to demolish many of the slums. Many of those who were made homeless never did come back to the East End.

In July 1940, the Battle of Britain began. As Hitler stepped up his campaign to annihilate the RAF Fighter Command as a necessary prelude to his planned invasion of Britain, we witnessed more and more aerial activity. Within viewing distance of the action in the skies over Biggin Hill we watched encounters between German and British planes. We followed many a dogfight between Messerschmitts and Spitfires, sometimes directly overhead, cheering whenever an enemy plane was chased off or shot down. Dad was stationed at Kenley airfield, not too far away. He worked as an aircraft mechanic. During the Battle of Britain the ground crews were frantically busy, refuelling and repairing planes between sorties. As the conflict intensified, ground crews and pilots alike were perpetually exhausted. When a Spitfire came to a stop one day at the airfield, no one climbed out. 'Something's wrong!' shouted Dad to the other ground staff. They ran over and Dad climbed up onto the wing. The pilot was fast asleep. Sometimes the pilots were so worn out; they fell asleep as they ate.

As the battle in the skies escalated we learned to identify the different aircraft. 'See the glazed nose of the Heinkel, there? That's one of theirs.' We became adept at recognising the different planes before we saw their identification marks. The Spitfires were our favourites; they moved with such speed and panache. We watched in awe one day in August when nine Dornier 17s swept in to bomb the airfield at Biggin Hill. They were intercepted by two Hurricane squadrons and a great fight ensued. Two of the Dormers were downed and the rest were driven off. Throughout that month the Luftwaffe launched a thousand planes a day across the channel. On 15 August, they mounted their maximum effort with eighteen hundred sorties. The skies seemed always to be filled with planes and the noise was tremendous. It was a different world from the peaceful skies of Sussex we had known.

In September Clare and I started back to school at Hawes Down Junior. If the air raid siren sounded while school was in session, we picked up our books and marched down the steps into the underground shelter to continue our work. The light was dim and when winter came it was bitterly cold with water running down the bare brick walls. A dank smell permeated everything. Air raids were frequent. One day we went to the shelter three times... If there was an air raid at night and the all clear sounded before midnight then school was open as usual next day. If the raid occurred after midnight, school was closed. Mother always sent us to school. Several times Clare and I walked the mile to school, only to find it closed. Once the school was closed for two days because of an unexploded bomb in The Mead, a nearby street. It was all very stressful and confusing. As the assaults on London escalated, we ceased going to school very much at all.

On 7 September hundreds of bombers targeted the London docks, setting them ablaze, lighting the way for more destruction throughout the night. We lay listening to wave after wave of bombers passing overhead. The racket of the anti-aircraft barrage was tremendous, but we found it comforting. The noise gave us the impression that something, at least, was being done to deter the bombers. Because of the din we couldn't hear the noise of the bombs whistling down, but neither could we sleep. The morning after a raid, Clare and

'The skies seemed always to be filled with planes and the noise was tremendous. It was a different world from the peaceful skies of Sussex we had known.' (Ralph Hull)

'The race to the 'planes when the scramble starts…' (Author)

'As the conflict intensified, ground crews and pilots alike were perpetually exhausted. When a Spitfire came to a stop one day at the airfield, no one climbed out. "Something's wrong!" shouted Dad to the other ground staff. They ran over and Dad climbed up onto the wing. The pilot was fast asleep. Sometimes the pilots were so worn out; they fell asleep as they ate.' (IWM)

I would rush outside to pick up pieces of shrapnel. We vied with each other to see who had the more interesting shapes.

West Wickham didn't escape damage. A bomb fell in the High Street, completely demolishing one shop and damaging several others. Houses on residential streets were bombed. There was great excitement when a Messerschmitt was shot down and the pilot captured. On the afternoon of 15 September, when every plane that the RAF could muster was flown to fight off the Luftwaffe attacks on London, the Battle of Britain was on its way to being won. Two days later, Hitler postponed the invasion of Britain. It never did take place...

Annette June Coppard, East London schoolgirl

I have told the Führer that the RAF will be destroyed in time for Operation Sea Lion to be launched on 15 September, when our German soldiers will land on British soil.

Hermann Goering, 6 August 1940

At approximately 1440 hrs AA fire was sighted to the south and at the same time a formation of about thirty Do 215s was seen. I climbed up astern of the enemy aircraft to engage the fighter escort, which could be seen above the bombers at about 30,000ft. Three Me 109s dived on our formation and I turned to starboard. A loose dogfight ensued with more Me 109s coming down. I could not get near to any enemy aircraft so I climbed up and engaged a formation of Me 110s without result. I then sighted ten Me 109s just above me and attacked one of them. I got on his tail and fired several bursts of about two seconds. The enemy aircraft

'The Spitfires were our favourites; they moved with such speed and panache.' (IWM)

Hurricane pilots of 310 (Czechoslovakian) Squadron at Duxford during the BoB. (IWM)

was taking violent evasive action and made for cloud level. I managed to get in another burst of about five seconds before it flicked over inverted and entered cloud in a shallow dive, apparently out of control. I then flew south and attacked two further formations of about thirty Do 215s from astern and head on. The enemy aircraft did not appear to like the head-on attack as they jumped about a bit as I passed through. I observed no result from these attacks. Fire from the rear of the enemy aircraft was opened at 1,000 yards. Me 110s opened fire at similar range but appeared to have no idea of deflection shooting.

Squadron Leader Brian J. 'Sandy' Lane DFC, CO, 19 Squadron Spitfires, Duxford, 15 September 1940. Flight Sergeant George 'Grumpy' Unwin, Lane's Red 3, reported sighting 'thousands of 109s'. At close range 'Grumpy' fired a three-second burst at a 109 which half-rolled and dived steeply into the clouds. Although the Spitfire pilot pursued his prey, he lost the 109 at 6,000ft when his windscreen froze up. Climbing back up to 25,000ft, a rotte of 109s appeared above him, flying south. Unwin gave chase and caught both over Lydd. The first consequently burst into flames and went down vertically, and the second crashed into the sea. It is likely that these two 109s were from I/JG77: Oberleutnant Kunze, of the Geschwaderstabschwarm, was killed when his aircraft crashed at Lympne, as was Unteroffizier Meixner, who crashed into the sea off Dungeness. This brought Unwin's total of Me 109s destroyed this day to three.

The thin blue line. (IWM)

'As we crossed the English coast, Henrici and I saw about four or five Hurricanes approaching us. We left the formation and attacked the British aircraft. During the battle, I found myself behind a Hurricane and opened fire. At that same moment, I was hit in the back, at the level of my shoulder harness.' (BAe)

The gratitude of every home in our island, in our Empire and indeed throughout the world, except in the abodes of the guilty, goes out to the British airmen, who, undaunted by odds, unweary in their constant challenge and mortal danger, are turning the tide of the world war by their prowess and their devotion. Never in the field of human conflict was so much owed by so many to so few.

Winston Churchill, 20 August 1940

Squadron Leader Douglas Robert Stewart Bader (centre) with P/O William Lidstone McKnight DFC from Edmonton, Canada, to his right and F/L George Eric Ball to his left at RAF Duxford in September 1940, when he commanded 242 Squadron. Willie McKnight received a bar to his DFC on 8 October 1940 and was promoted Flying Officer in November. He was KIA on 12 January 1941 during one of the first low-level 'Rhubarb' sorties over France. He was twenty-twoand had scored seventeen victories. George Ball, from Tankerton, Kent, who had joined the RAF in April 1937, scored six outright victories in 1940 and received a DFC on 1 October 1940 before being posted to the Middle East. He spent the rest of the war in a German POW camp after flying into a sandstorm in April 1941. In October 1945 he was promoted Squadron Leader and took command of a Meteor jet squadron. He was killed in a flying accident on 1 February 1946. He was twenty-seven. (IWM)

The Blitz began in earnest that autumn. For fifty-six nights in a row London was bombarded from dusk to dawn. In our dining room we had a Morrison shelter. It was like a steel table, and we slept underneath on a mattress. After a while we didn't even bother to go to our beds upstairs because we'd always have to come down to the shelter when the siren sounded. Night after night Clare and I lay either side of Jennifer as she cried in fright at the noise. It was okay to cry when you were only three. Clare and I were frightened, too, but we took comfort in the fact that we were all together. Another 'safe' sleeping area was made in the big cupboard under the stairs, which Granddad reinforced, with solid wooden beams. An additional sleeping place was under the heavy oak dining room table. Along with the Morrison these places would have provided protection from falling debris had our house been damaged. London got a temporary respite when the Luftwaffe began attacks on other areas of England and then one night in May 1941, the worst raid of all on London killed and injured more than 3,000 people. Over 2,000 fires were started. From 10 miles away we could see London burning. As we looked at the red glow in the sky over the capital we wondered if there would be anything left of London at all. It took almost two weeks to put out the last of the fires.

Annette June Coppard, East London schoolgirl

Ops Room. (Author)

Above left: *'I have just seen that the RAF flyers have a life-saving jacket they call a "Mae West", because it bulges in all the right places. Well, I consider it a swell honour to have such great guys wrapped up in you, know what I mean?' (Author)*

Above right: *Called to action. (Author)*

Punch]   [Pont

" But you must remember that I outnumbered them by one to three."

'I then sighted ten Me 109s just above me and attacked one of them. I got on his tail and fired several bursts of about two seconds. The enemy aircraft was taking violent evasive action and made for cloud level. I managed to get in another burst of about five seconds before it flicked over inverted and entered cloud in a shallow dive, apparently out of control.' Squadron Leader Brian J. 'Sandy' Lane DFC, CO, 19 Squadron Spitfires, Duxford, 15 September 1940 (left, on wing). Flight Sergeant George 'Grumpy' Unwin (beside Lane), Lane's Red 3. (IWM)

'At close range "Grumpy" fired a three-second burst at a 109 which half-rolled and dived steeply into the clouds'. (IWM)

Flight Sergeant George 'Grumpy' Unwin. (IWM)

THREE

ERKS

I didn't want to join the Air Force,
I didn't want my bollocks shot away.
I'd rather hang around
Piccadilly Underground,
Living off the earnings of a high-born lady.

The lower ranks of airmen in ascending order were: Aircraftsman Second Class (AC2); AC1 (First class); Leading Aircraftsman (LAC); Corporal (Junior NCO [non-commissioned officer]). Prior to the automatic promotion in 1940 of all aircraftsmen to sergeant, air gunners might have held any of the lower ranks. I was an AC1 at the time. The pilot of a Blenheim (if an officer, as were the majority), the navigator (normally a senior NCO) and the air gunner lived in three entirely separate social worlds. The only time the SNCOs and the officers met was once a month on invitation to the opposite mess. The airmen only met the officers at the annual airman's Xmas dinner when the officers traditionally served the meal. The SNCOs and officers enjoyed a high standard of living in their respective messes. The wireless operator/air gunners lived in barrack rooms together with the lowest AC1s who might have cleaned the toilets. The only extra remuneration the ACs got was 6d a day for the Flying Bullet badge and 1s a day flying pay! Even when waiting for the take-off during standby we would he in separate crew rooms in the hangar. In my training days at West Raynham I would be flying by day but not excused a night guard duty, having to carry a rifle all night guarding dispersed Blenheims during that bitter winter. So there we were – three virtual strangers probably in most cases very soon to die together!
  Jack Bartley, RAF 626100

In June 1940 I went to the RAF Recruiting Office in Kingsway, London. I was eighteen years old and had been a photographer in Civvy Street. The pilot officer asked me what

I wanted to do. I said I wanted to fly aeroplanes. I was wearing glasses because I was shortsighted and had been since the age of six; he told me that because of my poor eyesight I would have to consider my responsibility to other crewmembers.

He said: 'We can't let you fly.'

I said: 'What responsibility to other crewmembers? I want to fly Spitfires or Hurricanes!'

He said that if a bullet shot my glasses off, they would lose a valuable aircraft. So I said that if I had perfect vision and a bullet came that close, they would lose a valuable aircraft anyway.

So that got me nowhere. The pilot officer said: 'Well, what would you like to do in the RAF on the ground?'

I said: 'I would like to be an aerial photographer.'

To which he asked: 'What do you understand by a circle of confusion?'

I said: 'As far as I understood it was three pilot officers discussing a technical point!'

They made me an electrician.

Dennis 'Joe' Davis, 515 Squadron

It was early morning and we were gearing ourselves up to face yet another breakfast of bubble and squeak, some hellish concoction involving leftover cabbage. We could smell it wafting up the stairs from the kitchens.

'Hey, lads, do you see what I see?' It was Len, who was standing at the window, insisting that he get some fresh air before facing breakfast. As we crowded to the window he pointed to a bundle, which was bobbing gently on the incoming tide. It was a body, dressed in RAF blue, floating face down in spite of the Mae West. We weren't the only ones who had seen it as a boat was slowly approaching the beach and a sailor stood with

" Why do I want to join the R.A.F.? Oh, because I owe so much to so many."

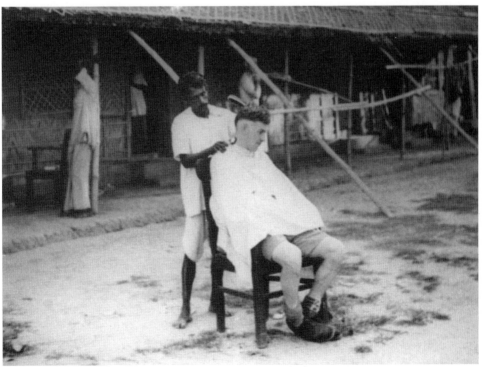

'Aircut, You! (G/C Jones Collection)

"Come along there—put some bloody life into it!"

a boat hook held ready to haul the corpse from the water They were approaching the beach cautiously, as it was strewn with anti-personnel mines. We watched the scene in silence, although someone did remark that, after four weeks in Brighton, the only airman we had seen was a dead one. The scene we watched didn't enhance our appetite for the bubble and squeak, which was flopped on our plates in the mess.

When we formed up in pairs for the usual ritual of parade, the flight sergeant, no less, told six of us to fall out and stand to one side. He came over to us.
'You're all 6ft and over, ain't yous?' he growled.

On receiving the assurance that at the last count we all had topped the 6ft, he marched us round to a side street and announced in a stage whisper which reverberated up and down the street: 'Right, you're all on a funeral party tomorrow, you're the pall bearers. I'm goin' to teach you all about it, understand?'

Leading Aircraftsman Johnnie Clark, later a Mosquito pilot, awarded the DFC. From One Man's War.

An aircraftsman walking across the Parade Ground passed an officer whom he failed to salute.
'Don't you know that when you meet an officer you are supposed to salute him?' asked the officer.
'No, sir', replied the aircraftsman, nearly in tears.
'What? How long have you been in the RAF?'
'The whole blinking day, sir.'

This is my story, this is my song;
I've been in this Air Force just too flaming long.

The high spot of the RAF activities during the Second World War occurred at RAF Castle Bromwich in 1943. When airmen heard a plane landing late at night, they assumed it was one of many Spitfires tested there. Switching on an Aldis lamp, however, Aircraftsman R. Morgan observed that it was a German bomber. As it taxied down the runway he expressed the intention of having a crack at it with the Lewis gun and went off to get permission.

While the German plane revved its engines, Aircraftsman Morgan tried to ring through to control. 'We had to crank like fury on the field telephone for permission to fire', he said. By the time he got through the 'plane had taken off and was en route for Germany'.

From The Least Successful Attempt to Shoot Down Enemy Planes: The Book of Heroic Failures *by Stephen Pile*

A party of ATC cadets was suddenly let loose in the hangar. The novelty of visitors soon wore off as we tried to get on with our work. I was working in the dinghy stowage area and came up for air to see a cadet sitting on the pilot's seat. A rigger had already told the cadet not to mess about with switches or controls. As I rested for a minute or two I heard the cadet ask 'What's this?', as he held up the chromium plated item with flexible tube. He received the perfectly serious reply: 'That's to plug the oxygen into.' Whereupon he took several deep sniffs and said: 'I didn't know oxygen smelt like that.'

Leading Aircraftsman W.G. 'Bill' Cooper, electrician

'Don't trust the erks to clean your Perspex surfaces: check them yourself during daylight, before an operation.' Pilot Officer Prune, a cartoon character in the RAF's surprisingly light-of-touch training magazine, *Tee Emm*, was once shown hanging by his straps during violent evasive action occasioned by a spot on his cockpit canopy which he had mistaken for a Hun in the Sun.

Graham Harrison, gunner

Pilot Officer Prune says—
" Take Tee Emm regularly !
Prevents that Thinking
feeling ! "

"Just once over with the grease-gun, Sir, and she's all ready to drive away after tea."

AC2 plonk was the lowest form of animal life in the Service, they used to say.
Pat Holmes

Pembrey in Wales for my Air Gunners Course on Bristol Blenheims was my first experience of the cramped conditions in a bomber aircraft. How on earth would I even get into that gun turret and more pointedly, how on earth would I get out in an emergency? The stark reality of being a member of aircrew wasn't so appealing now.

Finally, I passed the course and became a Sergeant WOP/AG. My uniform took on a more glamorous appearance now but somehow it didn't seem the same as when Ted first appeared after being made up. I seemed to remember my brother being the only one of his kind. When I travelled by train or bus, it seemed that every other person was a WOP/AG. AC 'plonks' appeared few and far between.

My next port of call was 15 OTU at Harwell. I saw this as the 'Grand Hotel' where pilots, navigators, bomb aimers, wireless operators and air gunners were thrown together for a 'getting to know you' programme. This was where crews were assembled, entirely from your own choosing and not influenced by the establishment. From my point of view, the priority was going to be the skipper (captain) and so I went looking for an Errol Flynn or James Stewart, but on my first survey all I saw was a Danny La Rue or Franklin Pangbourne (comedy film star of the '40s). Because I was so anxious to be selective and discriminating, most crews had been made up and I was left with little choice. Of the two remaining pilots, one was a 'dead ringer' for Stan Laurel (of Laurel & Hardy fame) and the other a cut-down version of Clark Gable. I chose the latter who turned out to be a Sergeant W.A. Molyneux ('Molly') and so I was fixed up and duly introduced to Dave Davison (navigator), Pilot Officer Joe Campbell (bomb aimer) and Jimmy Velzian (rear gunner). They seemed a great bunch of guys and turned out to be very good at their jobs.

After a week's ground training and classroom work, we started our cross-country flying exercises in daylight on Wellington ICs. We soon found out that the 'Wimpy' was a super aircraft for all crewmembers, certainly more comfortable than the Blenheim. There was so much more room to move about and with easy access to the 'Elsan', which subsequently became a very important piece of equipment as far as Dave, our navigator, was concerned. He was very often airsick and spent a lot of time sitting on the 'Elsan'. Our only comfort was that we were assured of a warm seat!... Our daytime exercise went off quite well with a few bumpy landings but on one occasion we did six overshoots to land in very bad visibility. Night flying was next and this went quite well. Our last night exercise over a celebration was the order of the day and the WAAFs in the Mess put on a farewell supper for us consisting of eggs, bacon and fried bread; a rarity, but of course no booze.

Twelve crews were passing out at OTU to join operational squadrons and one of these crews had a problem that came to light before a take-off. The rear-gunner of the crew, named 'Curly' (because he was as 'bald as a badger') was worried about his pilot, stating that he had been seen to be drinking double whiskies in the sergeants' mess earlier after learning of his wife's association with another man. When we saw him we too were aware that he had been drinking excessively and the concern of his gunner was shared by us all. Nobody would confront him with the dangers that lay ahead and I failed to understand why it was not reported. Such was the misplaced loyalty of the day, but it was considered disloyal to inform on another crewmember and to do so would mean being shunned by the others. We were ushered out to the lorries to take us to the aircraft on the dispersal areas and saw ironically that the sergeant was due to take off first. I would

THE SEVEN DEADLY SINS OF NAVIGATORS.
No. 7.

Over-familiarity with the Route.

'I WISH I could remember whether the red goes inside or outside.'

Hickey

gamble that fifty-nine pairs of fingers were crossed as he lined up his aircraft on the runway. The run up of the engines, the green light from control, the release of brakes, then the familiar sound of full power saw him move forward. The roar of the engines got fainter as he sped forward. The navigational lights were clearly visible for what seemed an eternity but slowly they lifted into the dark sky, banking as they went. Fingers uncrossed, everybody was happy for 'Curly' and at least his skipper had three hours or so to recover before facing a landing.

We had a straightforward exercise and on returning were called by the control tower and advised not to land but to join the circuit at Harwell. This became obvious when we saw a Wellington burning fiercely yards short of the runway. No chance of there being survivors – we hadn't kept our fingers crossed long enough for 'Curly' and other members of the sergeant's crew.

Sergeant Harry Wheeler

FOUR
SPROGS

A 'Sprog' was what they at first called me
Meaning that on an Op I had never flown.

Sergeant George 'Ole' Olson RCAF

We were to scatter-bomb Mannheim in a 'town blitz'. Aircraft were dispatched to the target singly. At this time we could not afford crew losses from collision or bombs falling on each other's aircraft, so this was the only practical way. It was cold and lonely in the front turret but my Brownings never froze up on any of the operations I would fly. However, if one carried an apple, we were warned not to eat it; it would break your teeth!

From a safety point of view, the front turret was preferable to the rear, which could be an exhausting trek to reach in our flight gear. The rear gunner was protected by two slabs of armour plate which could be joined together to protect the rear gunner's chest. However, in the front turret I could only rely on armour plate behind the pilots to stop bullets hitting me from the rear. The primary function of an air gunner at this time was to be a heavy flak spotter for the captain. He told us to keep our eyes peeled and report enemy aircraft and flak gun flashes immediately.

We dropped our bombs on Mannheim from about 12,000ft and although it was my first experience of flak, we came through all right. We landed back at Newmarket after being in the air for six hours and ten minutes.

Sergeant Alfred Jenner, Wellington WOP/AG, 99 Squadron at Newmarket Heath, 16–17 December 1940. His first operational trip, Operation Abigail, was in retaliation for the German bombing of Coventry and Southampton. In all, some 134 bombers, including sixty-one Wellingtons, were dispatched. It was the first 'area' bombing raid on a German industrial target

Sprog crews, for their few operations, were assigned to any spare aircraft available and we were to do six ops before being allocated our 'own' aircraft, namely a Halifax BIII with Hercules WI engines and lettered 'F'. So many aircraft with the letter 'F' had been lost that it was felt that an unlucky name for this one would not make any difference anyway and it was 'Jumbo' Smith, the pilot who handed over to us on completion of his tour, who named it *Friday 13th*. This name, plus skull and crossbones, an upside-down horseshoe and the words 'As Ye Sow, So Shall Ye Reap' were painted on the nose of the fuselage, with a 'bomb' to represent each completed operation.

I think most of us harbour some superstition, although not always ready to admit it, but I had miraculously survived Course No.13 at Mesa, Arizona, home of 4 British Flying Training School, better known as Falcon Field. *Friday 13th* had safely completed a total of forty-two operations by the time we took it over and so our delight in having our own aircraft must have outweighed any doubts we may have felt.

Again the magic No.13 had proved lucky for me as we flew twenty-six operations on *Friday 13th* to complete our tour. We handed over to 'Doc' Gordon, an RCAF pilot and his crew, who were to complete their tour on it and by the end of the war in Europe a few other crews took it to the quite remarkable total of 128 full operations. It was then exhibited in Oxford Street, London, before being scrapped.

'So much for superstition?'

Derek Waterman DFC, pilot, 158 Squadron. An Australian lad attempted to purchase the aircraft, but he was too late. He did, however, manage to obtain the fuselage panels bearing the name and bombing tally and these remained under his house until 1972, when they were flown back to the UK for display in the RAF Museum, Hendon, where they still remain in a glass case, together with our crew photo

The actual flying conversion to Whitley IIIs was quite a step. A real heavyweight was my first impression, but in practice it was not too difficult to fly once the delayed action control response was accepted. Take-off produced a distinct swerve to port and was something to get accustomed to. A large part of the training was devoted to navigation involving quite long cross-country flights. Cross-country exercises at night at first were quite taxing – it was a different world entirely, finding one's way around in the dark, but at the age of twenty one soon learns and the whole experience becomes second nature. Much of our flying was carried out from a satellite airfield – Stanton Harcourt. There was such a thing as the Harcourt medal, a fictitious gong awarded to the biggest clot of the week and I have to report that my rear gunner managed to deliver a burst from his four Brownings over the village. Fortunately, nobody was hurt, but apparently the village horse-drawn cart was last seen disappearing at great speed, milk flowing freely from holes in the churn.

Basil S. Craske, RAFVR, Whitley pilot, OTU Abingdon, Oxon, 1940

The Christmas 1941 school holidays were not yet over when Mrs Isaac knocked on our door that winter morning. It was my first experience of grief. I was almost eight years old and knew something serious had happened but it was something between my mother and our neighbour so I took myself into another room with my Christmas presents.

The war had been raging for over two years. We had won the Battle of Britain and were now beginning to hit back at the Nazi war machine. My overwhelming interest was in aeroplanes. I couldn't get enough books on Allied and enemy aircraft and reckoned that I could recognise anything flying, some merely by their sound. Across the road in a smart semi lived the Isaac family, whose eldest boy, Peter, had left Victoria School and joined the Royal Air Force Volunteer Reserve. I envied him as I saw him coming home on leave, his forage cap to one side, his gas mask case slung on his back. Then one day he came home with the three stripes of a sergeant on his sleeve and the half wings of a wireless operator/air gunner on his breast.

" **Dummy pops off and attacks the docks at Brest—O.K.?** "

[Punch

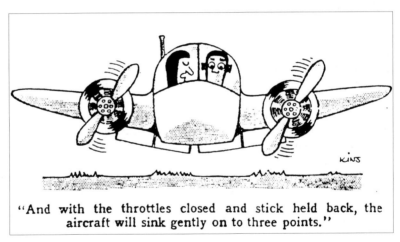

"**And with the throttles closed and stick held back, the aircraft will sink gently on to three points.**"

On the morning of the penultimate day of 1941, a Post Office telegram boy pedalled up Kelmscott Crescent in Watford and walked up to the front door opposite our house. Mrs Isaac was shocked when she saw the lad. Feeling sick in the pit of her stomach, she took the flimsy envelope, tore it open to read the cryptic message and shook her head at the boy. There would be no reply. He turned and hurried away, knowing from recent experience what bad news he had brought.

When a tearful Mrs Isaac left our house, my mother told me that Peter had been on a raid and had not got back. He was reported as missing, so everyone lived in hope that he might be alive somewhere. I was told he had been flying in a Handley Page Hampden twin-engined bomber. I got out my books to read about this aircraft. Medium bomber, crew of four, two rearward-facing gun turrets, one on top and one below the fuselage. I wondered which one Peter had been in.

Some time later, Mrs Isaac told my mother that Peter's body had been found in Holland. There was some story about it being found in a dyke and, as he had been a very

'. . . As I was saying just before we took off . . .'

Brockbank, *Punch*

strong swimmer, there was speculation that he might have been wounded and bailed out. It was sad that my hero had died so soon but the war didn't allow much sentimentality and, in any case, an eight-year-old has plenty to occupy himself with.

Fredric Boyce, who fifty years later began investigating Peter Isaac's final sortie. Nineteen-year-old Sergeant Peter F. Isaac was the WOP/AG on P1165, a 408 'Goose' Squadron RCAF Hampden from Balderton, which was shot down over Holland on 28/29 December 1941 by a German night-fighter. That night sixty-one Hampdens of the eighty-one detailed reached their target, the Chemische Werke, a synthetic rubber plant at Hüls, west of Duisburg. The target was clearly identified in the moonlight and the factory was thoroughly bombed, fired and photographed. Four Hampdens were lost, including P1165, piloted by Pilot Officer Stuart Bruce K. Brackenbury who, like Peter Isaac, was on his eighth trip. Oberleutnant Helmut Woltersdorf of III/NJG1, operating from Deelen, claimed the Hampden, which crashed near Winterswijk (Gelderland). The Hampden had reached the target and bombed it. The flare they could have used to illuminate the target had not been needed so they were still carrying it when a Bf 110 night-fighter attacked them while at 15,000ft. The flare was hit and ignited. Brackenbury bailed out and was free for four hours before being found by some Dutchmen who led him down back streets to the police station, which was manned by Germans. He was taken to meet Major Wolfgang Falck, kommandeur NJG1 at Twente, who claimed to have shot him down. Falck apologised, treated him well and told him that he was his thirteenth victim. Hampden AD804 of 144 Squadron crash-landed only 30km from the site of the crash of P1165. The emergency landing was made to save the life of Sergeant Cheesman, who was seriously wounded by enemy action over Germany. Unfortunately, he died in hospital shortly after his arrival. Woltersdorf was killed at Twente on 2 June 1942 when he crashed into parked aircraft after being attacked by an enemy aircraft while landing with his wounded wireless operator, Heino Pape. Peter Isaac is buried in Winterswijk General Cemetery. His headstone has the engraving, 'In sweetest memory of our dear son Peter. "Till we meet again", Mum and Dad'

We were finally getting closer to the real thing. We would be flying the Wellington twin-engined bomber for our operational training operations. Earlier that year, changes were made to the makeup of the bomber crews. First, the observer had been responsible for both navigation and bomb aiming. This had caused difficulties of concentration over the target – just too much to do and from different crew positions. Anyway the old observer job was divided into navigator and bomb aimer or air bomber. At the same time the requirement for a second pilot was dropped. Some other member of the crew would be given enough training to fly the aircraft in an emergency. The size of the crew remained at five.

So all the observers had to decide what new job they wanted. I chose air bomber. I tend to be lazy and I thought this would be the easier of the two jobs. In a way this was only partially right but more on this later. I think the Navigator jobs filled up faster. Consequently some who wanted to be navs became bomb aimers. Crewing up was an interesting experience. The RAF method was very hit-or-miss but it seemed to work. You were all put into a room and told to crew up.

The food at Pershore was miserable, monotonous servings of stringy mutton and Brussels sprouts. There was one day I still remember. The whole unit was formed into a hollow square on the parade-square. The object of attention was a rear-gunner who had fallen asleep on operations. He was stripped of his wings and rank badges in a slow impressive ceremony – which was the whole idea I guess. The parade had been dismissed and the young sergeant continued to stand there, alone in the middle of the square, head bowed, eyes averted, absently picking at the strands of thread where his NCO stripes had been. No one approached to offer him comfort. Very sad.

Sergeant Jack Woodrow (promoted to Flight Sergeant on 28 August 1942), 23 OTU, Pershore, Worcs, 16 July–30 September 1942

9 September. We have done two trips now, so I can just about call myself operational again. It's good to be back on the job again. On Tuesday night we went to Hannover. It was a very easy trip and we had no trouble at all. On Wednesday night all the squadron aircrew departed for Cambridge and we all had a good time. Thursday night we went to Karlsruhe and had very little opposition. Of course, now we have got most of France we don't spend a lot of time over enemy territory when on southern targets. As we did not get to bed until 6 o'clock yesterday morning we spent last night on camp. We went to the camp cinema and saw Bette Davis and Paul Lukas in *Watch on the Rhine*, which was very good.

Letter home, 1944, from Derek Smith, Mosquito navigator, 692 Squadron, 8 Group

FIVE

THE STATELY 'DROMES OF ENGLAND

The Stately 'dromes of England are just a trifle bleak,
From Biggin Hill to Thurso, from Finningley to Speke.

The Stately 'Dromes of England, Flight Lieutenant John Mark, 1943

Over 1,000 airfields were used by the RAF in the UK alone during the Second World War, so it is not without some justification that Britain was referred to as 'a vast aircraft carrier anchored off the north-west coast of Europe'. By the end of the war some 360,000 acres of land had been occupied by airfields and a staggering 160 million square yards of concrete and tarmac had been laid down.

Chris Hobson, senior librarian, RAF Staff College, Bracknell, writing in 1995

As I settled into squadron life at Topcliffe I found that the best way to keep your sanity was to separate your pleasures from your work. I didn't want to become one of those casualties found walking around the airfield talking to himself. There was the odd one who cracked up mentally and you really couldn't blame him. For relaxation we would frequent the pubs in the village of Topcliffe and Thirsk, Ripon and Harrogate. Weldon MacMurray, a school friend of mine from Moncton, was stationed at RAF Dishforth. This was about 2 miles from Topcliffe, as the crow flies. We'd get together once in a while and exchange news from home. The nearest meeting place was the Black Swan pub, or as we called it, the Mucky Duck, in the village of Topcliffe. On one such meeting he informed me that Johnny Humphrey bought it. Another time that Graham Roger's number came up. This was followed by news that Brian Filliter was missing in action. One day at lunchtime I answered the phone in the sergeant's mess and it was Weldon inquiring about me. He'd heard that I'd bought it the previous night. A few weeks later, friends of Weldon phoned me from Dishforth to say that he had failed to return from a trip. I found out later that he was a prisoner of war. Boy! Was I getting demoralised! Would I be next?

Joyce Shaw of Harrogate and I became acquainted while I was operating out of Topcliffe. I would visit her home and parents for a meal and an overnight stay once in a while. Joyce was later to become a member of the WAAF (Women's Auxiliary Air Force). The inconvenience of having their toilet facilities in a separate brick building at the rear of their row house, located in the centre of this large city, never ceased to amaze me. This arrangement, after an evening at the pubs, left a lot to be desired. And, speaking of pubs, after the familiar 'time gentlemen please' was heard, one usually headed for the fish and chip shop. They were easily found as one could usually smell their tantalising aroma for blocks and we were always hungry. They were most often served in a paper cone made out of newspapers and liberally sprinkled with salt and vinegar. I still felt that good taste was due in part to the newsprint on the paper. It gave them that extra element of refinement!

While visiting a pub in the country one night, I offered to give a girl a lift home on the crossbar of my bicycle. We took a shortcut along a narrow path and ended up in a deep ditch. I became a casualty, with a cracked bone in my ankle and had to wear a walking cast, which was only knee-high, for a couple of weeks. I managed quite well with the cast, especially on a bicycle. I collected quite a few signatures on my cast and quite a few free drinks from those who may have thought I'd pranged in an aircraft. I never bothered to straighten them out. Using the supporting wire from inside my officer's hat eased the horrible itching inside the cast. We usually took this metal reinforcement band out of the hat and sloshed some beer inside to give it the droopy professional look.

After I was posted to 76 Squadron at Middleton St George, off duty we would frequent the pubs and dance halls in Darlington and York. A few memories of these places come to mind, like the night we stole the stuffed ram's head from the Fleece, a pub in Darlington, with which to decorate our sergeant's mess. And how we 'sheepishly' had to return it the following day after a complaint was made to our commanding officer. Also remembering the old walls around the city of York where the Minster Cathedral was visible from almost anywhere. Betty's Bar with its long mirror behind the bar on which dozens and dozens of signatures had been scrawled. It would be interesting to know how many of these signatures belonged to men no longer in this world. The Shambles, where the upper storeys of the houses bulged out over the road. These and other fond memories are deeply cherished.

A night on the town would sure look good, even though we sometimes missed the last bus back to our base. But then there was always the air raid shelter or a convenient haystack as sleeping accommodation. We were young and the first early morning transportation back to the squadron would suffice.

Pilot Officer J. Ralph Wood DFC CD RCAF, 102 Squadron, Topcliffe and 76 Squadron, Middleton St George

At Chipping Warden we were introduced to another lifestyle. On the wartime RAF stations, the Nissen hut reigned supreme. We shared a ten bed Nissen hut, ate in a Nissen hutted mess, took ground school in a Nissen hut and went into a Nissen hut at flights. At first sight, a Nissen looked anything but cosy. However, as wartime servicemen we could settle down anywhere and a Nissen wasn't too bad, although we certainly missed the comforts of the permanent buildings at Leconfield. It was summertime though, so we escaped the condensation on the walls and the water on the floor that affected winter dwellers. Outside, the aircraft were old Vickers Wellingtons, the Wimpy. I know they said: 'If you can't take a joke, you shouldn't have joined.' But this was beyond a joke. It was my nightmare scenario and it was here.

Ron Read, pilot, 12 OTU Chipping Warden, June 1942

'On 2 June I was promoted to Flight Sergeant. Great rejoicing and a couple of beers in the mess bar that night.' (Hammersley)

When the two local pubs, the Red Lion in East Kirkby and the Red Lion at Revesby had beer available and we were not flying, the lads would go along and spend an enjoyable evening drinking and singing. Sometimes the Red Lion at Revesby would run out of glasses and we drank out of jam jars. I am sure we enjoyed our beer more when we were drinking from jam jars than when we had normal beer glasses. These evenings relaxed the tension and for a while we could forget the war and our flying missions.

Sergeant Roland A. Hammersley DFM, 57 Squadron Lancaster WOP/AG

Being on a squadron was to be quite remote from the rest of the world. It became your whole way of life, an enclave that occupied every member of it. Although we shared the airfield with a squadron of Lancasters, they might have been in the next county as far as we were concerned. We met them for a pint or two in the mess from time to time and swapped experiences, but other than that their existence there might have been purely coincidental. I suppose they felt the same about us. There was a life going on outside the main gates of the airfield but we, the members of the squadron, knew little of it. Our days revolved around the Battle Order, which was circulated each morning. Our days off were spent mainly in catching up with sleep or roistering in the mess or in our favourite pubs. One night an Aussie said: 'Let's have a party tonight.'

'Why tonight?'

'Why not? It's Monday,' replied the 'blue orchid', 'there's only one Monday in the week.' We had a party.

The squadron, by mutual acclaim, had decided that Cambridge was the place to go and the Baron of Beef was the Eight Group's pub. The Bath Hotel in that academic town had become the drinking joint of the American Air Force. We each had our own watering hole and stuck to it. Occasionally the Pathfinder members met the Eighth Air Corps in the Blue Boar. Sometimes there was an air of conviviality; sometimes it descended to fisticuffs. When the latter happened I did a smart 180 degree turn and left. I had signed on to fight the Germans, not the Americans. One enemy was enough for me.

Sergeant Johnnie Clark, Mosquito navigator. From One Man's War

One hundred mighty bombers, returning from a raid,
Their target, the most distant that they had ever made;
Diverted to an airfield in the region of Exmoor
Without a place to sleep them save on a hangar floor
And there, with palliasses as apology for beds,
Seven hundred flyers lay down their weary heads.
They had sucked in oxygen for many, many an hour
Which now released as tummy-gas was noxious in odour
And as they'd also eaten hasty, gaseous food
The atmosphere was soon described as anything but good;
Thus tired, exhausted flyers combined to make a rattle,
Said to confuse some passer-by in thinking it was battle.
'Twas just a wartime incident which never made the press
And I would never know about but for a friend's distress
One who was a flyer in the story that I tell,
Who, having damage to his back, experienced some Hell;
Of course the doctor drugged him to modify the pain,
This drug has a side-effect: hallucinates the brain.
Now, in this semi-conscious state, his mind went to-and-fro
To where he was reliving that night so long ago
When sleeping in discomfort with a hangar for abode;
This time, they had one toilet: his invalid commode!
And seven hundred backsides all needing to discharge
Within this bedside 'office' which was not very large.
He viewed the scene with humour for, as one might expect,
Each and every backside desired that it be next;
Seven hundred bottoms all fighting to let free
Provided him a vision, it seems he watched with glee.
I understand it ended in an utter mad confusion,
He 'woke in helpless laughter and gone was his illusion
But he can still remember the details of that sight
With seven hundred flyers in toilet seeking fight
He told me the story, knowing I'm the rhyming kind
And, like most other poets, have a naughty mind
So I've employed my talent to put his tale to verse,
Confirming all suspicion that I can be perverse.
Now I have dreamed of wondrous sights whilst sleeping like a log,
But ne'er a horde of backsides in combat for one bog.

'Ode of Commode', Jasper Miles

The buildings in which we lived and worked were all very temporary, many of them Nissen huts with tin roofs. Hot in summer and freezing cold in winter, despite their stoves for which there was never enough coal; and not very comfortable at the best of times. And yet, I really cannot remember anybody moaning about them. One thing I do remember was the quiet that prevailed in the Mess Ante Room when the 9 o'clock news came on the radio. Very often, we would hear reports of what Bomber Command had done the night before and sometimes we would hear the words of Winston Churchill castigating the Germans and urging and encouraging us all on towards the brighter horizons of the future. People actually applauded his words as they came through the loudspeaker.

Squadron Leader (later Group Captain) A.F. Wallace., 'B' Flight CO, 620 Squadron, June 1943–September 1944

On 16 May 1944 we all flew in from Sculthorpe to Oulton, a few miles outside Aylsham. Oulton was one of the many temporary stations in Bomber Command – no permanent buildings, no fancy messes or barrack blocks. Most of the officers were billeted in Blickling Hall, previously owned by Lord Lothian who had been Ambassador in Washington 1939-40 and renowned for its historical association with Henry VIII and Anne Boleyn. I ran Music Club meetings in one of the ground floor panelled rooms of the Hall. A number of airmen and airwomen attended to hear me talk to a programme of 78s played on a wind-up gramophone with a sharpener at the ready for the fibre needles. In the grounds of the Hall, many temporary Nissen huts had been constructed, including one acting as the Officers' Mess.

On the very evening of our arrival, some of us drove into Aylsham to survey the local pubs, and after a few beers I wandered across to the blacked-out town hall to look in on a dance being held there. Without hesitation I made a beeline towards a lovely girl dressed in a pink V-neck dress standing across the floor from me. I had known girls at each place before, but there was always the acknowledgement that there would be nothing permanent about a relationship. I somehow knew this might be different. Her name was Patricia; she was nineteen, just a month away from her twentieth birthday. She had a divine figure. She had a pretty face. She was an excellent dancer, easily able to follow my somewhat jerky steps (I whispered two lines in Spanish of Besame Mucho as we danced). She loved classical music and played the piano, with a distinguished pass in Grade 8 behind her. She lived in the town square, just a few yards from the town hall. Pat told me some time later that her mother had almost dissuaded her from coming over to the dance that evening (you're out too often my girl). When her father heard us talking below her rooms in Aylsham Square, I understand he said to her mother, 'It's all right, they're talking about Beethoven'.

Flight Lieutenant (later Air Vice Marshal CBE DFC AFC) Jack Furner, 214 Squadron. Jack and Pat married on 7 February 1948

SIX
GARDENING FOR BEGINNERS

Laying sea mines carried the code name 'Gardening'.

There was lots of squadron training to be done before we were ready for operations. New crews were often put on mine-laying trips to help them get experience. This was especially true for Wellington crews because of its shorter range. A favourite target was the Friesian Islands off the coast of Holland and Germany. There was a lot of enemy coastal shipping and the mines caused a lot of damage. The normal load was two 1,500lb mines, which were also called 'Vegetables'. Our first trip was cancelled twice because of weather and we finally went on the third night. However our station did not have the capability of loading the mines, so we were sent to Middleton-St George to be loaded up. Right after planting our two 1,500lb mines, the captain asked me to take over the navigator's job. I ended up navigating the aircraft home. A satisfactory and a very memorable trip, but which ended in a blaze of ignominy. Each day as part of our flying rations we were given two chocolate bars. So when we finally went on our trip, I had six chocolate bars. Anyway, through normal excitement and nervousness from it being our first trip, and a problem with our navigator, I ate all six bars on the way home. Then I started to feel pretty sick. Right after landing, I jumped out of the aircraft and immediately upchucked on the dispersal pad. Very embarrassing.

Flight Sergeant Jack Woodrow RCAF, observer, 425 'Les Alouettes' Squadron

Our crew was detailed for a minelaying operation off Norway on 28 April 1943. We left Snaith at about 2030 hours in Halifax MH-Z with two sea mines on board and flew at about 1,500ft over the North Sea towards the Skagerrak, a body of water which separates Norway from Denmark at that point. Arriving about midnight, the aircraft entered the Skagerrak, nearer to the Danish coastline. White lights formed an entrance channel from the North Sea to the Danish coastline. We altered course to starboard and crossed the northern tip of the Danish mainland, which juts out into the confluence of the Skagerrak and Kattegat. The aircraft entered the Kattegat, slightly north of the Danish seaport of Frederikshavn, on the north-eastern coastline of the country. Climbing to an altitude of 2,000ft, the height-set for the release of the two 1,500lb sea mines, the aircraft again altered course, to starboard, to fly down the Kattegat, towards the release point, slightly north of the capital Copenhagen on the island of Zealand. This area was always dangerous on gardening operations because German night-fighters patrolled the 'Schakay' box area of the Kammhuber Line defence system looking to intercept the 'courier' aircraft, generally Mosquito aircraft, flying between Britain and Sweden. The weather at this time was 10/10ths cloud. The Halifax approached the release point for the mines at Area 'Verbena', calculated by Peter Finnett, the navigator, from indications on the DR compass and other navigational aids.

Suddenly, two streams of light flak appeared either side of the mid-upper turret. The aircraft was on the release run-in so Claude Wilson, the pilot, had to keep the aircraft straight and level at a steady altitude of about 1,000ft, at a predetermined speed and course, to where the two sea mines would float down by parachute and enter the waters of the Kattegat. I turned the mid-upper turret to starboard and then to port, lowering the aim of the four gun barrels as far as possible and fired blindly through the low dense cloud in an attempt to thwart the aim and source of the gunfire. I was unable to observe the source of the light anti-aircraft gunfire, but as we were over the Kattegat, I presumed that it was from one or more flak-ships. After a few bursts of machinegun fire in either direction, the light anti-aircraft fire ceased, but I was unaware if my return fire had anything to do with it. By luck, or some other reason, we did not encounter the night-fighter aircraft, based at Aalborg, although we passed over the base. We returned several hours later without further incident but Snaith was fog-bound and goose-necked paraffin burning flares were used (this was before FIDO – Fog Intensive Dispersal Organisation) to facilitate landing at the airfield.

Flight Sergeant Louis Patrick Wooldridge DFC, Halifax mid-upper gunner, 51 and 578 Squadrons, Snaith and Burn, Yorks, 4 Group Bomber Command, 1943–44

On the night of 25/26 February 1944 we set off for our eleventh operational flight, which was to be another mine-laying operation, dropping our mines by parachute into the Kiel Canal. It was the normal late evening take off, with all aircraft queuing up to take their turn, with the ground staff and any aircrew not taking part in that raid cheering and waving us off. On take-off, we 'Tail End Charlies', the rear gunners, used to have our turrets facing the beam and not astern. The idea being, should the aircraft *not* manage to take off for any reason and crash, we might be able to quickly open our turret doors and bail out backwards – if the full bomb and petrol load didn't beat us to it and give us a helping hand!

Having taken off and set course on the first leg of the journey, we would, whilst there was still some daylight left, see other aircraft from our squadron and other nearby 'dromes, all making their way in the same direction. When the night closed in, we were then entirely on our own and it was then we gunners had to be most thorough in our searching the skies, particularly underneath our rear. German night-fighters could be directed towards us with their radar, and that was the most likely position from where they would attack us. We had the usual searchlights and anti-aircraft gunfire at times, and a couple of scares of night-fighters trailing us, and took evasive action, but no actual attacks. We reached our target and dropped our mines. On our way home over the North Sea we passed too close to a German flak-ship (or perhaps it was one of ours) and received some damage from anti-aircraft gunfire but it was examined by our flight engineer and mid-upper gunner and not considered very serious.

Our pilot called up to report our return. We heard on the intercom that we were 'Turn 4', which meant three other aircraft had beaten us back to base and were to land before us. We also heard the weather had closed in; the cloud down almost to ground level. This was always a very dangerous time because Tuddenham, Mildenhall and Lakenheath airfields were so close together and so many aircraft were circling, waiting to land. We started down through the lower levels of cloud and suddenly found ourselves in a clear space, sandwiched between layers of thick cloud above and below. Many other aircraft were staying in this clear space as long as possible before they too had to go down lower. It was then our turn to start descending through this lower level of cloud, to try to find our runway approach. We had just started doing so, when we hit something. I thought we had crashed into another aircraft. We were far too low to be able to pull out and there was no chance for me to swing my turret round, reach into the fuselage, grab my chute and bail out. I was going to die and I wondered how it was going to happen.

I must have been knocked out for I 'came to' and found everything had stopped moving. Our aircraft was on the ground in pieces. I was still in my turret and it seemed to be in one piece. When I tried to move my right arm to pull on the wire just behind my right shoulder to open my turret doors I found I couldn't do so. My right arm was broken and I hadn't felt any pain. I called out but there was no reply. I was trapped in my turret and I could smell and hear burning. I had to get out quickly. The rear part of the plane had snapped off and my turret had broken away for I was looking down between my four machine guns, straight to the ground. Our tail turrets had recently had a large hole cut into the perspex, which a British scientist had found was the best way to deal with our icing up problem. We called it our 'clear vision panel', which of course it was. Thankfully our thickly padded, electrically heated flying gear stopped us from being frozen to death; it probably saved my life, by protecting me in the crash.

In my panic to get out, I tried falling forward to see if I could squeeze out through this hole in the turret. I could not do so because of my heavy flying gear, I was stuck there. Believing the fire was close, I called out again, much louder! This time my call was heard by our mid-upper gunner, Robbie Roberts. He had 'come to' on the ground outside the aircraft, he didn't know how he got there. He heard me calling out, came over and opened my turret doors and I popped out like a cork from a bottle, in spite of the broken arm. Robbie had been hurt with a blow to the chest. I had to help hold him up, whilst we staggered around looking for the other five of the crew. The front of the aircraft had been smashed beyond recognition. We saw only two of them. There was nothing we could do for either. There were several fires burning and plenty of live ammunition around. We had crashed into an orchard, near to a farmhouse from where some people came running to help us. They took us into their home and made us comfortable. Shortly afterwards a RAF ambulance and emergency crew arrived and we were in safe hands. Robbie and I were sent off to different hospitals. After a couple of spells of hospital treatment, I was helping to train other aircrew, when there was a need to replace an air gunner, on a new crew then passing through. I joined that crew and once again it was an Australian pilot, Clem Arkins, and the rest were British. We completed our training, on Lancaster bombers.

Sergeant Frank Tasker, rear gunner of Stirling III EF198, 90 Squadron, Tuddenham, Gardening sortie in the Baltic, 25/26 February 1944. In all, 131 aircraft were dispatched on minelaying operations in Kiel Bay, while the main force of 594 aircraft attacked Augsburg. Three Halifaxes and EF198 were lost. Losses were: Australian pilot, Flight Sergeant Allan Edward Dearlove Davey RAAF, from Fullarton, South Australia; Canadian navigator, WO2 George Stringer RCAF, from Ottawa, French-Canadian bomb aimer; WO2 John Jean Adrian Paul Rodrigue RCAF, from Montreal, Quebec; flight engineer Sergeant Edward Parrish, wireless operator; Flight Sergeant Dave Eaton, mid-upper gunner. Sergeant E.B. 'Robbie' Roberts was awarded the BEM (Military Division) for helping Tasker out by opening his turret doors

'The loss rate was especially high among Stirling crews. It was slow and with a load could reach about 16,000ft whilst with evasive action over occupied territory it was at around 12,000 over a Ruhr city. At that height it was also vulnerable from above if a Lancaster at 20,000ft released bombs. Bombing times were set to prevent this but not every crew kept to its time slot. The first of the four-engined bombers, its wingspan was 9ft less than the original design. This was by special request to Short Bros, the makers, to allow it to pass through the doors of the standard RAF hangar! This fundamental change caused problems. It had to have a huge undercarriage, which meant that the cockpit window was 20ft from the ground. The Stirling was slower and had a much lower ceiling than the Lancaster or the Halifax, both of which came later and replaced the Stirling towards the end of 1943.' Frank Diamond, Stirling navigator. (Shorts)

'All six aircraft dropped their mines and headed straight out to sea for home… An inferno erupted on what was a peaceful night. Right in the middle of it all a Liberator had been hit. It caught fire, keeled over and went in with one big explosion.' (IWM)

Laying sea mines was ordered for the night 31 May/1 June. My own crew with three other crews was briefed for the task. We carried out air-to-air and air-to-sea firing from the gun turrets. At the same time all equipment was checked ready for the minelaying operation we would be carrying out that night. The firing and testing took forty-five minutes after taking off at 1440 hrs. Laying sea mines carried the code name 'gardening'. At briefing there was invariably an officer from the Royal Navy who specialised in minelaying. We were to carry six Mk VI mines which had to be dropped following a timed flight from a point given at briefing and based on the reading given by the *H2S* radar equipment. The whole flight would be at low level so as to avoid the enemy radar detection equipment. The target was in the Kattegat, well down this waterway between Denmark and Sweden and not far from Kiel Bay. The altitude for the bombing run right up to dropping the mines was to be at 4,000ft.

We were away at 2135 hrs in fine weather. There was no opposition and all the mines were dropped into place as briefed, after which all the crews returned safely to base. We landed at 0520 hrs, a total of seven hours forty-five minutes flying time. Later the *Wall Newspaper* reported: 'A long low level flight in near daylight conditions by four aircraft of 57 Squadron is worthy of note – these four took off into the fading sun of double summer time at 2340 hrs to fly at 500ft around the northern tip of Denmark and down the Kattegat to drop their sea mines off Allborg, returning by the same route. The late sunset and early dawn were linked by the midnight sun and for the whole flight it was possible to see clear to the horizon. From 2 miles out we could see clearly Gothenburg's neutral waterfront ablaze with street and house lights, this was a rare sight after the experience of a blacked-out Europe.

Whilst the four crews that had flown the minelaying operation were sleeping during the daytime on 1 June, the squadron was preparing for a night attack on the Saumur

Warsaw Concerto. In vain, in August 1944 RAF, Polish and SAAF Liberator crews in Italy flew the almost suicidal 1,750-mile round trip over enemy territory to drop supplies to the beleaguered Polish Home Army fighting for survival. (SAAF)

railway junction. Fifteen crews took part in the attack and all returned safely to base. On 2 June I was promoted to flight sergeant. Great rejoicing and a couple of beers in the mess bar that night.

Sergeant Ronald A. Hammersley DFM, Lancaster air gunner, 57 Squadron, East Kirkby, gardening operation to the Kattegat, 31 May/1 June 1944

It was a well-planned operation with a diversionary raid laid on at high altitude to soak up any fighter opposition. We six flew at low level over the Golden Pagoda, which was our initial point for the mining operation. At timed intervals each Liberator dropped a string of mines almost on the Pagoda's doorstep, all the way along the river and almost up to Elephant Point at the river's mouth. We flew position No.5 in the dropping order. All six aircraft dropped their mines and headed straight out to sea for home... An inferno erupted on what was a peaceful night. Right in the middle of it all a Liberator had been hit. It caught fire, keeled over and went in with one big explosion. It was only on our return, about 100 miles from base, when we broke radio silence and the call signs came through, that I realised I had witnessed the destruction of my crew, with whom I had flown twenty-three operations.

John Hardeman, Liberator air gunner, 159 Squadron, describing a minelaying operation in the river approaches to Rangoon on the night of 29 December 1944

In the Far East the fall of Malaya and Singapore in February 1942 had been a major blow, and the RAF was hard-pressed to offer any effective resistance to the well-equipped and tenacious Japanese invasion forces. After reorganising and re-equipping with more modern aircraft, including Spitfires, Hurricanes, Beaufighters, Thunderbolts and Liberators, the RAF fought back, often in the most grueling conditions imaginable, from its bases in India, Ceylon and Burma and in conjunction with the SAAF turned the tide of war against the Japanese. By 1945 the RAF element of the Air Command SE Asia consisted of ten groups with seventy-five squadrons.

SEVEN

HEAVIES

We are the heavy bombers, we try to do our bit,
We fly through concentrations of flak with sky all lit,
And when we drop our cargoes, we do not give a damn,
The eggs may miss the goods yard, but they muck up poor old Hamm.

'The Heavy Bombers', Airmen's Song Book

It would be the bankruptcy of statesmanship to admit that [the bomber] is a legitimate form of warfare to destroy its rival's capital from the air.
　The Times, *1933*

The first of the RAF's four-engined bombers, the Short Stirling, entered service on 10/11 February 1941. In March 1941 it was joined by the Handley Page Halifax. Exactly a year later these were joined by the Avro Lancaster. By mid-1943 the four-engined 'heavies', using rudimentary forms of electronic warfare equipment, were beginning to achieve a greater measure of success than hitherto possible. The last two years of the war saw Bomber Command grow into an immensely powerful force of some 2,000 bombers. From 1942 onwards, bombing 'round-the-clock' with the USAAF, Bomber Command took the war to the heart of Germany, causing vast destruction to the German war effort. By May 1945 Bomber Command consisted of seven groups controlling seventy-eight operational squadrons of Lancasters, Halifaxes and Mosquitos.

We shall bomb Germany by day as well as night in ever-increasing measure, casting upon them month by month a heavier discharge of bombs and making the German people taste and gulp each month a sharper dose of the miseries they have showered upon mankind.
　Winston S. Churchill, 22 June 1941

'The cloud had cleared and off to starboard a Lanc was caught by at least fourteen searchlight beams. We could see him twist and turn and finally break out. But still the whole thing had a quality of unreality about it…' (Penny Riches)

The Germans entered this war under the rather childish delusion that they were going to bomb everybody else and nobody was going to bomb them. At Rotterdam, London, Warsaw and half a hundred other places, they put that rather naïve theory into operation. They sowed the wind and now they are going to reap the whirlwind.

We cannot send a thousand bombers a time over Germany every time as yet, but the time will come when we can do so. Let the Nazis take good note of the western horizon, where they will see a cloud as yet no bigger than a man's hand, but behind that cloud lies the whole massive power of the United States of America. When this storm bursts over Germany they will look back to the days of Lubeck and Rostock and Cologne as a man caught in the blasts of a hurricane will look back to the gentle zephyrs of last summer. It may take a year, it may take two, but to the Nazis the writing is on the wall. Let them look out for themselves. The cure is in their own hands.

There are a lot of people who say that bombing can never win a war. Well, my answer to that it has never been tried yet and we shall see.

Germany, clinging more and more desperately to her widespread conquests, whilst even seeking foolishly for more, will make a most interesting initial experiment. Japan will provide the confirmation.

Air Marshal Sir Arthur Harris

As soon as we beat England, we shall make an end of you Englishmen once and for all. Able-bodied men and women will be exported as slaves to the Continent. The old and weak will be exterminated. All men remaining in Britain as slaves will be sterilised; a million or two of the young women of the Nordic type will be segregated in a number of stud farms where, with the assistance of picked German sires, during a period of ten or twelve years, they will produce annually a series of Nordic infants to be brought up in every way as Germans. These infants will form the future population of Britain… Thus, in a generation or two, the British will disappear.

Walter Darre, German Minister of Agriculture, April 1942

There have been many arguments for and against the indiscriminate bombing of civilian targets. For what it is worth, I have reason to believe that the High Command on either side knew that this course of events was inevitable even before the war started. Germany commenced this 'terror' tactic as long ago as 1936 with the wholesale bombing of civilians in the Spanish Civil War against Guernica. Both Germany and England avoided this during the early war years. In my year of bombing in 1941, we were briefed in the 'ops' room to hit military targets only. In 1942, no army was ready to invade the Continent, the Navy dare not put to sea in view of the *Scharnhorst, Gneisenau, Graf Spee, Tirpitz* etc. – being more concerned with the protection of convoys with food and ammunition from America. Therefore in logical terms – the only weapon we had to retaliate was our own Bomber Command. In other words the Germans were hitting us badly with their raids so England had no recourse except to fight with the only weapon we had – the bomber.

Flight Lieutenant John Price, Wellington wireless operator, 150 Squadron, 1941–42

Like most aircrew I don't remember feeling any particular emotion toward the Germans. I had ended up as a bomb aimer and it was my duty to drop the bombs as accurately as possible. It was all sort of remote and impersonal. Our operations encouraged the Brits who had suffered so much and seen so much damage to their country. I had relatives living in the East End of London which suffered greatly. I was staying with them once in 1944 when a V1 buzz bomb came over and hit not very far away. On leave in London, I was always being thanked by the Londoners for giving it back to the Germans. I've never lost a moment's sleep from feeling guilty about bombing German civilians. They started it.

Flight Sergeant Jack Woodrow RCAF, observer, 425 'Les Alouettes' Squadron

A word about the Stirling: we called it the Queen of the Skies. On the ground the cockpit was an awesome couple of storeys high. It was a beauty to fly at low level and it looked magnificent. But its height performance was abysmal. It was a struggle to reach 14,000 feet. In consequence we had the uncomfortable feeling that the Halifaxes and the Lancasters - up at 20,000 feet - were always dropping their loads through us. Not nice. The problem with the Stirling was the wingspan. Had it been designed a few feet wider then the height performance would have improved. But hangar width demanded that wingspan should be less than 100 feet. And so that is how Short Brothers built them.

Pilot Officer (later Air Vice Marshal CBE DFC AFC) Jack Furner, 214 Squadron, Chedburgh

If I were pressed to describe specific raids, the highlights were Wuppertal on a brilliant night seemingly going up in one awful pillar of smoke, the chaos below of Hamburg's 'firestorm' and the extraordinary beauty of the Alps in moonlight en route to Turin. But the one that stands out above all others is Peenemunde, 17 August 1943 - and for a number of reasons. It was to be our last but two, although we didn't know that at the time. We were certainly reaching the slightly twitchy stage in the 20s. We were briefed that it was a scientific establishment making something or other that did not bode well for the UK. The briefing was highly unusual. Not a major city, with an aiming point somewhere in the centre, designed to take out as much industry as possible, but a strange place on the Baltic coast, which none of us had ever heard of. 'It's a secret place where new experimental equipments are being developed', the briefers said. There were a number of discrete aiming points (another unusual feature). Ours was a particular part of the Experimental Establishment and other Groups would be targeting the actual living quarters of the scientists involved. We were to fly Stirling Z/EF404. We were to go in over the target at a much lower level than usual, at about 8,000ft. And there was moonlight. 'But there are only light flak defences', the briefers said. The route looked nice. A quick dash across Denmark, through the Baltic and turn on to the target from a headland to the north of it; just a few miles from coast. A snip we thought. Not exactly. The intensive flak over the target was far worse than briefed. We were bouncing around on a dense carpet of it and on the way home, flak ships accurately placed all the way along our track, or so it seemed to us. It proved all very tiring for skipper John Verrall. He lined up the aircraft for the final approach to Chedburgh exactly 8 hours after take-off and ever so slightly misjudged his touchdown point on the runway. Proud old EF404 ran off the end of the runway and into a ditch. We were shaken but unhurt. It was some time before we realised the importance of Peenemunde. It was engaged in the development of the VI and V2 rockets. At least, on the night of 17 August 1943, we must have delayed their programme somewhat and ensured that London did not receive as many of them as Hitler would have liked. As an afterthought to the raid, I suppose it was useful to the US space programme that we missed Werner von Braun.

Pilot Officer (later Air Vice Marshal CBE DFC AFC) Jack Furner, navigator on Sergeant John Verrall's Stirling crew, 214 Squadron, Chedburgh

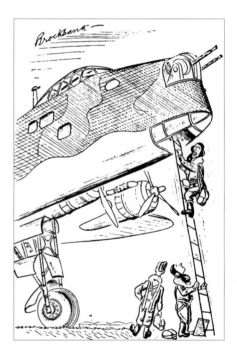

'Of course, I'm all right when it's in the air; it's climbing into it that makes me dizzy.' (Brockbank, Punch)

Life was not all flying and operations. We were granted a week's leave every six weeks, which I believe was unique amongst all the Services. Harris insisted on it. In the Mess on evenings without flying, an extremely casual and happy-go-lucky atmosphere pervaded, particularly since Chedburgh was a temporary, wartime only station with semi-circular corrugated iron Nissen huts for all offices and accommodation. There were favourite pubs in Bury St Edmunds, to which one or other of our broken-down jalopies would carry us. One of the pubs looked exactly like the studio version in *The Way to the Stars*. There were frequent losses. Faces would come and go only too quickly but there was little point in dwelling on that. We young men wouldn't wonder until we were some years older what the resulting sad administration was doing to our kindly 'uncle', the Squadron Adjutant George Wright. It was he who would be charged with informing relatives, dealing with personal effects, and clearing rooms ready for later arrivals. Jack Dixon's and John Verrall's were the only two crews to survive the whole period March to September 1943. Later statistics would show that 600 Stirling bombers were lost out of 1,750 built; 62 were lost in our last month - August 1943 – alone.

Pilot Officer (later Air Vice Marshal CBE DFC AFC) Jack Furner, navigator on Sergeant John Verrall's Stirling crew, 214 Squadron, Chedburgh

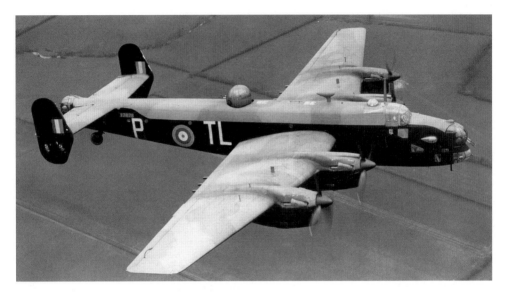

'Essen again. You begin wondering how much more it can take… The normal crew of a Hallybag being seven, three aircraft missing meant twenty-one wouldn't be around any more.' (IWM)

'Having taken off and set course on the first leg of the journey, we would, whilst there was still some daylight left, see other aircraft from our squadron and other nearby dromes, all making their way in the same direction. When the night closed in, we were then entirely on our own and it was then we gunners had to be most thorough in our searching the skies, particularly underneath our rear.' (IWM)

I had no qualms. It didn't worry me. I was briefed on targets in which I knew that civilians must become engrossed. I was briefed on lots of targets in which we were specifically told: 'Hit that point or don't bomb at all.' But the whole future of civilisation, I believed, was at stake. We didn't set the code for the pattern of war or the behaviour – that was set by Germany when they blew Warsaw over and walked across and smashed Rotterdam and Coventry and London. It was only then that the British followed the area-bombing concept. Prior to that it had been more of a direct target attack. But again, in life, you sometimes have to make a choice where it isn't black or white. You have to take the lesser of the two evils. The lesser of the two evils to me was to get the thing over, hit as hard as you could and get the people, who were in the concentration camps and in countries that were overrun, get them freed as soon as you possibly could. So I personally had no qualms whatever about what I was doing in Bomber Command.

Squadron Leader Arthur William Doubleday DFC RAAF, 'B' Flight CO, 467 Squadron RAAF in 5 Group at Waddington

Lie in the dark and listen,
It's clear tonight so they're flying high,
Hundreds of them, thousands perhaps,
Riding the icy, moonlit sky,
Men, machinery, bombs and maps,
Altimeters and guns and charts,
Coffee, sandwiches, fleece-lined boots,
Bones and muscles, minds and hearts.
English saplings with English roots
Deep in the earth they've left below,
Lie in the dark and let them go;
Lie in the dark and listen.

Lie in the dark and listen
They're going over in waves and waves
High above villages, hills and streams
Country churches and little graves
And little citizens' worried dreams;
Very soon they'll have reached the sea
And far below them will lie the bays
And cliffs and sands where they used to be
Taken for summer holidays,
Lie in the dark and let them go;
Theirs is a world we'll never know,
Lie in the dark and listen.

Lie in the dark and listen.
City magnates and steel contractors
Factory workers and politicians,
Soft hysterical little actors,
Ballet dancers, reserved musicians,
Safe in your warm civilian beds,
Count your profits and count your sheep
Life is passing above your heads,
Just turn over and try to sleep.
Lie in the dark and let them go;
There's one debt you'll forever owe.
Lie in the dark and listen.

Noël Coward

'The aircraft hit with a hell of a crash. The props flew off; engines ran away and quickly caught fire...'
(Via Mick Jennings)

Night bomber. (Author)

One night as l lay on my pillow,
My batman awoke me and said:
'I say there are ships in the Channel,
But there's bags of black cloud overhead.'
Chorus: Bring back, bring back,
Oh bring back my Bomber to me, to me.
Bring back, bring back,
Oh bring back my bomber to me.

So I climbed in my old heavy bomber
And I took off right dead into wind.
And I searched the whole of the Channel
But not a damned ship could I find.

So I turned round and headed for England,
Just thinking of coffee and bed.
The controller said: 'How can you miss them?'
I'll leave you to guess what I said!

'Bring Back My Bomber'

He walked a Devon lane and made some praise
Of God in England, for it was holiday time,
His peacetime job was safe and there were ways
Of lifting up his heart in youthful prime.

Oh! there were cloud and sky and golden fields,
Strange little coverts and pigeons on the wing,
Red earth and growing corn and all that yields
Beauty and blessedness for whom may sing.

He sang. He raised his lusty voice and sang
'Uncle Tom Cobleigh', because it seemed to fill
All the high Heaven and the echoes rang
Down the steep valley. There they echo still.

He will not sing again this half of light,
They stilled his voice one night above Cologne.
But when the Devon sun in spring is bright,
There is a valley with a voice its own.

'There Was An Air Gunner', Flight Lieutenant Anthony Richardson RAFVR

Eastward they climb, black shapes against the grey
Of failing dusk, gone with the nodding day
From English fields.
Not theirs the sudden glow
Of triumph that their fighter brothers know;
Only to fly though the cloud, through storm, through night,
Unerring and to keep their purpose bright,
Nor turn until, their dreadful duty done,
Westward they climb to race the awakened sun.

'Night Bombers', Anon

I was part of the Lancaster's seven-man crew and my job was to aim the bomb and drop it at the right time – and get home as quickly as possible because we were constantly at risk from flak and enemy planes. Once in the air we were a self-contained unit with no outside communication and, as a result, the crew became extremely close. At the back of our minds, we knew each operation might be our last. People from other crews always went missing. One night you'd be out drinking with them and the next they weren't there. Their beds would be empty and someone would come the next day and collect their kit.

Flight Sergeant John Aldridge, 49 Squadron Lancaster bomb aimer. Nine of the thirty-three operations he flew as a bomb aimer in 49 Squadron from September 1944–April 1945 were on built-up areas

EIGHT

OPS

We had been flying all day long at a hundred effing feet;
The weather effing awful, effing rain and effing sleet.
The compass it was swinging effing south and effing north,
But we made an effing landfall in the Firth of effing Forth.

Chorus: Ain't the Air Force effing awful? (repeat twice)
We made an effing landfall in the Firth of effing Forth.

We joined the effing Air Force 'cos we thought it effing right,
But don't care if we effing fly or if we effing fight.
But what we do object to are those efjing Ops Room twats,
Who sit there sewing stripes on at a rate of effing knots.

It is held now in some quarters that saturation bombing of German cities with large scale civilian casualties should not have been carried out but few of us at that time felt any remorse. It was all too impersonal for that. Germany was simply a large blacked-out area which had to be crossed to find the target, to avoid flak, searchlights and night-fighters, to release the bombs and get away as soon as possible. We had no thoughts of people being killed or cities being devastated. The only Germans we thought about were night-fighter pilots, flak gunners and searchlight operators. They were our contacts, often with unfortunate results to ourselves. It is difficult to describe but for five or six hours you entered a different world in which you were completely cut off from your normal life. On landing back at base you suddenly switched back to real life – the next op.
Sergeant Bill Rae, Wellington rear gunner, 142 Squadron, then POW from 16 November 1942

Life on the squadron was pretty hectic – frightening – due to fear of imminent death, scary because when we returned from raids on Germany, one looked at the ops board and

'The sky was steel blue and everywhere below, there was the restless criss-cross pattern of long white beams, the bright pinpoints of the bursting heavy flak shells at our level, leaving big, dark smoke puffs... the long strings of red tracers from the light flak guns being hosed up like liquid cork-screws...'
(IWM)

saw the number of aircraft who did not return and wondered when it would be my turn. In between were visits to all the local pubs and the enjoyment of comradeship amongst the crews. One of my friend's aircraft with some bombs on board crashed and caught fire when returning from Germany one night. We all rushed to help, but the heat from the fire drove us back. I could only stand and watch my friend turn black as he turned to a cinder. We turned and ran just before the bombs exploded.

Flight Lieutenant John Price, Wellington wireless operator, 150 Squadron 1941–42

A day on an operational bomber squadron would begin when brought to readiness by Group HQ's Teleprinter message that operations were 'on' for that night and there would be noticeable activity throughout the Station. Ground crews, encompassing all trades, would swarm around the aircraft to bring them to full operational standard. Engine and air-frame fitters carrying out their inspections and tests, wireless and electrical engineers checking their equipment and changing batteries, armourers replenishing ammunition, checking rotation of turrets, installing bomb-sights. Instrument technicians testing and checking dials and instruments, oxygen bottles being replaced, each aircraft was a hive of industry. All were under the watchful eye of the engineering NCO in charge who was responsible for reporting to the captain of aircraft that all was in order.

The loading of fuel and the bomb-load would be the last task, this being dependent on the target and distance involved. The aircrew would then undertake an air-test, usually taking about twenty minutes or so. On landing, the captain would be presented with Form 700 for signature to confirm acceptance of the aircraft's serviceability, or he would advise the chief engineer of any faults needing to be rectified. The aircrew would then disperse to relax prior to being called for briefing. On many occasions, the crews would be 'stood down' and they would heave sighs of relief that at least they would survive one further night. However, when it was 'all systems go' Group HQ would send by Teleprinter details of aircraft required, the target, route to be taken in both directions, bomb loads and any relevant information. Whereupon the squadron navigation leader would plot the flight, determine the fuel load, times of take-off to reach the target at the time specified by group. He would also list possible diversion aerodromes in the event of adverse weather conditions prevailing at base on return. Operation briefing time would be communicated to the officers' and sergeant's messes together with times of pre-flight meals. In-flight rations and flasks of coffee would be prepared.

Late activity on the airfield would see the huge petrol bowsers moving from one aircraft to the next and long trailers hauling their bomb-loads from the bomb dump to dispersal points with gangs of armourers waiting to winch them into the aircraft bomb-bays. It was fascinating to watch the efficiency with which these lads fitted nose and tail fuses and then winched the bombs, sometimes up to 12,000lb, into position, then moving on to the next plane.

'The shell bursts made a squeaky, gritty noise. The smell of cordite was strong and you had the feeling that someone was underneath kicking your undercarriage, keeping time with the bursts.' (Via Mick Jennings)

'Where are the bombers, the Lancs on the runways,/Snub-nosed and roaring and black-faced and dour,/Full up with aircrew and window and ammo/And dirty great cookies to drop on the Ruhr?' (Jack Hamilton 463 Squadron RAAF Collection via Theo Boiten)

Aircrews would be relaxing in many ways before briefing, some playing cards, snooker or darts, others quietly reading or writing letters and some just staring into space. Came the time to attend briefing, the operations room was a hubbub of noise until the squadron commander entered, followed by his specialist officers, when everybody sprang to attention. Waved down by the CO, the cloth that covered the target map would be removed. Some targets were better received than others. Berlin for instance drew groans from the crews, whereas Italian trips brought little reaction. The heavily defended Ruhr area was always dreaded. Each specialist officer spoke on his particular aspect of the operation, after which the CO would invite: 'Any questions?' Then he would wish us luck and leave. Navigators and captains would remain behind to plot their courses on the maps, noting heavily defended areas en route and any special instructions. The other crewmembers withdrew to their various section leaders for their instructions. The wireless operator would be issued with the Verey cartridges for the colours of the day, to be fired off if challenged by friendly fighters or ack-ack defences. He would also be advised of radio frequencies to be used and enemy radio beacons that could assist our navigation. Bomb aimers would be instructed as to the strategy to be adopted in reaching their aiming points and gunners advised as to whether and when they could test their guns in flight, tactics to be adopted against fighter interception. The dining halls were a hubbub of conversation as the pre-flight meal was served. Many were the times you would hear: 'Can I have your eggs and bacon if you don't come back?' Many flippant remarks disguised the nervousness among crews prior to take-off but once in the air this tended to disappear once fully engaged with the task in hand.

The crew rooms were a hive of activity as gunners donned their heavy electrically heated suits. Flying boots were pulled on; parachute harnesses put on over voluminous coverings of warm clothing and Mae Wests, helmets and oxygen masks examined. Navigators with their hold-alls carrying maps, charts and sextant. Wireless operators with their code books and radio frequency tables. Gunners carrying the coffee flasks and packets of confectionery comprising chocolate and fruit sweets and cans of orange juice would all troop out to the waiting transport to take them to their aircraft out on the far dispersal areas. Jocular remarks were made by one crew to another and the inevitable two-finger signs were predominant.

At dispersal, the faithful ground-crews were waiting to give a helping hand to the aircrews boarding the plane and then standing by the starter motors until starting-up time was signalled by the captain. The first engines would burst into life and one by one the others would follow until the air was filled with the roar of possibly twenty or so aircraft. After run-up, chocks were removed from the wheels and the long procession of aircraft would move out on the perimeter track to take up their position at the end of the runway. With maximum load, great care had to be exercised in keeping the plane on the concrete perimeter, running off onto the softer grassy areas could so easily have caused an aircraft to become bogged down and consequently abort the take-off of those taxiing behind.

Radio silence was maintained to prevent the enemy's listening posts gaining prior knowledge of an impending attack and take-off was indicated by a green Aldis lamp flashed from the air traffic control caravan sited by the side of the runway. Facing into the wind, the captain would call for 'full boost' and then, releasing the brakes, the aircraft would gather increasing speed nose-down to lift off its massive load just before the end of the runway. The impression was that we were not going to clear the trees at the airfield perimeter. Fortunately we always did and we would all so slowly gather height before setting course on the first leg of the route out. The navigator would call 'first course 090 degrees' or whatever and the compass would be set accordingly. As soon as sufficient height was gained the wireless operator proceeded to the rear of the plane to let out the trailing aerial to gain maximum radio signal strength. In the case of four-engined aircraft, the flight engineer ensured that the landing wheels were securely locked up after take-off and would then check the instrument panels to ensure that all systems were functioning satisfactorily. The gunners would be on full alert against possible enemy intruders, there was never really a time to relax. Climbing through cloud with such volume of aircraft involved was always hazardous and a sharp lookout was vital. The bomb-aimer and rear gunner would co-operate with the navigator in determining wind drifts, the wireless op would keep a listening-out watch on the group frequency and the pilot would adhere to the pre-determined height and speeds to reach the target at the right time.

As we approached the enemy coast, an even fuller alert was necessary, as interceptions and engagements with enemy fighters tended to be all over within seconds. Over the coastline, invariably searchlights would begin their probing and, near to sensitive and defended areas, the flak would start bursting around the aircraft. Puffs of black smoke would be seen and the crump of bursting shells heard above the noise of the engines. The pilot would maintain his course and speed unless the situation became untenable and he was forced to vary his height and speed. Guns would have been switched from 'safe' to 'fire' in readiness for any attack. The navigator would fix his position from time to time by use of his *Gee* radar set, in earlier times when radar assistance was not available he would use his sextant for this purpose, providing the stars were visible. Help was on occasions forthcoming from the W/OP when D/E loop bearings were obtained from enemy radio beacons. On occasions, dependent on the target, searchlight belts up to 50 miles in depth would be encountered and it seemed that the plane was perpetually illuminated, which was quite frightening.

Approaching the target area, the bomb aimer took up his position in the nose of the aircraft and checked his bombsight and the fuse switches on the master panel. The wireless op went into the astrodome position to provide another pair of eyes. Other friendly aircraft would probably be sighted above, below or on either side. Timing of an attack

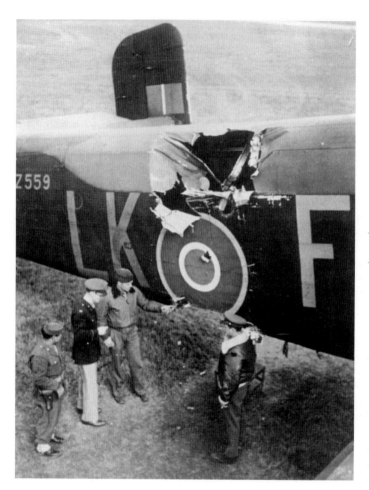

'... on 3 September 1944 at 17,500ft on the bombing run for Venlo airfield in Holland... At 1700hrs I remember my bomb aimer, Sergeant P.E. Wells, saying "Bombs Gone", when there was an almighty crash. My first thought was that we had taken a direct hit by flak, which was supported by the top gunner saying: "There's a f****** big hole in the top of the fuselage about 10ft aft of my turret." However, when the first moments of panic had died down a bit, I found that the aircraft was behaving normally. This, despite the news that there was an equally big hole in the floor of the fuselage and that the chemical closet and the flare chute had disappeared!' (Sqd Ldr Bob Davies)

was all-important, one did not wish to arrive too early with the prospect of having to go round again. The flight engineer would cast a critical eye on the fuel gauges and there would be great tension until the considerable bomb loads were released. Varying amounts of damage could be sustained en route to the target without drastically affecting the efficiency of the flight; nevertheless this could be very perplexing. The excitement had a distinct effect on the bowels at times and a tightening of stomach muscles always seemed prevalent. The run-up to bomb release appeared interminable, with the bomb aimer calling for 'bomb doors open' and the captain's response, then a lengthy 'Right, right, steady' – a pregnant pause, final directional adjustments until you heard the magic words 'Bombs gone!' With flak bursting around, a direct hit could be the end!

In front of the radio set I had a bucket seat in which I placed my parachute to give me more height to see the dials and on occasions it was very difficult to remove it. I used to ponder on this problem during our run-up to the target and often felt uneasy about the time factor should I need to leave the aircraft in a hurry. The rear gunner too had a problem as there was insufficient space in the turret to store his 'chute and he stacked it in the main fuselage near his turret doors. The turret door locks were known to be suspect on occasions – some gunners were sucked out when the doors burst open on full rotation of the turret. In one attack on a squadron aircraft, the rear guns jammed and in the heat of the moment the gunner unwittingly removed his heated gloves to clear the blockage but as soon as he touched the bare metal his skin became welded to it and he consequently suffered severe frostbite. Once having released the bombs, the aimer would check to establish that all had gone and that there were no hang-ups to cause further problems. The pilot would then leave the target area at speed to evade the defences and turn on to a course given by the navigator.

Many occasions saw encounters by other aircraft with enemy fighters and plots were made and times noted of aircraft destroyed or seen to be going down. Calculations were made of remaining fuel to ensure economical use on the return flight in order to reach base safely. Encounters with enemy fighters could create long diversions with the danger of using up precious fuel and thus failing to achieve landfall and having to face a possible ditching in the North Sea. That prospect gave little hope of survival.

The hot coffee in our flasks, which was usually drunk somewhere on the homeward run when things seemed quiet, relieved parched throats. In the sometimes excessive heat of the cabin or in the extreme cold if the heating failed, the coffee was a welcome relief. It was a great feeling just to unbutton the rubbery oxygen mask for a minute or so. When nature called, a journey was made in the darkness to the Elsan toilet located behind the main spar but all gun positions had to be covered by the wireless operator or flight engineer until the gunners returned. The pilot was not so lucky and had to use a bottle or tin which proved difficult when one hand remained on the controls. Many the curses when their aim was not accurate!

Crossing the enemy coast was no guarantee of safety. Flak-ships would give a sharp reminder of their presence and of course there were the marauding fighters anxious to wreak their havoc on unsuspecting crews. Nearing the home coast, the wireless operator would switch on the IFF apparatus to identify us as a 'friendly' to the UK defences. However, there were many trigger-happy naval types who were taking no chances, banging away at anything in the air causing us to fire off the colours of the day. Without relaxing fully, it was a relief to make landfall and we hoped that weather conditions at base were favourable and that there was no intruder alarm in force. A radio listening-out brief was maintained and we groaned whenever we were diverted to another station. We only looked forward to our own beds. Eventually we would make our final approach, say a small prayer that we would land safely and with the screech of the tyres on the runway we would congratulate ourselves

'We shall bomb Germany by day as well as night in ever-increasing measure, casting upon them month by month a heavier discharge of bombs and making the German people taste and gulp each month a sharper dose of the miseries they have showered upon mankind.' (Jack Hamilton, 463 Squadron RAAF Collection via Theo Boiten)

'... on the law of averages it would be completely impossible to survive thirty operations.' (Jack Hamilton, 463 Squadron RAAF Collection via Theo Boiten)

on having completed one more operation. Thoughts would then move on to other crews, hoping they had been as fortunate as we were. With the aid of torches, the ground crews would guide us into our parking spots, the engines would be switched off and chocks placed in front of the main wheels. With final checks to ensure all equipment was switched off, we would descend onto the tarmac to be warmly greeted by our ground crew who were on first name terms. They would be anxious to know if we had experienced any problems with the aircraft or equipment, or whether we had sustained any damage. The smokers among the crew would light up their cigarettes, take a first lengthy draw and make comments on how they thought the flight had gone. Within minutes the aircrew bus, invariably driven by a pretty WAAF would arrive to take us back to the Operations Block for de-briefing by the Intelligence staff who had probably been sitting around for hours awaiting our return. We would be greeted by the CO and the chaplain, who would be first to offer us a cup of tea or coffee and biscuits, asking if all were well with us. Signs of weariness showed on the faces of all crewmembers whether the flight duration had been four or ten hours. Intelligence officers would ply their questions concerning the defences both en route and return, all aspects of the raid, combats, time of bombing and observed results, time and position of aircraft seen destroyed or going down, weather conditions at all stages, how radar worked etc. etc. The logs were handed over to the Navigation and Signals Leaders, whereupon we would take a last look at the Operations Board to see who had not yet returned. There were sometimes some comments like *'Mayday'* signals heard. Off to the Crew Rooms then to discard flying clothing, parachutes and harnesses, then back to the Officers or Sergeants Messes for our usual eggs and bacon breakfast. Whilst hungrily consuming this meal, the crews would talk about their own particular experiences. Some would then wait in the Mess for absent friends, others would be away to bed, wondering if the experience was to be repeated again that night. Such was an 'uneventful' trip!

It was strange how crews related to their own particular aircraft and they were never so confident on the occasions that they had to use an alternative machine, for whatever reasons. Even the smells in their aircraft could be identified, strange, as that may seem. Smells were very dominant, particularly in the heat of battle. There was the combination emanating

from the heating system, creating body odours, the smell from the dope covering various patches of the fuselage from previous damage, the strong pungent cordite smells when one had experienced a heavy flak barrage or after the plane's guns had been fired. Additionally, there was a constant smell of fear about the aircraft during flight, emphasized by the odd trips to the Elsan toilet. The rubber oxygen mask too created its problems with the sweat and condensation. After landing, the crew would delight in taking great gulps of fresh air, even if some then proceeded to light up cigarettes to relax jaded nerves. The sweetest smell of all was when one entered the Mess after de-briefing to that marvellous aroma of fried bacon and coffee. Or was it the realization that one was a survivor?
  Warrant Officer Eddie Wheeler, Lancaster WOP/AG, 97 Squadron

If an enemy bomber reaches the Ruhr, you can call me Meier!
  Hermann Goering

The Battle of the Ruhr was fought over ninety-nine nights and fifty-five days, 5/6 March–23/24 July 1943, and 24,355 sorties were flown at a cost of 1,038 aircraft (4.3 per cent). Approximately 57,034 tons of bombs were dropped.

If I could hermetically seal off the Ruhr, if there were no such things as letters or telephones, then I would not have allowed a word to be published about the air offensive. Not a word!
  Diary entry, Hermann Göebbels, Nazi propaganda minister

Ops were often scrubbed at the last minute. I think this happened close to half the time.
  Flight Sergeant Jack Woodrow, 425 Squadron, Dishforth, Yorkshire, 7 October 1942–4 June 1943

On 5 June I completed my twentieth op, to Essen. It was a hot one and they were ready for us. The damn flak was like lightning flashing in daylight all about us as the searchlights grabbed us over the target. The shell bursts made a squeaky, gritty noise. The smell of cordite was strong and you had the feeling that someone was underneath kicking your undercarriage, keeping time with the bursts. We were glad to get back without too much damage.
  Pilot Officer J. Ralph Wood DFC CD RCAF, Halifax navigator, 76 Squadron, RAF Middleton St George, Durham

In half an hour on Saturday night Bomber Command made one of its heaviest attacks this year – on the U-boat building centre of Hamburg. Four-ton bombs were dropped, so were two-tonners, so were tens of thousands of incendiaries. And most of the bombs fell in the new 'thunderbolt' fashion in less than fifteen minutes.

So it was that our crews, many miles on their way home, could see the glow of the enormous fires they had caused. Over the target the sky was clear and the pilots could see the Aussen-Alster and Binnen-Alster lakes pointing the way to the great docks a mile or so away across the Elbe river.

Several pilots reported that they saw the four-tonners burst among buildings and that the target area became completely obscured by incendiaries.

Hamburg has the reputation of being one of the most heavily defended cities in Germany, but on Saturday night the flak was only moderate and there were no reports of night-fighters.

The dock area extends for 9 miles along the Elbe.

It was Hamburg's ninety-fourth raid; the last one was in November.

The RAF on Saturday also bombed objectives in Western Germany and from the night's raids five planes did not return.
  Daily Express *account of the Hamburg raid, 30/31 January 1943, the first* H2S *raid of the war*

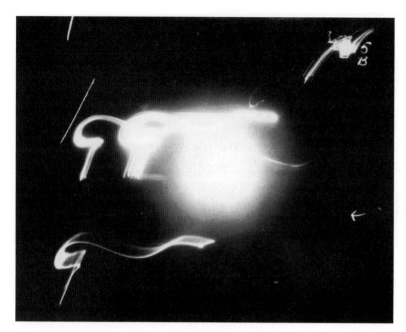

'... the brilliant flares that hang interminably between heaven and earth and never seem to move, the photo flashes exploding near the ground with a piercing blue-white light, then the long strings of incendiaries being laid out in geometrical patterns among the buildings and the great red mushroom explosions of the 4,000-pounders.' (IWM)

On the 16th we had been to Pilsen [16/17 April 1943] in a full moon and had lost 16 per cent of the 300 plus aircraft. With the moon still full it was with some trepidation that we realised from the petrol and bomb loads that we were in for another long trip. With briefing came enlightenment. Bomber Command had come up with a new plan to beat the German GCI – a low-level trip. We climbed on take-off and crossed the North Sea at 10,000ft, reaching the Danish coast somewhere around Esbjerg, where we descended to 700ft. Now began one of the most exhilarating trips I took part in as 350 heavy bombers streamed across Denmark between 400 and 700ft. Lying in the nose, map-reading did feel a bit hairy as we were constantly being hit by the slipstream from other unseen aircraft. In the brilliant moonlight all the ground detail was clear and Danes came out of their houses flashing torches and waving. Occasionally, a little light flak came up to port or starboard as aircraft strayed off course or the sky was lit up as an aircraft hit the deck.

We continued low level across the Baltic doing a cruise among the islands until, on our last leg with the North German coast on our starboard, we climbed to a bombing height of 14,000ft. As we approached the target, Stettin was well alight and in the glare from the fires below and the brilliant moonlight, it was like carrying out an aircraft recognition test. It was the first time I had seen Fw 190s and Me 109s flitting about among the silhouettes of Lancs and Halifaxes, as well as 110s and Ju 88s, all clearly visible. Somehow we were not singled out for attention as we went in and bombed. Immediately after completing the bomb run we dived for the deck and went out the same way we had come. For such a long-range target, over 600 miles from England and well outside the range of 'Oboe', it was probably the most successful raid during the Battle of the Ruhr. There were a lot of very tired pilots when we got home. We still lost between 6 and 7 per cent that night, which was the going rate for the job, so presumably Harris felt there was nothing to be gained by repeating the exercise. As far as I know this was a one-off and the tactic was never used again on such a large scale.

The Most Exhilarating Trip, Sergeant Tom Wingham DFC, bomb-aimer, Halifax II, 102 Squadron, 20/21 April 1943, sixteenth op, Stettin. Eight and a half hours – 339 aircraft were dispatched, twenty-one Lancasters and Halifaxes were lost

NINE
GOT THE CHOP – GONE FOR A BURTON

My brief sweet life is over, my eyes no longer see,
No summer walks, no Christmas trees, no pretty girls for me,
I've got the chop, I've had it, my nightly ops are done,
Yet in a hundred years from now, I'll still be twenty-one.

'Requiem for a Rear Gunner', Sergeant R.W. Gilbert, from his book of the same title

One day a Blenheim appeared in the circuit firing red Verey cartridges and taxied in at a fair rate, being marshalled into the hangar and under the crane. The MO and ambulance were standing by and it could be seen that the one who was wounded was the rear gunner so the MO jumped up to attend to him. He disappeared into the aircraft through the hatch and no one else moved. Harry jumped up onto the wing to render what assistance was necessary. The gunner was sitting on the seat with his eyes closed and his head resting on the ring of the turret just as though he was asleep. The MO made his examination and the man was dead, killed by a bullet that had entered his back. With a hydraulic turret the seat went down as the guns were raised and conversely went up when the guns were depressed. They were in the latter position when the bullet entered the turret. When the MO tried to get the body out he found that it was jamming in a curved position. Harry shouted for him to press firmly down on the lip of the seat and it would then bleed down. This he did and the body fell back. The sling was attached and Harry called for the crane hook to be raised. Slowly the body started to come out but something was hindering the withdrawal. His foot was caught in the pedal of the turret and Harry had to call for the crane to lower again while the MO freed it. Then up again, only to halt again when it was found that the chap's helmet was still plugged into the wireless socket and was slung round his neck. Out came Harry's knife and the wire was cut through. Slowly the body came out and Harry guided it over the side and down where it was placed on a stretcher and put into the ambulance, which drove away. Harry slowly made his way down and outside where he lit a cigarette and sat, trying hard to stop shaking, which delayed shock had caused.

'Harry', 21 Squadron

Incendiary bombs were exploding in 99 Squadron's sleeping quarters when I arrived from Operational Training Unit on a cold, foggy November evening in 1940. They were going off in the open fireplace of the room under the grandstand on Newmarket Racecourse, which then served as NCO aircrew billets. Fortunately, the bombs were British incendiaries, or pieces of them, which bored airmen were throwing into the fire to enliven their lives after the previous night's raid on Gelsenkirchen. The talk was all of earlier raids, old comrades on other stations and those who had already 'gone for a Burton' (killed).

Sergeant Alfred Jenner, Wellington WOP/AG (front gunner), 99 Squadron, 1940

Every time we beetle down the runway I'm wondering if we're going to make it back. I guess I've seen too many guys go for a Burton this past year. 'Gone for a Burton' meaning, in barrack-room language, 'gone for a shit', a Burton being a strong ale which caused one's bowels to move rather freely, necessitating a quick trip to the can.

Pilot Officer Ralph Wood DFC CD RCAF, 76 Squadron Halifax navigator, Bremen, 3 June 1942. It was never said that 'old so and so was killed last night'. He had either 'got the chop' or had 'gone for a Burton'. The latter expression was derived from a Burton Ales advertisement, which always showed a group of people with one person obviously missing – the captain had gone for a Burton

We made enquiries to find out 'who had got the chop' and were told who they were. It is difficult to describe one's feelings after the loss of so many friends, for while we mourned their loss, we could not suppress a sense of elation at having survived. The only way you could carry on and retain your sanity was believing, no matter what, you would be the one to get back.

Sergeant (later Flight Lieutenant DFC) Jim 'Dinty' Moore, Blenheim WOP/AG, 18 Squadron

Our losses were running at approximately 5 per cent, so one believed one was living on luck after the twentieth trip. One was just as likely to 'buy it' on the first as on the 30th.

Sergeant Eric Masters, pilot, 99 Squadron, shot down on his thirtieth and final op, to Cologne, 7 July 1941

On our homeward journey we would get into our Thermos of coffee and sandwiches of spam. Of course, our real treat was the flying breakfast of bacon and eggs back at the base and our discussions of the attack with the other crews on the raid. Bacon and eggs were otherwise scarce as hen's teeth. At the ritual breakfast after every mission there were empty tables – chairs, dishes and silverware aligned – for the men who weren't coming back. Weldon MacMurray, a school friend of mine from Moncton, stationed at RAF Dishforth, about 2 miles from Topcliffe as the crow flies, once informed me that Johnny Humphrey bought it. Another time, Graham Roger's number came up. This was followed by the news that Brian Filliter was missing in action. One day at lunch I answered the 'phone in the sergeants mess and it was Weldon inquiring about me. He'd heard that I'd bought it the previous night. A few weeks later, friends of Weldon phoned me from Dishforth to say that he had failed to return from a trip. I found out later that he was a prisoner of war. Boy! Was I getting demoralized! Would I be next?

Pilot Officer J. Ralph Wood DFC CD RCAF, Whitley navigator, Hanover, 25 July 1941

'[Branse Burbridge and 'Red' Skelton] knew before they set out precisely where they will be at a certain time. They carry a picture in their head of the whole night's operation… the various bomber streams, times, targets. They try to read the enemy mind… they visualise at what time he will discover what is happening, how far he will be misled, what he will do, what airfields he will use, what times he will rise, whether he will fly, what his tactics will be. They act accordingly. If one expectation fails, they know which next to try. After they had shot down three Burbridge said: "Time we were starting for home, Bill." To which Skelton replied: "Well if you like, but I've got another Hun for you." They went round after him and destroyed him too. Then they had a further look round. "But," says Burbridge's combat report, "we found no joy and presumed we had outstayed our welcome."' (IWM)

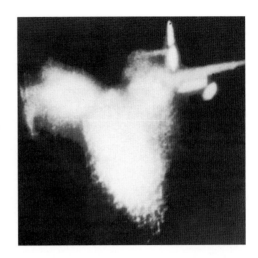

Height was slipping away badly. Instructions were given for all loose gear to be slung overboard to lessen weight, including guns and all ammunition belts. It was a blow to the three gunners to have to unlock their babies and drop them out into the night, for it robbed us of all protection. Fortunately, no German night-fighters spotted us.

The two functioning engines were being flogged to the limit and now they, too, began to lose revolutions and burn at a dangerous temperature.

I began to check on my parachute. In the air I seldom wore the pack on my body. Moving about and working over maps was easier without it. A special container was fixed to hold it on the starboard side of the aircraft and in an emergency I could quickly snatch it. When now I pulled it out, the silk fell listlessly, almost mockingly, about my feet. The rear of the pack had been badly ripped and the ripcord elastic binders completely severed. I examined the folds. A piece of shell had drilled itself through and through the folded silk and, looking at the side of the cabin where the chute had been attached, I saw a hole as big as my fist. The wind blew in, agitating the loose white silk about my feet. I was seething and rebelliously furious. But my safety valve, cursing, did not let me down and I managed to stabilise my feelings.

I went to the tail of the bomber and then worked my way back to the fore part of the aircraft. Seven perspiring and exhausted faces managed to pucker up a grin. Each man knew full well that 'Special Target Berlin' was almost over. Each man must have speculated on just how much longer we could remain aloft and silently conjectured on just how many of the crew would remain alive when the engines cut out.

Returning to the main cabin, I collected my damaged parachute, pressed it into a tight ball and stuffed it out of sight under the pilot's seat. What did it matter? What did anything matter any more? I was sky dreaming when the pilot spoke. I hardly noticed his voice. With astounding clarity I visualised details of familiar pubs in the vicinity of our Huntingdonshire aerodrome and the pencil gripped between my lips was as soothing as the rim of a whisky glass. I sucked at the drippings of sweat, which trickled continuously from my upper lip and let my imagination happily believe that the moisture was whisky-flavoured rather than salty.

I thought of Blondie in the parachute-packing section. She had always made the packing of my particular 'chute one of especial attention and had kissed it good luck whenever I collected it. When Blondie had packed my parachute earlier that day her face had gone white and her lips had quivered. Somehow, because of the love between us, she knew my own fear that I would not return. She tried to persuade me to go sick, the

Stirling by name and sterling by nature. (Shorts)

first time she had ever attempted to transgress the flying man's code. I had brushed her concerns aside saying blandly: 'I'll make it.' I had even managed a smile and added: 'You know me. I'm damned lucky.' That night we met for the last time. We lay together on my thick flying-coat on some wasteland alongside the bomb dump. I stroked her small, oval face. The touch of her soft skin alive in my senses. I cupped her golden hair in my hands, smothering it into my face. A faint and personal fragrance sweetened the air. We lay there for a long time [until] a fighter plane droned across the sky, bringing me to my senses. I took her memory into the sky... She would never know that all her painstaking and affectionate work had been cancelled out by a single chunk of anti-aircraft shell. When the news came through that we were missing in action she would console herself with the belief that I had bailed out; she would be confident, too, that my 'chute had opened perfectly because she had methodically folded the silk so that it could not do otherwise.

'Pape... for Christ's sake!' Wallace-Terry yelled. 'Give me a position. What the hell's wrong with you?'

I reacted quickly, feeling ashamed that I was neglecting my duty in selfish concern over past niceties of life.

'20 to 30 miles from the Dutch-German border', I replied, after a couple of minutes' work on my charts.

Wallace-Terry, as if talking to himself, slowly muttered: 'I'll get this aircraft that far if this bloody, fantastic petrol from nowhere only continues a while longer.'

The petrol gauges stood at zero. From what the needles indicated we were bone dry and flying on nothing.

The inner port engine started to cough badly and kept spluttering.

'Swing back the escape hatch, somebody', called the pilot. 'Bail out while you have the chance, you chaps.'

I crept forward and down the short ladder into the Stirling's bombing well. As I passed the pilot's seat I raked up saliva and spat on my dud 'chute in respect of my feelings for the enemy; then I paused and touched the silk with a quiet thought in respect of my admiration and affection for Blondie, the Waaf.

As I released the escape hatch in the floor, the inrush of cool air was clean and refreshing. I peered into the darkness and instinctively felt the earth's close proximity. We were only 1,500ft above it. I could not see any sign of the dull lustre of water on which a possible pancake landing could be made.

And then it happened. In one choking sobbing struggle, the two functioning starboard engines died with a mechanical death rattle. Stirling by name and sterling by nature our bomber had steadfastly refused to give up the scrap. From the time it had received its mortal wounds it had struggled gamely to carry us as far as the Dutch-German border. Its engines had groaned and gasped, its petrol arteries, ripped and bleeding, had seen its vital spirit drain away. With wings listing and shaking it had stubbornly kept going, refusing to give up the ghost without a fight. But now our kite had had it. We started plunging earthwards. The wind moaned and hissed. One of the crew started to bawl: 'We'll meet again, don't know where, don't know when…'

The strong Scottish voice of Jock Moir burst in: 'And I'll be in Scotland afore ye and me and my true love…'

Wallace-Terry cut it short. 'You crazy idiots!' he bellowed. 'For Christ's sake bail out while you still have sufficient clearance. You've only a few hundred feet left.'

'If you're sticking to the controls, skipper,' piped up a voice which sounded like the kid gunner's, 'then I'm sticking to you and the kite.'

It was then that the inter-communication, with a short burring, went dead…

The ground was frighteningly close. I started to crawl back to the centre of the bomber, the safest place for the big dig-in. My hand was on the top of the ladder, which led into the cabin when a body hurtled forward, boots crunching my fingers. I turned to see head and shoulders slip from sight through the opening. Before I had time to move forward again, a second body leaped forward and disappeared through the hatch, out and down into the night. As I braced against a metal stanchion and drew up my knees for the impact with the ground I wondered which members of the crew had got out. In the short remaining time I attempted to bolster up my morale by a vicious tirade of cursing against God and the Germans. I screamed out hate and vituperation against the Almighty for my peppered parachute. I paused for a breath and started to swear again, then folded up like a pricked balloon. I was dead scared. I knew it was only a matter of seconds before we smashed a hole into the earth. 'A terrific shock… A blinding white flash… A realisation in the thousandth part of a second that it was the ground… hard, hard ground!'

Sergeant (later Warrant Officer) Richard Bernard Pape, a tough red-headed Stirling navigator in 15 Squadron at Wyton who had completed nine operational sorties since 7 July 1941, and part of Flight Lieutenant R.P. Wallace-Terry's crew of a Stirling of XV Squadron, which left Wyton on the evening of 7 September for a raid on Berlin. They were badly damaged by flak over Holland and had to crash-land near Hengelo. Seven men were captured. Although badly burned and suffering from head injuries, Pape evaded. He made his way on foot to Amsterdam where an organisation made arrangements for him to be shipped back to the UK but Pape was arrested and subjected to severe torture in an unsuccessful effort to obtain from him details of his helpers. Inspired by Douglas Bader, who he met in his first POW camp, Pape escaped from a coal mine in Poland and made his way on foot to Krakow. His health was in a poor state and he collapsed at the station while waiting for a train. He was re-arrested and, after a period in a concentration camp, was again put to work. Later, Pape again escaped and walked through Slovakia, attempting to reach Yugoslavia. He was re-arrested and afterwards developed meningitis, temporary blindness and pleurisy, which kept him in hospital for about a year. Whilst in hospital, he continued his underground activities. He also gave secret propaganda talks to the other inmates. Pape, who was captive for three and a half years, was awarded the Military Medal. After the war he wrote a book about his experiences called Boldness Be My Friend, *in which he recalls the fate of Blondie: 'Three months later, during a trip to London to seek information about Richard Pape, "missing, believed killed", a bomb destroyed her. The enemy did not even leave me a grave, for there was nothing left of her to bury. I learned the shattering news of Blondie's death through enemy action five months after we crashed in Holland, soon after I had been taken to Stalag VIIIb. It was a bleak winter morning in February 1942. I will never forget the day; the cold depression of it still haunts me. Her death changed everything. With Blondie alive I would never have taken such risks with my life as I did during the coming years.*

Over Bremen we received a direct hit from flak on our inner starboard engine, killing three of the crew and injuring the WOP, Hickley. The bombs were dropped live, a photo taken and we headed for home on three engines. Over the Zuider Zee a night fighter appeared. I can still recall the flash of his windscreen in the darkness as he opened fire. As I was speaking to the rear gunner, he was blown out of his turret. I was ringed with cannon shells and injured in the leg by shrapnel. Owing to the electrical cut-out which protected the tail of the aircraft from the mid-upper guns, I was unable to fire on the fighter attacking us. Fortunately, the turret became jammed in the rear position, allowing me to vacate it. Forward, the aircraft was burning like a torch. I could not contact any crewmember. The position was hopeless. I felt I had no option but to leave the aircraft. My parachute was not in its storage holder. I found it under the legs of the mid-upper turret with a cannon shell burn in it. I removed the rear escape hatch, clipped on the parachute and sat on the edge of the hatch. I pulled the ripcord and tumbled out. The parachute, having several holes from the shell burn, 'candlesticked' (twirled) as I descended and I landed in a canal. I was apprehended the following day and was taken to Leeuwarden airfield for interrogation. I met the pilot of the Messerschmitt 110 who claimed to have shot us down. I abused him in good Australian. He understood, having spent three years at Oxford University.

WOP/AG Warrant Officer Len Collins RAAF, the only survivor of a Stirling of 149 Squadron, Bremen raid, 29/30 June 1942, his thirty-third trip. His adversary was Leutnant Hans-Georg Bötel of 6/NJG2 (KIA 7.2/3.42, three victories)

> Here lies, beneath, with arms crossed on his breast
> A Sergeant-pilot, finally at rest,
> Not twenty Aprils sunshined his small life,
> Before he took dark maiden Death to wife.
> So often viewed before, with no surprise,
> He gazed, at last, too deeply in her eyes.
> He sleeps content. Familiar was her face
> As she enfolded him in her embrace!

'Epitaph', Flight Lieutenant Anthony Richardson RAFVR

The high casualty rate among aircrews tended to breed superstition. Young men who under normal circumstances would have had a highly rational outlook on life succumbed to the carrying of talisman and lucky charms. Any innocent member of the WAAF who happened to have two successive boyfriends who failed to return from operations would be labeled a 'chop girl' and shunned. Superstition even extended to members of the aircrew fraternity. Some aircrew could be considered unlucky to fly with and would be regarded as a jinx.

115 Squadron diarist

On 22 July 1942 we collected a brand new Wellington from Oxford factory. Had two flights checking the instruments, synchronising guns etc. and then a few hours rest and

"Late again, Parkinson."

off at about 10 p.m. to Duisburg in Ruhr. I flew as a tail Charlie (rear gunner) – the first to die, or first to live in a crash. With a full bomb load we climbed up to 22,000ft zig-zag fashion as beacons below were directing the fighters out to us. Over the target there was hell on earth. Heavy raid ack-ack plastered a 300ft cube box area on the Wimpys and Lancasters, which were caught in a searchlight. Just after we dropped the eggs and steadied to take the picture, a blue (master) searchlight focused on us with others coning on us. The pilot dived sharply in a hell of bursting shells which peppered the 'plane all over. One shell hit the 'plane, igniting the port engine. The wireless operator was wounded. He called for his mother. Suddenly, the whole 'plane exploded. At the time I had manually turned the turret to the right, shooting at the searchlight, but in the explosion I was thrown out. I floated down on the parachute, which I had on my chest. A short prayer for a lucky escape, a very sad prayer for those in the three burning remnants on the ground, a near miss of the factory chimney and a wallop with my feet on the railway line. In the morning near Aachen, where I knew a friend's address, I was caught and beaten by civilians and eventually taken with some Canadian airmen to Düsseldorf army camp for treatment. After *Dulag Luft* I was sent to *Stalag VIIIb* in Upper Silesia; home to 30,000 airmen and Army, half of them on working parties all over Germany. Many tunnels were dug in the sandy soil and escapes were made through the barbed wire or from working parties. After Dieppe invasion some 3,000 soldiers were caught and sent to our camp but on Hitler's orders they were chained for one year.

Joe Fusniak, Wellington gunner

I reported to Middleton St George to join 78 Squadron on 3 September 1942... We spent the day checking in and making ourselves familiar with the station. In the mess at lunchtime the squadron crews were just getting up after their previous night's operations. We eavesdropped on their talk, not daring to say a word. This was the stuff of experienced veterans. Soon we hoped we would be able to share these conversations, talking from our own experience. Two crews were missing, one who had completed twenty-five operations. We were a little shocked to realise that even at twenty-five you weren't immune from the 'Chop'. These matters had been thoughts harboured secretly but never considered openly. Here was stark reality… My rear gunner, sleepy old 'Sunshine' Smith, was loaned to Linton and went missing with a 76 Squadron crew. We would have to find a new gunner. Worse, my friend Geoff Hobbs had also gone missing, with an experienced pilot and crew on their twenty-eighth trip. Geoff was doing his obligatory 'second dickie' trip. Three Halifaxes were lost from the thirty-nine sent to Krefeld by 4 Group that night. I was shocked at the news of Geoff, the best pilot all the way through all our various courses from elementary at Calgary to heavy conversion at Riccall. We'd been best friends for over a year. Now he'd gone without even flying one operation as captain. What a waste! Now I knew ops were for real. A little chill ran down my spine. Morty Mortensen, my long-standing friend from our training days had completed his 'second dickie' trip and was about to start operations.

'You'd better hurry up Readey,' said Morty, 'or we'll all be chopped before you get here.'

… One day I had a long and controversial conversation with a couple of intelligence officers about 'Chop Rates'. They were averaging 4 per cent per sortie, I mused that with thirty sorties to complete the average crew had a minus 20 per cent chance of surviving. Their reply was instant and consoling but spoken from theory not experience. 'Oh no,' they said, 'it doesn't work like that. The statisticians say it starts from zero, for every trip. So it's only ever 4 per cent.'

'Nonsense,' I said, 'if you only had to go once, it would be 4 per cent, as long as you don't go again. If you go again your percentage chance of the chop must go up. I've got to find a way to get on to someone else's percentage.'

They laughed and tried to convince me by insisting the statisticians had proved it was only 4 per cent. I said if they'd find me a statistician who'd completed thirty operations I might believe it. Otherwise I believed myself. By this time into a tour one became quite cynical. The illusions of youth had fallen away. Gone were the images of single-engined knights of the air jousting in the blue skies fostered by the Battle of Britain. We saw the raw, ugly face of death and destruction all around us, when nightly flying those hostile skies across the North Sea… We were all aware that some of us wouldn't return. The self-protective aspects of human nature made us believe that it couldn't be us. Although sometimes a little secret, traitorous voice kept asking, 'Why not?' If I cared to think about it, I knew quite well why not. The chop rate was 4 per cent per sortie. Since you had to complete thirty sorties before being taken off operations for a rest, there was a strong mathematical probability that you wouldn't. So I didn't think about it. Take each day, and especially each flying night, as it came, was the common Bomber Command crew's attitude.

If You Can't Take a Joke, *Ron Read, Halifax pilot, 76 Squadron*

According to records 125,000 flew in Bomber Command. Fatal casualties, including those who died as POWs, were 55,000. When you add the other POWs and those wounded on operations or in accidents, the total casualty rate was nearly 74,000. It is a casualty rate that compares with the worst slaughters in the First World War trenches. To undertake thirty operations, which was the requirement for a tour in 1941–1943 and the first half of 1944, was to have only about a 50 per cent chance of surviving. The stats seemed to show that the chances of a crew surviving a first tour got much better if it could survive the first five or six operations. After all our training, the deciding factor for survival seemed to be experience. When we started, we had no idea of what we were getting into. Well into the tour, you started to count up the crews that had not returned since you had started. Then you began to realise the lousy odds you were fighting. Having said all that, perhaps the most remarkable fact is that despite the cold, the dark, the lousy weather conditions, the flak, fighters and searchlights, the loss of comrades, the constant strain and fear, the

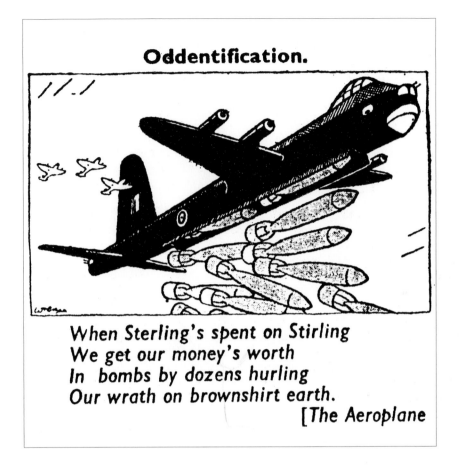

Oddentification.

When Sterling's spent on Stirling
We get our money's worth
In bombs by dozens hurling
Our wrath on brownshirt earth.
                    [The Aeroplane

general morale remained solid. I think most of us handled the strain well. We knew that ops were dangerous and stressful and that some crews would be lost but we also knew the trip was necessary.

Pilot Officer Jack Woodrow, Wellington observer, 425 Squadron RCAF, 1943

Very few crews ever completed their allocated number of thirty operations, which entitled them to be given a rest from the squadron and sent to training command. We were shocked when crews did not return but the effect was tempered by the knowledge that on this occasion we had made it. Perhaps we would last a bit longer after all. However callous this may seem, I think it must have been our defence against the knowledge that to have given the situation serious thought would have seriously damaged our morale. We accepted that losses were a factor that bombing heavily defended enemy targets involved. We called it 'getting the chop'. All the men knew that the odds against getting away with it were slim but we all believed that we could make it. The chances of this were much better for experienced crews but how to gain this experience without becoming a casualty was the great question. We all knew that in 1943 the average 'life' of a crew was ten operations so you can imagine that everyone was a bit jumpy at their 13th!

We all called Bomber Harris, our C-in-C, 'Chopper Harris', without any disrespect or animosity. We would have done whatever he asked of us.

Harry Barker, Stirling bomb aimer, 218 Squadron

'... gunners donned their heavy electrically heated suits. Flying boots were pulled on; parachute harnesses put on over voluminous coverings of warm clothing and Mae Wests, helmets and oxygen masks examined.' (IWM)

Oft this earth I leave behind,
And soar God's heavens.
Till sun and stars I find,
And fence the towering clouds
With others of my kind.
Fear not if I should lose my way,
Nor keep sad hearts
For my returning day.
'Tis that I flew the heavens too high
And reached God's guiding hand,
And heard him answer to my cry;
'Your journey's done – now land.'

'Last Landing', A. Burford Sleep

Burford Sleep wrote this poem two days before he 'flew the heavens too high'. A bomb aimer on Lancasters, he was killed returning from a bombing raid on Cologne. He had handed copies of this poem to each member of the crew the night of the raid and he was the only one killed in his aeroplane, although others were injured and wounded. Ironically, his brother, Squadron Leader R.M. Sleep (109 Squadron), marked the target on Cologne on that particular night.

To Hell with submarines
They get blown to smithereens
And keep your bayonet chargin'
It gives little safety margin,
Armoured tanks are very fine
'Til some idiot lays a mine
And fighting ships at sea
Would scare the pants off me.
If heroics are the need
The words that one should heed
Are 'Be backward coming forward'!
Be a calculating coward
And with methods of the day
Fight the safest way
And this by implication
I assess as aviation
Since Irvin was so cute
To invent his parachute.

'Thanks to Leslie Irvin', Jasper Miles

You would hear someone say, or overhear them saying that they didn't expect to see home again. I said, 'What's that? You make your own arrangements, I'm going home.'

You used to get remarks from some of these people.

'Oh, I can see you're going home. Everyone knows you're going home – but I won't.'
Fred Boys, RAAF

I don't really feel that anyone in Bomber Command in 1942 could feel that he was going to finish or that he had any right to. Certain people said 'Oh yes, I'll finish', and they did, but taken by and large I think the attitude was: 'No, I won't finish, but I won't go tonight and I won't go tomorrow night.'
Squadron Leader Arthur William Doubleday DFC RAAF, 'B' Flight CO, 467 Squadron RAAF in 5 Group at Waddington

I do not recall our losses affecting our morale; we were a happy confident crew. I remember going to funerals in the local cemetery of colleagues who were killed when their aircraft crashed on the base or were dead when their aircraft returned from an op. On a couple of occasions I was in the firing party, firing blanks over the open grave. As a crew we did not discuss the losses. I do not think this was deliberate. We would sometimes say 'so and so got the chop last night' but we were not affected by it and it was not on our minds when we were next on ops… We finished our tour with a trip on 13 May 1943 to the steelworks at Bochum, a routine one as ops went but we were all very much aware that it was not unusual for a crew to be lost on their last op. We were an experienced crew but many an experienced crew 'went for a Burton'. But we made it, and the following day we left 102 Squadron and went on leave.
Nineteen-year old John 'Jimmy' Anderson Hurst, Halifax II tail gunner, 102 Squadron, 4 Group, Pocklington, Yorkshire, 6 November 1942–13 May 1943

We were hit just like as if it was a three-ton truck. BANG! We held together for a minute then she screamed right across the port wing, hit the propellers and we went out of control. Both engines burst into flames. I got thrown to the floor and banged my head. I got up, or tried to get up. I could see Alan trying to get her straight. Then she dipped her nose and I went straight down into the nose with all the junk that was on the floor and landed on top of the bomb aimer. All of a sudden, the nose broke off. I just saw it start to crack. The bomb aimer and I fell out. I was surrounded by bits of plane – cowlings, pieces of metal – floating all around me. It was like standing on a bridge over a river when the bridge moves and the river doesn't. It was the same effect. I thought I was going up instead of the bits of metal going down. All the planes were coming in like little mosquitoes; line upon line of them. Gelsenkirchen was all lit up. It was a yellow light, from the fires that were just starting – something like a watery sunset. You could see the bombs coming down. They were like big golden darts, dropping in the yellow light. Of course I was right over the target and it was horrifying really because I had always wanted to escape out in the fields if I got shot down…

I was captured and told to climb into the back of the truck. Up I got and I saw boxes. It was dark of course. I thought, 'What's in the back of the truck?' I put my hand out and felt and came upon a flying boot. I thought, 'Gee, that's all right, I want a pair of flying boots'. I put it on and felt around for the other one. When I put them on, all of a sudden I realised that they were soaking wet. I could feel the water coming through my socks. I felt horrible because I thought it was blood. And then, of all a sudden, it hit me – I was sitting on top of coffins. I counted them. There were five on the top layer and six on the bottom. Afterwards I found out that four of them were members of my crew, seven of the other's.

The first stop on the train to my POW camp with two Luftwaffe guards, was Mülheim, which was still smouldering from a raid the previous Tuesday. There was a Red Cross train just opposite us, painted white with a red cross on it. There was a long ramp that disappeared out of sight and all of a sudden I saw these little children. They had bandages round their eyes and all had their hand on one another's shoulders. A nurse was in front and one was behind. They were leading them to the Red Cross train. That's the first time that I realised what war was really like. It was easy when you were dropping bombs up there. I turned to one of my guards, a good German and asked:

'Where's this?'

He said: 'Mülheim.'

I kept silent. I had been on that one too.

Sergeant J.S. 'Johnny' Johnston, Lancaster flight engineer, 103 Squadron at RAF Elsham Wolds, flown by Flight Sergeant Alan E. Egan RAAF, Gelsenkirchen raid, 25/26 June 1943

Every night a few of the chaps used to play a record by the Ink Spots called *For all you know, we may never meet again.* After briefing they played this over and over and over again. Until one night, one of the officers got so fed up with it, after briefing, that he took the record off the machine and smashed it over his knees. He didn't return from his next trip.

Squadron Leader Arthur William Doubleday DFC RAAF, 'B' Flight CO, 467 Squadron RAAF in 5 Group at Waddington

As the dark horizon of Germany rapidly climbs higher round you and *Z-Zebra* drops bumping into low cloud, rage grips you again this time at the thought of six men, six friends they are, riding with you and waiting for you to do something, hoping for the act of wizardry that will pull the rabbit out of the fire. Or is it the hat? You can't think which.

There's Billy, married, by a few months. You never did meet his wife. Don, due to be married in a fortnight. Joe, long since married and content. The rest of the boys, like yourself, with light-hearted dates for tomorrow night. A bloody fine skipper you turned out to be. Thoughts like these loom rapidly into your consciousness to vanish as quickly, pursued by wishful-thinking calculations of fuel and range.

'After breakfast the "station master" at Coltishall… told Bader about his new squadron [242] and was not comforting. The ground crews were about half English, three or four of the pilots were English and the rest were Canadians. Wild Canadians, the least tractable young officers he had ever seen, and most allergic to commanding officers! God knows what they would think when they heard that the new CO had no legs. Already unrest had affected the whole squadron. They needed someone pretty strong and active to discipline them.' (Bader was shot down and taken POW on 9 August 1941. He had scored twenty and four shared victories.) (IWM)

Like a stab in the back, the starboard inner engine suddenly screams and spews flame. Don reaches for the feathering and fire buttons. He might just as well have sat back and sung the Lord's Prayer. Faithfully he plays out the little game he was taught but, in the language of the times, you have had it.

Aching with the sheer muscular effort of holding up the plunging port wing, you feel the elevators tighten as the nose goes down with a lurch.

Too tired to think, you hear your voice giving the queer little order they taught you one drowsy summer day at the operational training unit in pastoral Oxfordshire; the absurd jingle you had never really thought you would ever use: 'Abracadabra, jump, jump. Abracadabra, jump, jump.'

Flight Sergeant Geoff Taylor RAAF, pilot of Lancaster Z–Zebra of 207 Squadron, which on 18/19 October 1943 failed to return from the raid on Hanover after taking off from Spilsby at 5.1p.m. Hptm Friedrich Karl 'Nose' Müller, a Wilde Sau pilot and a pre-war Lufthansa airline captain shot down Z–Zebra for his nineteenth victory. Taylor, Sergeants Don J. Duff, A.G. McLeod, C.R. Smith RCAF, A.R. Burton, W. Worthington and Flight Sergeant W.J. McCarthy RAAF were taken prisoner

When we first began flying ops in March 1943 losses were averaging 5 per cent a night but we believed we were special and would survive. We were sorry other crews didn't make it back but we accepted that this was the way things were. We didn't think it could happen to us. We were an above average crew and expected to go to Pathfinders after our tour. On return from leave in August our spirits were high. Casualty figures had got significantly lower. It came as a sharp jolt when the crew we had trained with failed to

'Outside, the aircraft were old Vickers Wellingtons, the Wimpy. I know they said "If you can't take a joke, shouldn't have joined". But this was beyond a joke. It was my nightmare scenario and it was here.' (IWM)

return from the raid on Mannheim on 9/10 August. Next day, however, was a beautiful day. The NFT went well. When we saw the fuel and bomb loading for *J-Johnny* we decided it would be a longish operation.

After the flying supper we went to briefing. The target was Nürnburg with the MAN diesel factory at Furth being the aiming point. As it was in south Germany the route was over lightly defended territory as much as possible. Climbing to a height of 21,000ft on track, we crossed the enemy coast at Le Treport, then flew on over France, directly to Nürnburg. 'Window' was dropped at intervals on entering German airspace north of Trier. There was about eight-tenths cloud with tops at 14,000ft, which meant we would be silhouetted from above by the bright moonlight. We knew we were in trouble and we generally weaved to give a maximum sky search. All of a sudden, at about 0030hrs, near Wolfstein (south of Bad Kreuznach and NNW of Mannheim, where we could see the glow from our bombing the night before), we were attacked by a night-fighter. Terry Woods, the mid-upper gunner, spotted the incoming attack and shouted: 'Bandit 5 o'clock high!'

I abandoned scrabbling about on the floor dropping 'Window' and stood at my guns (being 6ft 1in I could work the turret better standing than sitting). Cannon and tracer fire hit our port wing and port outer engine, setting both on fire. Terry returned fire, followed by Ronnie Musson in the rear turret before he was put out of action because of the loss of the port outer, which produced hydraulic power for his turret.

As our attacker broke away over the nose, I got in a burst of thirty rounds from the front guns. It was a Ju 88. Johnny started taking violent evasive action to blow out the fire. Sammy Small, the WOP/AG, was standing in the astrodome coordinating the defences as we had practiced. Almost at once Ron Musson, the rear gunner, called out a second attack. It began at 6 o'clock level, dead aft. All hell was let loose. Shells were exploding 'crunk', 'crunk', 'crunk' against the armoured doors and the 4,000lb cookie in the bomb bay. There was a smell of cordite and fire broke out in the bomb bay and mainplane. I dropped down to the bomb aimer's compartment and could see the fire raging. I told Johnny and he gave the order to jettison. I did. The attack was still in progress. The Ju 88 was holding off at 600 yards, blazing away. He didn't close.

The fire persisted and Johnny gave the order to bail out: 'Abracadabra, jump, jump!'

From beginning to end it had lasted perhaps one to two seconds but it seemed like slow motion. The order was acknowledged, except for the rear gunner. I got my parachute on and pulled up, twisted and dropped the front escape hatch in order to bail out. Ernie Roden, the flight engineer, and David Jones, the navigator, were coming down the bomb aimer's bay. I dived out and fell clear and delayed opening my chute until I was below the cloud. I could still see red and yellow tracer flying by. It is possible that Ernie and David

Above: *Stirlings wearing D-Day invasion stripes. These maids of all work dropped bombs and towed gliders.*

" What's the weather like up your end ?'

[The Aeroplane

" For you the war is over."

Above: 'Our aircraft was on the ground in pieces. I was still in my turret and it seemed to be in one piece... I was trapped in my turret and I could smell and hear burning. I had to get out quickly. The rear part of the plane had snapped off and my turret had broken away for I was looking down between my four machine guns, straight to the ground.' (Via Mick Jennings)

were hit when they bailed out. As I broke cloud I could see several small fires, which reinforces the idea that *B-Baker* exploded.

On the ground I chucked my lucky woolly gollywog away. It was nothing personal (I had carried him on all my eighteen ops) but I thought it had failed me. He hadn't because later, when I was captured, when I asked about my crew I was told '*fünf tot*' (five dead). Johnny Moss was the only other survivor, probably blown clear when the Lancaster exploded. A Luftwaffe NCO told me that three four-engined bombers had been brought down in a 10km circle by his unit. At Dulag Luft interrogation centre I thought about the attack and concluded that a professional, a real 'tradesman' had shot us down.

Len Bradfield, bomb aimer of B-Baker, a 49 Squadron Lancaster flown by Johnny Moss, on 10/11 August 1943, one of six Lancasters lost, and which was shot down by Major Heinrich Wohlers, Kommandeur I./NJG6, flying a Bf 110 who claimed a Halifax to take his score to eighteen. Dave Jones died when he landed in a vineyard and was impaled in the throat

Over several days when the weather was fine, sitting or standing on a servicing ladder out on *Easy*'s dispersal pan I painted a tableau of St Peter using the basic colours available in the flight dope store. It represented a war operation: 'Dicing with Death'. Historically

'Over several days when the weather was fine, sitting or standing on a servicing ladder out on Easy's *dispersal pan I painted a tableau of St Peter using the basic colours available in the Flight dope store. It represented a war operation "Dicing with Death".' (Johnny Wynne Collection)*

it is interesting because it shows St Peter, who theologically is the keeper of the Gates of Heaven, with his 'Golden Chopper', with which he harvested the 'Good Boys' for Heaven. This was current Bomber Command mythology. Hence the expression to 'Get the Chop'. There was of course a third player in this game of Crap. That was *Easy* herself who took care of us. Hence the exhortation 'Take it Easy'.

Flight Lieutenant Johnny Wynne DFC, pilot of Fortress III E-Easy, 214 Squadron, 100 Group, 1945. On the night of 14/15 March 1945 Wynne's Fortress III was hit during a support operation over Germany and, thinking the bomber was doomed, he ordered his crew of nine to bail out. Wynne somehow managed to level the aircraft off and, amazingly, reached England, where he crash-landed at Bassingbourn in Cambridgeshire. Wynne was sent on leave to await the return of his crew from France. However, five of the nine men who bailed out never returned. They were murdered in cold blood. In 1946 the Nazi ringleader was hanged following war crimes proceedings.

I was sitting with my back against the port side with my feet up against the starboard side, which was not the approved method, when we were jumped by the fighters. A shell came up under my legs and went out through the wireless. It might have hit my right leg. The aileron controls were shot away and we went into a dive. The pilot pulled it out on the tail trim. The gunner had been hit. I went back to get him out of the turret. I had trouble in getting the turret doors open because of the jagged metal and I got frostbite because I only had mittens on and it was 48 degrees below zero. When we eventually got Paddy out we didn't know what to do at that stage. We thought we would try and get behind our lines and land but the skipper realised that we wouldn't be able to land, as we didn't have any aileron control. The gunner said:

'Take your foot off my balls Blondie.'

I called to Blondie and said: 'What are you doing?'

Blondie said: 'I'm nowhere near him, I'm in the turret.'

So when we reported this when we got back the doctor said he thought that indicated he may have been hit in the kidney and this would have been giving him a restriction. So we bailed Paddy out on a static line. Well, the static line was supposed to have been over the rest bed position and wasn't. I used the trailing aerial. I wound it in and then brought it inside the aircraft and took it down the middle of the plane. We attached it to Paddy's ripcord and pushed him out the back. Jimmy, the bomb aimer, went out the front at the same time, the hope being that they would land together and he could attend to Paddy. Trouble was, it was about half past twelve at night in the middle of winter. There was snow everywhere. Jimmy ended up landing in barbed wire entanglements and injured himself. They didn't find Paddy for about another thirty-six hours. He was dead when they found him.

Sergeant Monty Carroll RAAF WOP/AG, oil plant raid near Leipzig, winter 1945

TEN
KRIEGSGEFANGENEN

You think I know f★★★ing nothing, in fact I know f★★★ all!

German POW camp 'goon' (guard)

To me, his adoring younger brother, Edward seemed to be not merely a brilliant pilot, but quite indestructible. He had survived a crash at Brooklands before the war when his car went over the top of the banking. He had also survived when, separated from his squadron in a dogfight, he was pounced on by upwards of twelve Messerschmitts. He shot one of these down and fought his way back to England, though wounded in the head and in a state of collapse from loss of blood. As to his last mission, it went tragically wrong and not only for him. He was shot down by anti-aircraft fire and, since the cockpit canopy had jammed, went into the ground at over 200mph. How he was not killed instantly I will never know, although he was severely injured. He recovered from his injuries remarkably quickly and was sent to Stalag Luft III.

He escaped certainly two or three times. Even then the Germans were thinking of making an example. He and a friend were travelling to Munich by train, as French workers. Unfortunately the RAF began a raid and the train was stopped and then searched. The two of them were arrested as suspected French agents. They had to admit who they were and they were taken before a Luftwaffe officer. He asked them why they wanted to escape. They replied that they considered it their duty to do so. He banged the table and said: 'Yes, it is your duty to do so!' After a time and some phoning, he told them: 'Gentlemen, you are lucky. I am to return you to your camp.' It sounds like the Luftwaffe officer had orders to hand them over to the SS or Gestapo and it also sounds as though, perhaps, he managed to talk someone out of it.

Terence Brettell. Edward Brettell was one of seventy-six prisoners who escaped from the North Compound of Stalag Luft III on the night of 24/25 March 1944, before 'Harry' (the name of the tunnel) was discovered ('Tom' had been discovered in the summer of 1943 and was blown up by

" . . . and how is your Wing-Commander's eldest daughter Penelope?"

the Germans. 'Dick' was used subsequently to store tools and equipment for 'Harry'). Fifty of the escapers who were captured, including Squadron Leader Roger Bushell SAAF – who, as 'Big X', organised the successful escape – and Brettell, who was caught together with Flight Lieutenants R. Marcinus, H.A. Pickard and G.W. Walenn near Danzig, were taken to remote spots and shot in the back of the head by the Gestapo. Only Bram van der Stok, Royal Netherlands Navy, Flight Lieutenant Jens Einar Mueller, Royal Norwegian Air Force, and Flight Lieutenant Peter Rockland RAF made 'home runs'

I remember Dixie Deans, our camp leader, saying at a parade in December 1944: 'I've been here for six Christmases and it looks as if I'm going to be here for another bugger'... The RAF were kept in the special 'escape-proof' camp at Heydekrug in East Prussia. This was Stalag Luft VI, and also at Luft I, Barth. Heydekrug was the camp especially built for NCO prisoners. If promotion came through during internment you were promoted from a Stalag to an Oflag. The Germans were very punctilious about this sort of thing; they gave me a receipt for a fountain pen! Heydekrug was supposed to be more escape-proof and nasty than Colditz but sixteen NCOs made 'home runs' as against fourteen officers in the whole of the war. I built a mental bridge that made no sense whatsoever. I told myself that the war would be over in nine months. There was no logical reason for thinking this in September 1943. The Invasion was almost unheard of. No one spoke about it or thought about it. We saw ourselves bombing Germany into submission. We knew nothing of the paratroops or gliders being prepared in readiness, although there were books published in 1943 that actually mentioned these preparations!

Geoff Parnell, air gunner, POW, Heydekrug, 1943–45

Above: 'Write a big
letter/Send it to me/
Send it in care of Stalag
Luft Three.' (IWM)

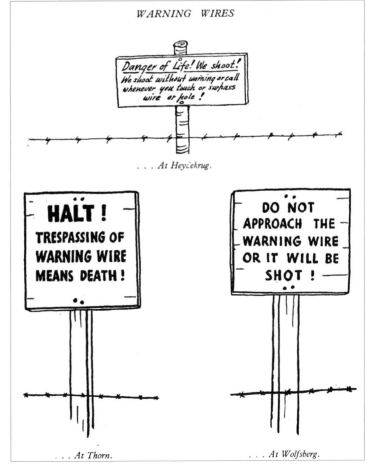

WARNING WIRES

Danger of Life! We shoot!
We shoot without warning or call
whenever you touch or surpass
wire or hole!

. . . At Heydekrug.

HALT !

TRESPASSING OF
WARNING WIRE
MEANS DEATH !

. . . At Thorn.

DO NOT
APPROACH THE
WARNING WIRE
OR IT WILL BE
SHOT !

. . . At Wolfsberg.

" I'm sorry, I can't understand a word you say."

Potato peelings are saved and boiled up again as soup for an evening meal. From the two slices of black bread which, with half-a-dozen rotting potatoes and a mug of turnip or millet soup, is your ration each for twenty-four hours of sub-zero cold, you cut the crusts and shred them into crumbs… Mixed with water and a hoarded spoonful of *ersatz* German jam made from turnips, the crumb pudding is a weekly treat. Generally we have it on Sunday night. It's very important that the pudding should be eaten at night, for it's becoming increasingly difficult to sleep at nights… There are of course, fleas and bed bugs and lice, but then they have always been with us. Bouts of dysentery on a diet of rotting potatoes also disturb the night with hasty visits to the stinking, frozen latrine pit inside the barrack door.

Piece of Cake, *Geoff Taylor RAAF, POW, Stalag IVb, Mulhlberg-on-Elbe*

ELEVEN
MILLENNIUM

The C-in-C moved at last. Slowly he pulled an American cigarette carton from his pocket and, flicking the bottom with his thumb, selected the protruding Lucky Strike. He lit the cigarette and then drew from his right breast pocket a short, stocky cigarette holder. Very deliberately he pressed the cigarette into the end of the holder and grasped it firmly between his teeth. He continued to stare at the charts and then slowly his forefinger moved across the continent of Europe and came to rest on a town in Germany. The pressure on his finger bent back the end joint and drove the blood from the top of his fingernail, leaving a half circle of white. He turned to the SASO, his face still expressionless.

'The 1,000 Plan tonight.'

His finger was pressing on Cologne.

Group Captain Dudley Saward OBE, Operation Millennium, the thousand-bomber raid on Cologne, 30/31 May 1942

The force of which you form a part tonight is at least twice the size and has more than four times the carrying capacity of the largest air force ever before concentrated on one objective. You have an opportunity, therefore, to strike a blow at the enemy, which will resound, not only throughout Germany but throughout the world.

In your hands lie the means of destroying a major part of the resources by which the enemy's war effort is maintained. It depends, however, upon each individual crew whether full concentration is achieved.

Press home your attack to your precise objective with the utmost determination and resolution in the foreknowledge that, if you individually succeed, the most shattering and devastating blow will have been delivered against the very vitals of the enemy. Let him have it – right on the chin.

Air Marshal Sir Arthur Harris, C-in-C RAF Bomber Command on the eve of the first thousand-bomber raid, 30 May 1942. Harris was of the opinion that saturation bombing would defeat Germany. On 28/29 March 1942, 234 bombers, mostly carrying incendiaries, had bombed Lubeck. Eight bombers were lost, but 191 aircraft claimed to have hit the target. About half the city, some 200 acres, was obliterated.

For four consecutive nights, beginning on 23/24 April, Rostock was devastated by incendiary bombs and by the end only 40 per cent of the city was left standing. The outcome led to Harris wanting to send more bombers to German cities, and a force of 1,046 aircraft was sent to Cologne for the 30 May 'Millennium' raid. Of these, 599 were Wellingtons, including four belonging to Flying Training Command, and 338 other bombers, of which sixty-six were Stirlings, 131 were Halifaxes and seventy-three were Lancasters. The rest of the force was made up of Whitleys, Hampdens and Manchesters. Operational Training Units (OTUs) provided 367 aircraft. For ninety-eight minutes a procession of bombers passed over Cologne. A total of 898 crews claimed to have reached and attacked the target. They dropped 1,455 tons of bombs, two thirds of them incendiaries. More than 600 acres of the city were destroyed. In all, forty bombers and two Intruders were lost, a 3.8 per cent loss rate; 116 were damaged, twelve so badly that they were written off. The fires burned for days and 59,100 people were made homeless.

We had only 700 first-line bombers. To make up the difference, the other 300 were drawn from the OTUs. I was doing my usual so-called 'rest' period of six months between ops, the idea being to give seasoned aircrew a brief respite from real operations and also to teach others. I found it ironic that so many of us got killed on these OTUs. Pilot error (the pupil was flying), navigational errors, bad weather over England in wintertime – the losses were horrendous… The target area was the centre of Cologne and the map clearly showed the red crosses of every hospital in the city. I would have nightmares after the war thinking about all the women and babies we killed that night. It is now obvious to me that we in England were determined to save our land at whatever the cost and killing the enemy, of whatever gender, was the only answer.
Flight Lieutenant John Price, instructor at 10 OTU

All bomber bases throughout England were at a high state of readiness to get all available aircraft airborne for the raid on Cologne. 12 Squadron at Binbrook, for instance, managed to put a record twenty-eight Wellington IIs into the air. To accomplish this task, however, all aircraft had to fly without second pilots and this placed added strain on the crews. Many aircraft came from OTUs and were flown by instructors. At Mildenhall, 419 Squadron had eighteen first line Wellingtons ready. 419 were wholly equipped with Wellington MkIIIs and there were crews for every aircraft. 'Moose' was not one to take over someone else's aircraft, so he borrowed an elderly IC from the Blind Approach Training Flight. This normally spent its time flying along our Lorenz beam – training pilots to use it.

We took off at 2325 hours. Although 419 were in the first wave, we were not. At approximately 50mph slower than the MkIIIs, our IC was also handicapped by trying to get to the briefed height of 18,000ft, some 4,000ft higher than I had ever been before in a Wellington. We made visual identification on arrival at Cologne and made one circuit of the city before our attack. We then flew round the target again as 'Moose' had a pair of night binoculars, which were remarkably effective, but I made no notes of what I could see. I think I must have been more interested in looking down from what seemed such a great height, this being the occasion on which I had dropped bombs from over 10,000ft. Our attack was made as ordered; height 17,500ft; night photograph taken and later plotted within 800 yards of the aiming point. The weather over the target was remarkably clear and not as we had come to expect from the Ruhr area.
Flight Lieutenant the Honorable Terence Mansfield, 419 Squadron Bombing Leader, who flew with his CO, Wing Commander 'Moose' Fulton, on the thousand-bomber raid on Cologne, 30/31 May 1942. A quarter of the 1,046 aircraft dispatched came from 3 Group, which operated in a fire-raising capacity, carrying loads of 4lb incendiary canisters. One of the chief hazards for each crew was the risk of mid-air collision in the highly congested target area. The second 'thousand-bomber raid', against Essen, took place on the night of 1/2 June with a force of 956 bombers, including

347 from the OTUs. Some bombers returned early with mechanical and engine problems. Thirty-one aircraft failed to return. A third 'thousand-bomber raid' took place on the night of 25/26 June, when 1,006 aircraft, including 102 Wellingtons of Coastal Command, attacked Bremen.

We took part in the first three 'thousand-bomber raids'. Cologne was my seventeenth op and we really pranged the target, leaving it looking like red-hot embers of a huge bonfire. Within an hour and a half 1,445 tons of bombs were unloaded – two-thirds of them incendiaries – and 600 acres of the city were devastated. With all these aircraft over the target during a short period of time, one wonders how many may have collided! Bomber Command had gathered up every bomber that could fly, even the Whitleys, some of which had been retired to submarine patrol over the bays in southern England. The second 'thousand-bomber raid', on Essen, was another spectacular raid, reminding one of paintings of the Great Fire of London. It was a vision of hell, a vision I would never forget. There was plenty of opposition over this target, which is part of the industrial centre of Germany. Those long cold hours sweating it out in the navigator's and bomb-aimer's compartment always chilled you through, even with heavy flying boots, extra socks, thick gloves and your flying suit. The usual 'cold sweat' didn't help much, either.

Pilot Officer J. Ralph Wood DFC CD RCAF, Halifax navigator, 76 Squadron, RAF Middleton St George

At briefing for the 'thousand-bomber raid' on Essen we were told our part in the operation was to kill as many of the workers as possible. Other bombers would go for the Krupps factory itself. Real bombs were not used on an OTU station, so I was a bit shaken to see them come rolling on to our airfield at Harwell. We had Whitley aircraft, unbelievably slow: We climbed at about 125mph with a full bomb load. The same turrets as the Wellington – no protection for the poor old air gunners front and rear; just Perspex. I felt very sad. As an instructor I had been ordered to go but as there were not enough instructors to fill the aircraft, pupil pilots were called upon, ditto navigators and air gunners. I was besieged by my pupils, pleading with me to let them go. I knew that half of them would not come back but I chose my dozen or so, then prayed for their safety. None came back – eighteen-year-old boys!

Flight Lieutenant John Price, an instructor at 10 OTU

The first day we were at Chipping Warden, excitement pervaded the station. They were preparing for the third of the 'thousand-bomber raids' Harris put on to show the enemy and British alike just what he meant to do with Bomber Command. The first 'thousand raid' on Cologne had been a success. The next night Essen had escaped almost entirely. Essen as usual was well hidden by broken low cloud, the industrial haze that always covered the Ruhr, plus the artificial smoke the Germans poured out when warnings sounded. The bombing effort was so dispersed the Germans didn't even know it was the target. The next effort was the one that all at Chippy were preparing for on 25 June. It was to be Bremen. The aircraft were manned by mixed complements of instructor pilots and navigators flying with trainee crews in order to reach the magic figure of 1,000 aircraft, the last time he would do so as the subsequent disruption to training programmes was too costly. We watched our aircraft take off with mixed feelings. It would have been nice to be taking part, but in a clapped out old training Wimpy, well, perhaps it was as well we weren't. Again it wasn't a good result; many aircraft failed to reach the target and losses at forty-four aircraft were high. We lost two aircraft from Chippy. One resident from our hut, a Canadian wireless operator, didn't return. We watched his effects being collected the following morning. A first indication that operations weren't going to be all fun.

Ron Read, pilot, 12 OTU Chipping Warden, June 1942

One of the series of stained glass windows at RAF Mildenhall, which commemorates 419 'Moose' Squadron RCAF. (Author)

I often wondered why the RAF Bomber Command did not continue their thousand-plane raids on our cities. Had they been able to do so the morale of the German population and the German labour force might have been significantly weakened. Of course, one reason why the burning of Bremen did not hurt the morale of our people more was because they did not know at the time the full measure of that catastrophe. Hitler's propaganda ministry had full control over all communications. Naturally, they did not play up bad news. I myself did not know the full extent of the fire-bombing of Bremen, the horrible loss of civilian life, until much later.

Albert Speer, Hitler's minister of armaments production, after the night bombing raids on the war industry in the Ruhr and especially heavy raids on coastal cities like Bremen and Hamburg, was directed to concentrate on night-fighter production. Eventually, the night-fighters began to take a heavy toll of the RAF night-bomber force as a result of devising tactics and techniques and developing equipment to deal with the night bombing effort

TWELVE
SHAKY DOs

But as our twisted arms embrace
The desert where our cities stood,
Death's family likeness in each face
Must show, at last, our brotherhood.

'The Long War', Laurie Lee

This trip was no better than the rest. You'd think by now we'd be used to it. We were all getting the 'twitch' as we experienced one 'shaky do' after another. A rough translation of 'shaky do' is 'a very frightening affair'. I must admit I was absolutely petrified on many occasions. You had to live with it, control it, but I was lucky. Once the danger was over I got over it fairly fast, until the next op. One of our Hallybags crashed in landing back at the base. The crew and aircraft were a mixture of broken bodies and metal. My morale was sure taking a beating.
   Op No.22, 19 June 1942. Pilot Officer J. Ralph Wood DFC CD RCAF, Halifax navigator,
   76 Squadron. He completed two tours (seventy-seven ops) by November 1944

There are many different grades of fear
From simple fright to scared-severe
And each can cause the bowels to itch
This, vulgar airman call 'Ring-Twitch'.
The twitch, too, has its much or slight
According to degree of fright;
You really know it's dicey flying
If your ring's like an egg that's frying.

'The Twitch', Jasper Miles

"*Fairly shaky do.*"

I know how I felt after a briefing until the time we climbed into the aircraft for an operation. The tension affected all of us. You couldn't stand still, you told stupid jokes and laughed loudly at other pathetic attempts at humour. There is a regular procession to the toilets, a condition we used to refer to as 'operational twitch'. You are really hyped up all because, although you would never admit it to a soul, you are scared. However, once you are in the aircraft, the engines are started and you feel OK, as you are able to concentrate on the job in hand.

Twenty-eight-year-old Sergeant Jim 'Dinty' Moore, Boston air gunner, 88 Squadron

On 12/13 May 1943 one of our best young pilots, Sgt Clay, came back from Duisburg with an odd tale to tell. His mid–upper gunner had bailed out near the target. When the wireless operator went back to the rear he found no gunner, just his helmet and gloves folded against the side of the open rear hatch. There was no apparent motive for the defection. We assumed that he might have had enough of ops, and was taking the easy way to a prisoner of war camp. The Special Investigation Branch made an inquiry on the basis that he might have been a spy but they found nothing. Clay and his crew, who had taken it in their stride, unfortunately went missing the very next night on a trip to nearby Bochum.

It was 51 years before I found the explanation to Clay's mystery. It was at the 1994 Squadron reunion in York. I asked Clay about his disappearing gunner. Apparently they had been heavily engaged by flak over Duisburg on the first occasion and Clay yelled, almost to himself but with intercom on, "We've got to get out of here quick". His gunner, whose intercom wasn't working too well, thought it was the order to bail out, wasted no time and went. Meanwhile Clay recovered the aircraft, escaped the flak and flew on home. His crew were debriefed, had their bacon and eggs and went to bed.

The next day they were briefed again and took off that evening for Bochum. Meanwhile their missing gunner was taken to a Dulag Luft, interrogation centre. He was not surprised when next morning, his crew turned up. He thought they had been held separately since being shot down with him over Duisburg. It took them a long time to convince him, that after he'd landed in Germany they'd flown home, had a nights sleep, a day at base, then being briefed for Bochum, had taken off again and were really shot down one night later. Another of those funny stories that could only happen to aircrew, this time with a reasonable ending.

Flight Lieutenant Ron Read DFC, 78 Squadron Halifax pilot, from his autobiography, If You Can't Take A Joke

The aircraft hit with a hell of a crash. The props flew off; engines ran away and quickly caught fire. We bounced on some high ground, became airborne again. The next contact with the ground was a rail embankment, into which we nose-dived. We had 1,500 gallons of high-octane fuel aboard. The fuel tanks exploded on impact and, lit by the engines, became a wall of flaming petrol. The aircraft broke its back just behind the second spar, flipped over the embankment and Sergeant Michael Read, the bomb aimer and myself were airborne for about 70 yards. We passed through the wall of petrol and became flaming torches, landing in a foot of mud, water and lots of bullrushes, where we burned quite furiously. Fortunately an old carpenter working nearby ran to the crash as fast as his seventy-two years would allow. He looked at the carnage, decided there was no hope of survivors and came over to investigate the two columns of smoke some distance away. He found us and rolled us into the mud to put out our fires. Apparently my uniform by now was almost completely burnt off. Read was in slightly better shape, although his arm was broken in two places. I had lost my helmet and was fairly well singed about my face and hands. My shoulder blade and about six ribs were broken. A sizeable lump of flesh was grounched out of my groin and a perfect print of a Lancaster spar, including two bolt heads, was imprinted on my back.

It seems incredible that a Red Cross nurse should be waiting for a train half a mile away with her emergency kit. She was soon on the spot and administered injections. I was apparently quite violent, insisting she shouldn't waste her bloody time on me, but concentrate her efforts on the rest of the crew, who were much worse off.

There seems no doubt that we would have burned to death if the carpenter had not been there. He had picked me by my 'Kiwi' accent. I insisted I was out cold, but he said: 'Oh no boy, your language, it were real thick. It were real bad.' Most of it was directed at the nurse for wasting her time on me. I hung my head, a little ashamed, but I had no idea about all this. We were taken to Ely hospital and I was an in-patient for two months. Officers of the investigating committee questioned me. Apparently the only part of the aircraft completely whole was the engineer's panel. I became one of Sir Archibald McIndoe's (a fellow New Zealander and father of skin grafts) 'guinea pigs' at East Grinstead hospital. I was photographed every morning and got a copy of my early grafts. I healed like a healthy animal and it wasn't long before I was disgracing myself getting a hard-on in my saline bath.

Life was cheap those pretty hard days. I went back to the squadron as a lost soul and crewed up twice with new crews but was taken off the battle order by Wing Commander Anmaud, a great airman, both times. Neither crew survived their first op. I later crewed up with a crew who had seven trips in Stirlings but the pilot and bomb aimer went LMF [Lacking Moral Fibre]. They were stripped of all rank and the crew were finally broken up after six trips, four of which were to Berlin. I went on with 75 (New Zealand) Squadron later and in all did forty-four operations. I had incredible luck all the way through. It would be no exaggeration to say I have missed death at least ten times during war and since.

Flight Sergeant Ivan Williamson DFC RNZAF W/T operator, 115 Squadron. His Lancaster MkII crashed at Magdalan, about 4 miles north of RAF Downham Market, after feathering two engines at 1,200ft during an air test on 14 September 1943. Flight Sergeant Bert Bradford, pilot, and the rest of the crew were killed

THIRTEEN
LMF

Notice how we often tell
Taste by knowledge of the smell?
Often both can be defined
As odour-flavour intertwined;
Of some, primeval and old
We never really need be told
But know their meaning right away
Experiencing their first display:
Ask a knowing man to jeer
About the taste and stink of fear?

'Instinct', Jasper Miles

He sat on the steps of the billet, his arms and hands moving through the air in a scatter motion as he fed the 'chickens'; except, of course, there were no chickens. They took him away a few days later.
Lancaster pilot

When we returned from leave we would ask who had gone missing whilst we were away and was 'our' aircraft still in one piece! The only case I recall of a crew member overcome by the losses and the almost nightly dangers of night bombing, was a pilot who had flown ten ops. One night while he sat at the controls and his crew in their positions at dispersal, waiting to join the queue of Halifaxes taxiing to the runway for take off, he burst into tears and told his crew he could not do it anymore. The crew was withdrawn from that night's op and the pilot taken to the medical section. He was quickly posted from the squadron and classed as LMF – Lacking Moral Fibre – that would be on his records for the rest of his time in the RAF and he would lose his rank!

Nineteen-year-old John 'Jimmy' Anderson Hurst, Halifax II tail gunner, 102 Squadron, 4 Group, Pocklington, Yorkshire, 6 November 1942–13 May 1943

> Into the heart of an air gunner there began to creep
> A feeling of fear which he would keep hidden deep
> The apprehensive feeling that he might not survive
> That the odds were against him finishing a tour alive.
>
> The foreboding realisation on him did gloomily dawn
> When a perception came, that good friends were gone
> On a tour of operations an air gunner's life is brief
> An alarming awareness which now caused him grief.
>
> The fear remained in him during the day and the night
> Going with him in the turret on each operational flight
> The constant fear would gnaw at him, deep in his inside
> And that is where he kept it, this fear he'd always hide.
>
> Continuing to fly on the Ops that he was ordered to
> While the fear he'd keep inside him continually grew
> Fear that any member of an aircrew can understand
> But apparently not understood by our Air Command.
>
> When orders came to fly missions, he'd have to obey
> A refusal to fly was a lack of 'Moral Fiber' they'd say
> Continued operations on his nerves would take a toll
> Flying on the missions in a squadron air gunner's role.
>
> Replacing the air gunners who on operations had died
> He couldn't tell crewmates who on him for safety relied
> The apprehension was never mentioned to even a friend
> It was kept deep inside him until his tour came to an end.

'Fear', November 28, 1944, Sergeant George 'Ole' Olson RCAF, air gunner. From No Place To Hide

Christmas 1941 was, for the Australians, the most miserable ever. The disquieting news of Japanese progress, the poor bombing results, the heavy losses in men and planes, the appalling weather, all contributed to create a feeling of gloom, frustration and defeat, a conviction that we were on the losing side and that on the law of avenges it would be completely impossible to survive thirty operations. By the New Year we had completed fifteen ops, which was halfway and we were looked upon as a veteran crew.

About this time, two incidents connected with crewmembers occurred which did not help to lift morale. The first concerned a little Cockney WAG, whose white, peaked-face skinny frame were the result of malnutrition from depression days, for it appears that from the age of ten to fifteen he had existed mainly on bread and dripping.

Despite the fact that he always had a prodigious appetite and ate at a breakneck speed he remained as pale and as skinny as ever. He was an inoffensive, quiet little fellow who should never have gone to war and we noticed as the ops increased, a nary little mannerism that developed, a kind of involuntary twitching of the muscles on the right side of his face.

Men got rid of their tensions in various ways, some drank, others became cantankerous, some brawled, but this little fellow seemed to have no outlet for his emotional stress except this continuous nervous twitching of his facial muscles. There was speculation as to how long he would last.

After a particularly tough op his plane was badly shot up by a fighter and the rear gunner killed. He had been instructed to go down and take over the dead gunner's place. We could readily imagine his nerve-wracking journey down the catwalk after the tension of the fighter's attack. It appears as he released the catch and groped in the darkness to remove the dead man, his hands had met a horrible ghastly mass of blood, guts and flesh. Despite the shock and horror of his find he had dragged the smashed remains back into the plane and crawled into the reeking battered turret and for three hours had taken over the dead man's duties.

We never discovered what transpired after they had landed but he had acted quite normally at interrogation. The first indication anything was wrong was while we were having our meal and he came into the dining room.

Blondie, who was sitting beside me facing the door, exclaimed: 'Christ, have a look at this joker. He looks as though he's seen a ghost.'

Suddenly he came over to our table, slumped into a seat and clutching his head in his hands began to rock backwards and forwards, at the same time uttering a high-pitched cry intermingled with some gibberish.

We had never seen a man's nerves break before. For a moment there was a shocked silence. Hally was the first to recover. 'He's broken down,' he declared, 'the poor bastard's nuts.'

They Hosed Them Out, *John Beede*

Of course we all pretended not to be afraid; in order to keep up the pretence we cracked jokes and sang dirty songs. Morale and discipline were everything. If you refused to go on a particularly dangerous operation, or cracked up on an operation, the RAF were much harsher than their American counterparts. US combatants were told by their doctors they were suffering from 'battle fatigue', given rest leave with their loved ones (Stateside USA) and eventually returned to duty after psychiatric help. In the RAF all aircrew (NCOs) were stripped of their rank and became an ordinary airman and whatever RAF station you were posted to you had to produce your flying log book with the dreaded words stamped in black letters: 'Lack of Moral Fibre'. Naturally, through the Orderly room, word spread throughout your new station, 'He's a coward'. It must have been hell on earth for some of these once brave aircrew whose nerves were stretched to breaking point. Thereafter they peeled potatoes in the kitchen or were forced to perform menial tasks.

Flight Lieutenant John Price, Wellington wireless operator, 150 Squadron, 1941–42

It was a remarkable standard of training that made it possible to take five different personalities and blend them into a single cohesive fighting unit, enabling us to accept, without equivocation, the dangers we were asked to face. We had arrived on the squadron sharing one unspoken fear – fear of the unknown. There are many kinds of fear but our training had been designed to make us aware of these – like the fear of injury, of burning in a crash or even death itself. These were all physical and tangible things which had affected us or our colleagues during our training. We knew what they were and consequently we knew how to combat them. The unknown fear was the fear of how we would react to flying over enemy territory to bomb a target – if we reached the target. What if this unknown fear should finally overwhelm us? How would we be regarded then? For next to the unknown our greatest fear was to be found to be lacking in moral fibre or LMF as it was euphemistically called. The layman has the harsher but more accurate word for it – cowardice. I am not ashamed to admit that after briefing for my first trip to Essen as second pilot on the night of 5/6 June 1942, I had to wash my underpants. That evening I knew the real meaning of fear, but after the trip it was no longer the fear of the unknown. Once the veil over the unknown is drawn to one side and its true nature revealed, you become aware of what it is that you have to combat and you can set about preparing yourself to cope with it. The night we flew to Bremen [29/30 June 1942], of the five of us in the aircraft I was the only one who knew what we had to fear. With the others it could be only speculation, yet Mike and Bruce overcame it with a magnificent demonstration of cool airmanship without which I am sure none of us would have survived. It should be remembered that the average age of a bomber crew was about twenty-three years which was not very old for the responsibility they were asked to assume.

Sergeant Neville Hockaday, Wellington pilot, 75 (RNZAF) Squadron, 1942

Stress and morale. I think everyone was affected by stress in some form, although most would not admit it or perhaps even realised its effect. I don't think that stress was affecting me though I remember and regret swearing at an Air Commodore after an operation. We had attacked Duisburg and were coned over the target by the big purple searchlight, radar controlled, which never wavered across the sky but came straight on the aeroplane and held it until a bank of usual searchlights flashed on and the flak intensified. We were badly hit before we could escape by violent manoeuvres. Our hydraulics were hit, the rear gunner couldn't move his turret, flaps and undercarriage were down and we plodded home at 110mph. Not knowing if our undercarriage would work, we circled away from our home base until dawn, then landed. The undercart did lock and we landed OK. After interrogation and having a cup of coffee, a visiting Air Commodore politely asked me, 'How did it go?'. I snapped, 'How the bloody hell do you think it went?' and walked away. I was known as a very quiet crew member and this was totally out of my normal behavior and I believe now was the result of stress. Next day the Wing Commander asked me why we had used more fuel than any other plane in Bomber Command that night. At that stage the average life expectancy of bomber crews was eight operations – a quarter of a tour. 75 Squadron at Feltwell had seventy crews shot down before one crew completed a tour in mid-1942.

I admired aircrew because I never knew of anyone breaking down or showing a lack of morale. The fear of being tagged LMF was ever present to some. I did speak to a sergeant on a squadron who said that when he had requested a break the Medical Officer had replied: 'What's wrong with you is you're yellow'. The lad had been the only survivor in a crash after an operation. He was killed a few nights later. I believe he was a genuine case of severe stress and had reached his breaking point. All aircrew were volunteers and some suffered greater stress on operations than others and reached their threshold of stress sooner. At a Goldfish reunion in Britain I met a member who had been unable to cope with continuous operational stress involving very high losses and could not continue flying. He was stripped of rank etc. and finished the war cleaning toilets.

Flying Officer Barney D'Ath-Weston RNZAF, Wellington air gunner, 115 Squadron, 1942/POW 26/27 July 1942

I don't really know what happened but it seems our navigator got into a 'blue-funk' and was not capable of doing the job. We returned to Dishforth and I never saw him again. Later on we heard he was accused of LMF and whisked off the station. I heard from him several months later. He told me he had been returned to Canada, discharged and then drafted into the Army. I never heard from him again and I feel very sorry that I did not make a greater effort to keep in touch. I have always felt disgusted with what the Air Force did with him. I think they should have been more understanding and compassionate instead of sending him home in disgrace as LMF. No rehabilitation was attempted. Maybe that first trip was an anomaly and he would have been OK with some help from the rest of us. But he never got the chance. I've always had the niggling thought that but for the grace of God, there go I. This was the saddest episode of my Air Force career. I heard very little talk about LMF while I was on operations and never had any connection with it other than our navigator. I think there is a fine line between battle fatigue and being a coward. There are of course two sides to the argument. The Air Force had to fight it because if you could get out of flying just by saying you didn't want to fly anymore, where would it all end? I think they had to have a strict policy but it should have been conducted with more compassion.

In my experience the number of aircrew who from loss of nerve were unable to continue operating was near zero on our squadron. Statistics show that it was less than one in 200 for the whole command. I think we went through stages. During the first few trips we realised that we had got ourselves into something very dangerous. I think our morale sagged a bit. Then we entered a stage of confidence. The enemy had done his best and we were still around. I think we all felt we had the measure of the job. Then came a stage of discouragement. We realised how lucky we had been so far and it was going to be tough to complete our tour. Then came the point that we might just complete the tour. By this time we had become highly experienced. We worked together as a highly efficient team. We each knew what to do and when. To my knowledge the main effect of the stress from operations was over-drinking – whether in the Mess, in the local pub or when on leave. It could have a long-term effect. A couple of squadron mates turned into alcoholics stretching into the post-war years. I don't know what finally happened to them. I certainly drank too much but luckily I suffered no long-term consequences. I think we all developed an attitude of fatalism. You always thought it would happen to someone else. Deaths were cases of bad luck or bad timing. I think our age helped. I was nineteen when I started on operations and finished by age twenty-one. A doctor told me that when you are on ops, your system is all keyed up and the op is your release. When you are off flying your system is still keyed up but there is no release. So most of us used drinking as the release. It made sense to me. I did notice some changes in a few of the guys. The odd one who was normally noisy became very quiet while a shy one would become boisterous.

Pilot Officer Jack Woodrow, Wellington observer, 425 Squadron RCAF, 1943

I was the observer on Sergeant Victor Page's crew, which arrived at Lakenheath on 14 February 1943 to fly Stirlings in 149 Squadron. On 10 March Vic went off on his second dickey trip, a mining expedition to Bordeaux. I hoped he was coming back because he wore my Irvine. It was a pretty rough do apparently. There was some flak through his kite but they got back OK and he flew a second op, to Stuttgart, on the 12th, poor swine. We were still waiting for a navigator when Vic went to Essen on 13 March. Poor old Vic never returned. We were quite stunned at the idea of never seeing the laddie again. I went for a long walk that night out along the Brandon road. On 27 March we left Lakenheath for 1657 Conversion Unit, Stradishall, to acquire a replacement pilot. We got there long after others had already 'crewed up' and when we were shown into a large room, there was only one pilot left. He looked rather thin and weedy but there was no-one else. We introduced ourselves. He said his name was

Bill. We asked him if he would be our pilot. He laughed and said, 'You'll regret it'. We laughed back, putting it down to typical British understatement.

Stradishall was the usual monotony of circuits and bumps, which were brightened only by a remarkable series of lousy landings. Bill's weak point was landing and we came pretty near to a prang on one landing. After bashing down in an unusually hearty manner on the deck, he suddenly decided to take off again (we were then about halfway up the runway) and in a series of sickly swerves we closely missed the roof of the hangars. However, on 18 April we were posted to Downham Market and 218 'Gold Coast' Squadron, also flying Stirlings. For seven days there was nothing much. Then they seemed to think it was time we did something and so we went 'gardening'. We stooged out to the island of Juiste in the Friesians. The cloud was pretty thick and Bill wouldn't go through the cloud to pinpoint (an essential thing on these efforts). He seemed to panic a bit when I said I saw some lights. I heard the short staccato directions in German over the R/T [and] knew a fighter was being vectored on to us but Jason falsed him up with 'tinsel' ['Window']. I saw these lights through a break in the cloud and I suppose this must have been Juiste. However, Bill wouldn't let me drop the mines though Shorty and I were all for it. I took over for about half an hour on the way back and got to bed about 0800 the next morning. On 1 May our kites went out mining in Stettin harbour and we lost three. We flew another 'gardening' op on 5 May and on the 11th we were briefed for the Ruhr but it was cancelled at the last minute. On 12 May we set out for Duisburg. It was a big effort. We had to turn back though because Jock and Len, the two gunners, couldn't get any oxygen through. They had forgotten to withdraw their bobbins. Shorty and I egged Bill on to complete the trip at 10 or 11,000ft but he was too windy to try it.

On 13 May we were off to Bochum, pretty well in the centre of the Ruhr, in *I-Ink* carrying all incendiaries. We were determined to get there at all costs. We crossed the Dutch coast off track and wandered pretty close to Antwerp. The searchlights and flak were pretty strong. It was a beautiful moonlit night and we managed to pinpoint quite easily. The *Gee* went u/s sometime before reaching target area and we turned up, all unaware, over Düsseldorf (on the way out I pinpointed our position exactly on the Dutch coast and gave a fix to Shorty, our navigator. Through a fault in his calculations, he then gave an incorrect course to our pilot. This meant that by the time we reached the Rhine we were some 20 miles north of the main force and this in turn meant that we approached the target from completely the wrong direction. It was fortunate for us that we didn't collide with one of our own aircraft, who, by the time we reached it, were leaving the target in a northerly direction). Being the only kite over the place, they gave us all they'd got. Did my best to pinpoint but dazzled by all the lights.

Bill panicked and circled about in a frantic endeavour to get out, losing height all the while. Before we left Düsseldorf we were at 6,000. Immense cones of thirty/forty searchlights picked us up at a time and we were a sitting target for light, medium and heavy flak. There was plenty of it. I should think that something like 200–300 guns were firing at us at any one time. It was at this point that Bill gave the order to bail out. I replied that if we did no one would reach the ground in one piece. Bill then said, 'You bloody well fly it then!' I went up the steps and grabbed the second pilot's controls and steered a straight course. In a few minutes we had left Düsseldorf behind. Some ten minutes after that Bill had recovered sufficiently to take over again. We then passed over the southern outskirts of Essen and for several minutes we were coned by searchlights and fired at continuously. When flak hit the aircraft there is a clap like thunder and a strong smell of cordite. Finally, we arrived at the target. The place was ablaze. Immense fires covered the ground and reflected red on a great pall of smoke, which hung above the town.

Meanwhile, Jock, our rear gunner, had obeyed the order to bail out but he had pulled the ripcord too early and his parachute had partially opened, jamming him in the escape hatch. In this position, with his head, shoulders and arms out of the aircraft, he had received the full blast of the explosions. Having bombed I tried to get Jock on the intercom and had no reply, so I went back to see how he was, to find him half in and half out of the hatch. He was in a dazed condition when I pulled him back in. I then sat next to Bill. *I-Ink* was shaking so badly that I had to hold the throttles in position from then on. At last we lost the searchlights and headed north into the seemingly quiet fighter belt that ran right the way from northern Denmark down to below Paris. *Gee* still u/s, but I managed to pinpoint the Zuider Zee. There was only just enough petrol to get home.

We arrived back at base in the half-light of early morning. The TR.9 was u/s so we landed without permission. Just as I thought everything was OK, I looked at Bill to find that he had let go the controls and had both hands over his eyes. The kite swerved suddenly to port and the next thing I knew we had cut a lorry in two, killing a couple of poor blokes just back from the raid who had disembarked from their aircraft and were about to enter the operations block for interrogation. We also knocked two cars for yards and partially demolished the briefing room, where de-briefing was taking place, before finally pranging into the operations room with our right wing. A few people in there were injured. *I-Ink* finally came to rest on the control tower. I headed for the hatch but Paddy, who was wielding an axe in a desperate attempt to hack his way out, blocked the way. I tapped him on the back and asked him if he had tried the door and with that we all ran out of the kite, fully expecting it to burst into flames. We all went to the MO who gave us two little yellow pills each, which all but knocked us out before we reached the billet! Next day we looked over our kite. It had had it. We walked round counting flak holes and there were about 100 – several extraordinarily close to where we were sitting. Len's turret had five or six holes in it, one piece of shrapnel grazing his nose on its way through. The astrodome was whipped away while Paddy was looking through it and Jock had a deep cut in his head. I was lucky to escape injury myself as shrapnel broke off a 6in piece of metal from my compartment, which hit me on the head, but fortunately my leather helmet saved my bacon.

After breakfast we were told to report to the CO. When we got to his office we gave him our account to do with the raid on Bochum. I told him that we had no confidence in Bill and did not wish to fly with him again. The CO looked at some papers on his desk and told us that we were Bill's sixth crew and that he had crashed the lot!

This was news to us, but the main thing was that he granted our request. We thought that Bill would have been grounded but later, at Stradishall, we found him with another crew. I will never know for sure what happened to Bill eventually. Some months later I was in a pub chatting with a bomb aimer from another squadron who told me that he thought he had seen Bill's Stirling heading into the Channel for no apparent reason with all guns firing.

As for Jock, in the month that followed, he went missing a few times and was found wandering around the fields near the aerodrome, barefoot and in his pajamas. We never saw him again.

Sergeant (later Warrant Officer) Arthur R. 'Spud' Taylor, 218 'Gold Coast' Squadron, Downham Market, observer, Stirling III I-Ink, *operation to Bochum, 13/14 May 1943.* I-Ink *was damaged beyond repair*

One morning the whole of the operational training course was summoned to present itself in the briefing room. The group captain with all the medals on his chest strode in and, without preamble, congratulated us on having completed the course. It was too bad that we had lost one crew during that time. It was unusual at an OTU. There had been no case of OTU-itis. Our postings were on the notice board outside the crew room. We were being spread among the other Mosquito Squadrons in the Eight Group. He left as abruptly as he had arrived.

'What on earth is OTU-itis?' I asked a seasoned-looking navigator.

'Haven't you heard of that?' he replied, raising his eyebrows. 'Well, to put it crudely, some of these intrepid birdmen like to wear a brevet,' he pointed to his wings, 'and pick up a few free beers in their local. However, when the chips are down, they suddenly discover that they have an incurable disease which their great uncles, or some other relative in the family, had picked up fighting in the Afghan wars or somewhere else in the British Empire. They call off flying before they have to face the flak and the fighters. The powers that be treat them pretty roughly. They're stripped of their rank and brevet, then their documents are stamped LMF – lack of moral fibre. They usually become shit-house-cleaners-out.

One Man's War, *Sergeant Johnnie Clark, Mosquito navigator*

LMF was something we'd heard little of during our training – a subject clouded in mystery and seldom referred to on squadrons. It was a phrase used to label people who officially 'had forfeited the confidence of the commanding officer in the face of danger in the air'. It was viewed as a disciplinary problem rather than an illness or mental condition. Men in the forces were expected to carry on going into battle as often as their commanders wished. Symptoms of fear leading to a refusal to fly on operations were viewed as simple cowardice and therefore suitable for punishment. All aircrew were volunteers but once you were accepted there was no way of transferring back to a less dangerous occupation. There was no acceptance that a person's mental state could be affected by their operational experiences and thus affect their willingness or ability to continue operations. It was not within any local medical officer's competence to consider such problems, so no one was available to listen, even if the individual plucked up the courage to discuss it. The average commanding officer was more concerned in stopping such un-British nonsense spreading and at pains to remove any sufferer/offender from his station before anyone knew about it. Once out of the way there was no machinery for treatment of the condition since it was not recognised as illness. Neither could anyone be officially treated with sympathy in case this led to other aircrew revealing their fears to avoid further operations. Stoicism in the face of mortal danger was the expected way of life for operational aircrews and, because of our upbringing, it was the way we expected to be treated. Much depended upon the views of the CO and the record of the individual. Some COs felt that imprisonment was the only suitable treatment. Others less militarily inclined, arranged for a quick posting to some unit as far away as possible.

Post-war research in revealing something of the problems appears not to have fully understood the way things were on squadrons. According to those solemn psychological studies conducted in hindsight, the symptoms indicating the early signs of stress were almost standard behavior in any operational mess. By their definition, we could all have been LMF. They mention increased excitability, something which rose and fell on squadrons as targets were revealed, visited and left behind. The nervous excitement prior to briefing was intense. Restlessness, irritability, or truculence were said to be other signs. Most aircrew on operations were restless souls, wanting to be doing something to take their minds off the problems of survival. Inevitably, some became irritable. In crowded messes, jostled together with non-aircrew, groups of people from different backgrounds and skill levels, someone, sometime, was bound to be irritable about something.

In the main, most aircrew were tolerant of their fellows, but it was easy now and again to 'blow one's top' over something. A cancelled leave, a failure in the repair of equipment or aircraft, the purloining of a favourite newspaper; all these could irritate sometimes. The other signs of stress were equally normal behavior for certain types, like unusual quietness, with a desire for solitude. Some souls were like that and retreated into themselves to avoid the hurly-burly of a crowded, lively, mess. Other symptoms were said to be changes in facial expression; looking tired or haggard, pale, worried, tense or nervy, miserable or depressed. I would defy any normal person not to look tired and haggard after four nights out of five flying for six, seven or longer hours over enemy territory. Haggardness could also be self-inflicted. Too many nights stand down, too many trips to town, too many drinks, too many girls, could make you look just as haggard as too many ops.

It was said, rather obviously, that LMF arose from stress; the fact is that all aircrews on operations were under severe stress. Not being sure whether you would survive the next twenty-four hours over a period of six to twelve months was a more stressful occupation than any other I've known. Like any human beings, crews were affected by immediate events. There were gloomy nights when the loss of close friends occurred, bad news from home, or of friends lost in action elsewhere. But these events were usually lost in the day-to-day drama of life on a bomber station. Spirits and morale rose and fell, as they do with any group of people, but, as befitted their occupation, bomber crews were volatile personalities and there were more spontaneous parties in bomber messes than most. Many more cases of LMF might have surfaced if we hadn't been of the generation we were. Self-disciplines, born to respect authority and obey orders. Above all we regarded any show of fear as an appalling breach of code. Another symptom was a consistent pattern of early returns with technical problems. This worried me more than anything. With my luck with aircraft I felt under increasing pressure when some failure occurred. Because of the fear of being thought LMF, I was torn between the urge to risk it and press in against my better judgement, and the commonsense of returning with an unserviceable aircraft, to live to fight another day.

I used to think of what must be going through people's minds, especially the COs, as I suffered once more a failed engine or another piece of equipment falling off, or malfunctioning. There were good reasons why they didn't think I was LMF but I was not to learn of these until after the war. Another indicator of stress was said to be, 'a loss of keenness for flying duties'. Apart from fatigue from too many operations in too few days, the natural keenness of the average crewmember tended to weaken, as the realisation of chances for survival became apparent. I know of few aircrew who actually loved going on operations, however keen they were on flying. Flying was a wonderful way to fight a war but operations were a nasty duty, repaying the debt one owed for that privilege. We all kept up some pretence of keenness for the morale of our own and junior crews. This was also part of the code. But keenness to fly operations, it was not.

If it was tough for the captains, it must have been ten times worse for the other crewmembers. They had little control of their destiny and were almost totally in the hands of their pilot captain. His skill, his reactions in an emergency, his keenness, his temperament decided their ultimate fate. The degrees of skill and capability of pilots varied widely, as did the speed of their reactions. The captain could be losing his morale but even if they did notice the symptoms it would be a brave crew who would make an official complaint about him. Even if they felt driven to there were no channels for such matters to be dealt with.

There was a classic case of a captain striving to hide his loss of nerve in 76 Squadron. He held out until his sixteenth trip when they were attacked by a night-fighter. The rear gunner called an attack warning with the standard instruction, 'Turn to port,

Turn to port, Go!' The captain froze on the controls and flew straight and level. The gunners kept firing. So did the fighter. The crew kept calling to the captain to weave. He stayed locked to the control column, flying straight and level, staring straight ahead. The aircraft was severely damaged and several crew were wounded; one of them died. Somehow, the fighter gave up and the captain recovered sufficiently to fly the aircraft home. He was treated sympathetically and sent to instruct on a conversion unit, never to fly operations again. It had happened because he'd been unable to admit to his fears and refuse to fly. The survivors of this unfortunate crew were crewed up with other captains and required to complete their tours.

The increasing tempo of operations in 1943 increased the incidence of LMF cases but they still remained a very low percentage of total numbers of Bomber Command. Throughout the war, 4,059 cases were considered – 746 officers and 3,313 NCOs. The 'charges' against most were dismissed and only 2,726 (389 officers, 2,337 NCOs) were actually classified as LMF; a total less than 0.4 per cent of all the aircrews of Bomber Command. The NCOs total was higher because there were more of them than officers. Many of us suffered a loss of confidence from time to time but somehow or other we would find some way to rationalise our problems and carry on until we reached the end of our tours or literally died in the attempt.

Ron Read, Halifax pilot, 78 Squadron, 12/13 March 1943, Essen

'Aircrew Refresher Centres' were for defaulters who were sent there for a variety of reasons involving breaches of discipline. These breaches could involve drunkenness where damage had been caused to the sergeants mess or by personnel who were found to have red-coloured 100 octane or blue-coloured 230 octane aviation petrol in their car petrol tanks. Other instances were flying accidents, which were deemed to have been avoidable by the person or persons concerned, and persons classed as LMF who requested to be removed from operational aircrew status. Not all LMF personnel were sent to the Aircrew Refresher Centres. Personnel in state of constant nervousness and fatigue brought on by continuous flying operations sometimes collapsed temporarily, generally about the middle to the end of a tour, i.e. between fifteen and thirty operations. Providing they survived that length of time, they were removed from an aircrew and sent to the RAF Convalescent Home at Matlock, Derbyshire. They returned to operational duties after a period of convalescence and a general medical examination. In the other instances of LMF, if he was a non-commissioned officer, he was stripped of his rank and generally sent to another RAF station and put on ground duties. In the case of a commissioned officer, rather than convene a court martial, which was necessary in order to strip them of their commissioned rank, the easy way out was to quietly arrange for the person to be transferred to ground duties. If the officer was subject to a court martial, which resulted in the loss of his commission, he was discharged from the RAF and was liable for military service in the Army.

Flight Sergeant Louis Patrick Wooldridge DFC, 578 Squadron, mid-upper gunner

There was suddenly an horrendous, blinding flash. The whole aircraft shook as if it was a fish in its final thrash of life. Something had passed clean through our forward perspex nose window, taking parts of the bomb aimer's equipment. I thought of all those famous last words, 'Keep calm, Don't panic.' I wondered if the person who couched those words had ever been in such a position. I tried to struggle into the bomb aimer's station. The pressure from the ice cold blast now entering the nose section was immense. I put on my oxygen mask, not for oxygen but to help me to some state of normal breathing. The wind tore at my Irvin jacket. Debris was everywhere. Odd bits and pieces tore at my face. This was an impossible task.

'Skipper. I am on the R/T.'This is bloody hopeless! I can't even stand up.

'There was another explosive crash somewhere aft in *G-George*.'How is Jim?'

'I can't get near him but I think he's had it, Skip. He's bleeding from ears, nose and mouth.'

With the added assistance from the unbelievable force of the wind coming through the damaged nose, I returned to the cockpit to find chaos reigning supreme. The skipper was as calm as always. He was a wonderful guy. There was glass, oil and various liquids everywhere. Several of the pilot's instruments were u/s but he just sat there as calm and collected as is humanely possible under the circumstances. For a moment our eyes met. Were we both thinking alike? Then one eye winked. I think there was a hint of a smile, perhaps of encouragement.

'Check the fuel levels, Den. I don't know what the situation is, you tell me.'

'I don't know if we have lost any. Poor old George is like a bloody sieve at the moment, holes everywhere.'

I hoped to God we'd got enough to get home. From hereon I am not truly aware of what happened. I do recall the inferno below us at the target area. I remember a Lanc', minus tail end, with all four engines on fire, hurtling to earth. From then on my mind was a blank... On landing it was confirmed that Jim was dead and I was taken from the kite by ambulance and I was taken to station sick quarters. I was there for four days. All the lads came to pay their respects but regrettably I was never aware of their presence. I learned eventually that I was as much a problem to the crew on their visits as I was to station medical officers. I was diagnosed as having no wounds, no broken bones and no physical disabilities but I was apparently quite content to remain in bed oblivious of anything and everything. I could not stand or sit. I ate and drank nothing. I did not seem to understand any sproken word and despite attempts by all medical staff, nothing would register in my mind. ... I was taken to an RAF pyschiatric hospital at Matlock [this institution with twin turrets, high on a hill overlooking the town had been the Rockside Hydro, a 160-bed spa hotel before the war] in Derbyshire (known to in-patients as 'Hatter's Castle', after the Mad Hatter in *Alice's Adveventures in Wonderland*) where air-crew types there were referred to by our RAF colleagues as 'A right load of nutters'! For many weeks my life was just a blank. A nurse accidentally knocked a steel dish of medical instruments from a trolley on to the floor and it seems I sprang to my feet, fell flat on the floor, because of my weak state, and screamed, 'There's another poor sod going down, let's get the hell out of here. Look at the flares, look at the flares, shoot the Bastard down, they're coming closer, for God's sake shoot the Bastard down!' ... My service life came to an abrupt end. I attended a RAF Discharge Medical Board and then a further medical board. I confirmed my name, rank and serial number but I had to admit that the previous years were a complete blank in my mind. I now find all this difficult to believe. There is no real end to this particular episode in my life. Even to this day the RAF remains prominent in my mind. I think of 'Skipper' and the 'boys' and of 'Hatter's Castle' with its abundance of broken lives.

Dennis 'Lofty' Wiltshire, Flight Engineer, G-George. During 1940-194 Lofty served as an Engine Fitter before he was posted overseas. In 1943 he remustered to flying duties and during training in Canada he survived a bad crash and remained in the wreck of the aircraft in sub-zero temperatures for two days before being rescued. He then spent two months in hospital recovering from frostbite and snow blindness. He recovered and became a Flight Engineer on Lancasters in 1944

FOURTEEN
MALTESE TIMES

After this war, when the name of Malta is mentioned, you will be able to say with pride, 'I was there'.

Air Vice-Marshal Sir Hugh Pughe Lloyd, 20 April 1942

They say there's a Lib leaving Malta for Gib',
Heavier than ever before,
Tight to the turrets with terrified troops,
Fifty or sixty or more.
There's many a Hun with a gun in the sun
As they trundle back home to the Rock.
In case of brake failures they're glad of the Sailors
As they ditch at the end of the dock!

'A Lib Leaving Malta For Gib', Airmen's Song Book

American built B–24 Liberators were used extensively by RAF Coastal, Special Duties, Transport and Bomber Commands in the Mediterranean and Middle and Far East. Coastal Command Liberators, Wellingtons, Hudsons, Catalinas and Sunderlands waged an unremitting and initially unrewarding war against the German U-boat menace. Through technological developments such as the Leigh light and radar, but mostly through the determination and courage of its aircrews, Coastal Command played a major role alongside surface forces in defeating the submarine threat. By May 1945 the Command consisted of seven groups with a total of twenty-four squadrons of long-range anti-submarine warfare (ASW) aircraft, flying boats and strike aircraft, which together had accounted for 191 U-boats over the previous six years. Other RAF bomber squadrons, some of them equipped with Liberators, also made attacks on German submarines.

Nearly a nasty accident. (Ken Westrope Collection)

Battle-scarred George Cross Malta stands firm, undaunted and undismayed, waiting for the time when she can call, 'Pass friend, all is well in the island fortress!'
    Governor, Lord Gort, Palace Square, Valletta, 13 September 1942

Throughout the Second World War the RAF's commitments overseas were considerable. In the Middle East and North Africa, after initial setbacks, the RAF played a major part in defeating the Axis forces. The RAF fought alongside units of the USAAF under the control of the combined Mediterranean Allied Air Forces and eventually swept through Italy, the Balkans and southern France. Having begun the war with meagre forces based mainly in Egypt, the RAF had come to dominate the region by 1945, with sixty-seven squadrons operating from major bases in Italy, North Africa, Greece, Malta, Egypt and Palestine.

It was in May 1942 that Denis Welfare and I were posted to our first operational squadron – 141 – at Tangmere in Sussex. The Squadron had recently been equipped with Beaufighter MkIIs for defensive night-fighting. They were armed with four cannon and six machine guns and, with the AI they carried, were the most effective night-fighters in service. These MkII were powered by two Rolls-Royce Merlin engines and unfortunately had a terrible reputation with aircrew. Pilots, particularly those who had flown the more sedate Blenheims previously, found them almost lethal on take-off and landing and few had a kind word to say about them.

    The CO of the squadron was Wing Commander G.F.W. Heycock DFC and it was a tribute to his energy, drive and enthusiasm that confidence in the aircraft grew and that newly joined aircrew like ourselves settled in and quickly became truly part of a squadron.

Our first few weeks in the squadron were taken up by training; Denis to become accustomed to the Beaufighter and myself to the operation of the radar to achieve successful camera gun 'attacks' on target aircraft that were much faster and more manoeuvrable than the Blenheims on which we had trained at OTU.

By the late summer of 1942, German bomber activity over the UK was negligible and Denis and I were posted to the Middle East and to 272 Squadron at its home base at Edcu near Alexandria. It was here that new arrivals were trained for long-range daylight fighting, before transfer to the main squadron at its forward base in Malta.

We were introduced to the latest MkVI Beaufighter, powered by Hercules engines and soon found that the extra power transformed it from 'the bloody cow' into a friendly and exhilarating aeroplane that was affectionately called the 'Beau' by all who flew in it. Denis soon mastered the plane and became enthusiastic about it. I took a w/t course and we spent hours flying over the desert and sea practicing navigation with the minimum of visual and radio aids.

The chief instructor at Edcu was Squadron Leader G.M. Coleman DFC; nicknamed 'Pop' because he must have been one of the oldest operational pilots in the RAF. He was a kind, shy gentleman, but one of the most skilful and knowledgeable pilots I have ever seen. Aircrew who completed their operational tours in Malta will know that their survival was in no small part due to what 'Pop' had taught them. 'Pop' returned to operational duties with 272 Squadron in 1943, but sadly was forced to 'ditch' in the Mediterranean and was unable to fly operationally afterwards.

By the end of 1942 Denis and I were ready for operations in Malta, but shortages of planes there meant that, first of all, we had to go to West Africa to pick up a new Beau. At that time the only feasible way to supply Beaus to Egypt or Malta was for them to be crated by sea to Takoradi, where they were assembled and flown across Africa. Thus on 1 January 1943 Denis and I, together with about six other crews were flown by Liberator to what is now Ghana. We arrived at Takoradi on the 5th, carried out an air test on our new Beau on the morning of the 6th and left that afternoon, finally arriving back at Edcu on the 10th.

I shall never forget that flight – east from Takoradi along the 'slave' coast to Lagos, then north over the tropical forests of the Niger Delta to the grasslands of Northern Nigeria. As we flew east the grasslands became sparser and were replaced by the desert of the Sudan. We refuelled at Maiduguri and El Fasher – surely the hottest place on earth. Then ever eastwards – the desert below us was devoid of landmarks or life of any sort. Denis and I became mesmerised by the featureless horizon – we were hot and fighting sleep and were exasperated by mirages that appeared and disappeared. Then in the distance we saw vegetation, which turned out not to be another mirage, but the Nile Valley. I was overwhelmed by two emotions. Firstly relief that my navigation had been OK and secondly, to experience what was for me the most beautiful view I had ever seen before or since. The Nile Valley was like a lush green ribbon stretching northwards though the desert, as far as eye could see from the confluence of the Blue and White Niles at Khartoum. After that it was easy – follow the Nile north, stay the night at Luxor, then on to Edcu with forty hours of flying in our log books and 10,000 miles behind us.

A few days rest and we were off to Malta. 272 Squadron, like its sister squadron, 252, was based at Takali – a 'grass' airfield near Rabat in the centre of the island and we were introduced to the CO of 272, Wing Commander J.M. Buchanan DSO DFC★. 'Buck' had been a Wellington pilot operating over Europe during the first year of the war, when he was awarded the DFC. He then saw action in Eritrea before moving to Egypt in 1941. He flew Blenheim IV bombers in the early desert campaigns and by 1942 had completed some 230 ops and awarded a bar to his DFC. He took command of 272 Squadron in Malta in November 1942, flying fighters for the first time.

Valetta. (Author)

Buck's exploits in the Middle East were legendary and were talked about over and over again during our period in Egypt. We heard how he had shot down about fifteen enemy planes during his first six weeks with 272 and was awarded a DSO. How he appeared to be indestructible even when attacking destroyers with cannon fire. How he escaped from operations over the Western Desert with half a squadron of Italian fighters on his tail. And how a blonde female correspondent from an American news magazine stood behind him in the cockpit while on ops. To my surprise, Buck was quite different to the mental picture we had of him – he turned out to be a small, slight man with long blonde hair and a trim moustache, who walked with short, mincing steps and was very quietly spoken. We soon found that looks were deceptive. It did not take many ops for us to realise that he was one of the bravest men I ever knew. He became the top-scoring Beaufighter pilot of the war but sadly Buck's aircraft was hit by light flak over Kos towards the end of the Mediterranean war. He was forced to 'ditch' out to sea and died from exposure in his dinghy.

Our operations fell into several categories: patrolling the German and Italian supply routes between Sicily and North Africa and attacking any planes or shipping that we saw; escorting Beaufort torpedo bombers that were attacking convoys and 'drawing' the fire from escorting destroyers to give the Beauforts a chance; escorting our own convoys coming to Malta and protecting them from attack by enemy bombers.

Life expectancy on such daytime operations was not high. Anti-aircraft fire from Italian destroyers was intense, while single-seater fighters based in Sicily were lurking nearby. The Beau, for all its plusses, was not a match in speed or manoeuvrability for the Me 109; indeed it was suicide to try to take it on.

Many of my close colleagues were shot down. I particularly remember a group of Canadians who came out with us to Egypt, back to Takoradi and on to 272 and with whom I spent hours playing poker and bridge. Amongst them were Gladbrook and Bradshaw, Cozette and Fletcher, who were shot down on 8 May by Me 109s just off Sicily and the fight they put up helped Buck and ourselves to escape back to Malta. Another Canadian crew, Grimes and Dawson, disappeared after a dawn operation on 23 March. We spent about four hours searching for a dinghy, but no luck. Dawson was a massive young man – a lumberjack at home – while his pilot Grimes had married a WAAF in the UK to whom he wrote a letter every day and always ended it with a poem that he composed on the spot.

Another op that needs mentioning had a happy and memorable ending. Buck, ourselves and two other crews went night-intruding into Sicily – shooting up anything that moved. The three of us landed safely, but by the time Buck returned, sea fog covered Takali. He was advised to try landing at Luqa but Buck was not the type to take the easy way out. The whole squadron came out to watch him doing a circuit with a 90-degree bank around the perimeter at about 50ft, before landing safely with only a few yards to spare. The story of that landing was told many times afterwards in the bar of the mess and each time the fog was thicker. The last time I heard it, Buck said: 'The fog was so thick when I landed that even the birds were walking!'

Supplies were always short in Malta – we were constantly hungry. If we could afford to do so, we could buy on the black market – I recall buying an egg for £1 – a lot of money in 1943. We had relief from the siege conditions when a Beau needed a major service and we took it in turns to take it to Egypt. This meant a couple of days in Cairo before it was ready to go back. Cairo meant unlimited food and bright lights and we filled up the Beau with personal supplies. Most welcome were new razor blades, after shaving with a blade three months old!

Our last nine days on our operational tour were memorable. On 14 May we shot down a Do 24 in the Bay of Naples and set an Italian F-boat on fire near Sicily. On the 16th four of us on patrol intercepted two Ju 52s off Sicily and shot them both down. On the 18th we escorted a convoy into Malta, while on the 19th flew a Beau to Cairo for a service and flew back with a new one on the 20th. On the 21st, I spoke to Dolores for the first and only time and on the 22nd was nearly killed. Dolores was a legend – she was an attractive, vivacious young Maltese brunette who lived not far from our mess. Aircrew went to any lengths to meet her and take her out – especially as she liked aircrew. However, there was one major snag. It was said that anyone who dated her was killed on ops soon afterwards. By May she apparently had six 'victims' to her credit – mostly new aircrew who did not take the advice of the old hands. Whether this was true or just a coincidence I do not know, but what I do know is that I was shot up on the day after I spoke to her for only a few minutes.

Wellington of 104 Squadron under attack. (IWM)

'We were introduced to the latest MkVI Beaufighter, powered by Hercules engines and soon found that the extra power transformed it from "The bloody cow" into a friendly and exhilarating aeroplane that was affectionately called the "Beau" by all who flew in it.' (IWM)

'Torbeau' – torpedo-carrying Beaufighter – 'a tough, dependable aircraft with a design that allowed it to be flown at wave height with perfect safety. There was another reason – perhaps the most important of all – the expertise and dedication of the ground staff… who maintained the Beaus in tip-top condition.' (IWM)

The op on 22 May was our thirty-sixth and last on 272 and also our last flight on a Beau. Four crews set off from Takali to patrol between Sicily and Tunis; Buck, ourselves and two new Australian crews. We spotted a Do 26 flying boat heading towards North Africa and went in to attack it. Unfortunately, we did not spot the six Me 109s that were escorting it – presumably it was carrying some VIPs. The two Australian crews were shot down. Two attacked us – we managed to damage one of them (it may not have got back to Sicily), but the other riddled us with machine gun fire. The Beau was badly damaged and I had a bullet through my shoulder. I waited for the next burst from the 109, which would have finished us off. We would crash into the sea and be killed instantly. I remember my last split-second thoughts – not fear but sadness – sad that my life was going to end, sad for my fiancée waiting for me back in Wales and sad for the children we would never have. But miraculously the final burst did not come. Maybe the 109 had run out of ammo or, more likely, we were flying too low for the comfort of the 109. No pilot likes flying at 300mph at about 10ft and looking into a gunsight at the same time. Buck, as usual, escaped unscathed, but Denis and I crash-landed near Carthage and our plane was written off. Examination showed it had thirty bullet holes in it. We had survived due to Denis' skill as a pilot and because the Beaufighter Mk VI was a tough, dependable aircraft with a design that allowed it to be flown at wave height with perfect safety. There was another reason – perhaps the most important of all: the expertise and dedication of the ground staff at Takali and back in Egypt, who maintained the Beaus in tip-top condition.

Some called the Beau an ugly and unglamorous plane, but these were not aircrew who had flown one. To Denis Welfare and myself it was a friend that never let us down. It carried us safely over the jungles of Nigeria, over the deserts of the Sudan and over the hostile seas and skies around Italy and Sicily. And finally, Beau 646, which we had picked up only four days before in Egypt, had enough resilience, in spite of being terminally damaged, to take us to safety at an obscure airfield in Tunisia, where it ended its days.

An Operational Tour on Beaufighters in Malta, *Taffy Bellis DFC. Flying Mosquitoes in 239 Squadron, Flight Lieutenant D. Welfare DFC★ and Flying Officer D.B. Bellis DFC★ destroyed seven enemy aircraft in air combat, 31 May–8/9 August 1944*

Wellington wrecked on Malta.

FIFTEEN
BOMBER'S MOON

The bombers are out in force tonight
A thousand strong is an awesome sight
High above the earth the bombers soar
Propellers spin and four engines roar.

To targets eastwards the bombers stream
Where the damage caused will be extreme
For a bomber's moon hangs in the sky
Lighting up targets to which they fly.

The landscape beneath them far below
Lays basking in the full moon's glow
This tranquil scene will quickly change
Soon they will enter night-fighter range.

Back at their bases is anxious concern
They know some bombers will not return
The operation tonight will have its cost
Some bombers and aircrew will be lost.

Many airmen will not see tomorrow's dawn
To their after-life they will have gone
That is the price many airmen will pay
They'll have no tomorrow and no today.

But every full moon when skies are clear
This awesome sight will once again appear
If each bomber's moon we always do send
A thousand planes out, this war will end.

'Bomber's Moon', 7 October 1944, Sergeant George 'Ole' Olson RCAF, air gunner

It was the moon, the German night-fighter's moon that we all thought about most. The moon it was, in all its phases, that governed the tide and tempo of our flying. Sunset had become the evening symbol of the beginning of one's own personal share in the war. The dawn had become the best part of the day. Triumphant over the Fenland mists that could shroud a flarepath while your back was turned on the downwind leg of the circuit; the dawn was the thing to warm your bones. You associated it with the incessant roar of engines spluttering and backfiring into a silence so peaceful and positive that it left you drowsy with the relaxation of strain and concentration; so drowsy that it took actual physical effort to slip off your sweaty helmet, slide back the altitude-chilled slide panel in the cockpit canopy and lean out to feel the fresh air on your face and welcome the pleasurable sounds and sights of earth…

Piece of Cake, Geoff Taylor, RAAF Lancaster pilot

I'll press the tit sir, I'll press the tit, sir,
I'll press the tit at the first flak we see.
'Cos I don't like the flak sir, I don't like the flak, sir,
I want nothing but plenty of height for me.

Essen again. You begin wondering how much more it can take. Our crew consists of two Englishmen, a Scotsman, an Irishman, a Welshman and myself as the Canadian. A very mixed crew and all nervous as hell. It must be remembered that each bomber was really a flying 25-ton bomb just looking for an excuse to blow up. The 5 tons or so of high-explosives and magnesium flares, plus another 3 or 4 tons of high-octane fuel, provided the ideal mixture for a violent explosion when hit in the right place by an explosive bullet or shell. We were losing too many of our friends. It was not very pleasant, when you awoke in the morning, to see them gathering up the personal effects of those who failed to return from last night's raid. The normal crew of a Hallybag being seven, three aircraft missing meant twenty-one wouldn't be around anymore. New replacements would soon arrive and fill these empty beds. And so the war goes on!

Pilot Officer J. Ralph Wood DFC CD RCAF, 76 Squadron Halifax navigator, Essen, 1942

White moon setting and red sun rising,
Bright as a searchlight and red as a flame,
Through the dawn wind her hard way making,
Rhythmless, riddled, the bomber came.
Men who had thought their last flight over,
All hoping gone, came limping back,
Marvelling, looked on bomb-scarred Dover,
Buttercup fields and white Down track.
Cottage and ploughland, green lanes weaving,
Working-folk stopping to stare overhead – Lovely, most lovely, past all believing
To eyes of men new-raised from the dead.

'The Bomber', Anon

SIXTEEN

FIGHTING FIRE WITH FIRE

In spite of all that happened at Hamburg, bombing proved a comparatively humane method.

Air Chief Marshal Sir Arthur Harris

You knew that the routine of the operational squadron operating mainly at night could start again at any time. You would get down to the flights and be told, 'We're on tonight'. Heavily laden navigators would disappear to the briefing rooms to prepare their maps and charts and their flight plans. The rest of us were not yet to be told the 'target for tonight' but rumours circulated in whispers and by lunchtime everybody knew. There was a feeling of excitement, inevitably tinged with apprehension. We did our air tests; the signallers, the engineers, the bomb aimers and the gunners went off for their own specialist briefings. And we all came together for main briefing, usually with our sister squadron who we all hated of course, perhaps at 6 p.m. to hear from the Met.-man (Cloudy Joe), the intelligence officer who used to tell us about the enemy defences en route and around the target. We would listen to the separate 'leaders' giving their own people the very latest information on call signs, fuel loads, bomb loads and so on.

There was usually a message of encouragement from the station commander, always delivered personally; sometimes even from Butch Harris. His messages, meant to be morale-boosting, didn't always have the impact he intended. I remember one, in particular, in which he referred to the previous night's raid on Hamburg when we used 'Window' for the first time to confuse the enemy's air defences. By normal Bomber Command standards, the raid had been an enormous success, since most of our aircraft bombed Hamburg very successfully and only about ten out of 800 were lost. But he used the words, 'Only a handful of our aircraft were lost, most of them stragglers off track'. Three of those 'stragglers' came from our station and Butch Harris's words that night went down like a lead balloon.

'In spite of all that happened at Hamburg, bombing proved a comparatively humane method.' (IWM)

It wasn't all bees and honey. The briefing would conclude with take-off times, radio silence, times on targets, recognition signals and pathfinder plans around the aiming point, and so on. Afterwards, we usually went back to the messes for our pre-flight meal and then, if there was time, perhaps to write a letter home (the bars would be closed all days on which we were operating, but opened after take off; nobody minded). As we left our sparsely furnished rooms to start our final preparations, we would take a last look around – perhaps at the bedside locker with its family photographs. Most of us were single; some would have a picture of the girlfriend or Betty Grable or 'Jayne' of the *Daily Mirror*. Some were married and the pictures would be of the wife and perhaps children and Betty Grable and 'Jayne'. There might just have been that lingering thought: 'I wonder if I'll see them again?'.

And then, it was back to the crew-rooms and to the lockers to get dressed for the night's work; to collect the 'flying rations' – usually a chocolate bar, some barley sugar, raisins, Horlicks tablets and, if you wanted them, two Benzadrene tablets to keep you awake. You knew it would be cold up there, so you were grateful for your warm flying clothing and your lambskin-lined boots, often worn with two or even three pairs of socks; for your gauntlets, with woollen gloves and silk liners to help you retain your sense of feel in the freezing cold at maximum height.

Then it was outside, into the crew bus, out to dispersal and to 'our' aircraft. As far as possible, crews used to like to stick to their 'own' aircraft. It was a bit of a thing really: we tended to be superstitious. What about the gremlins? We hated carrying passengers, especially padres. Most of us felt close enough to God without having them on board to cramp our styles!

We strained our ears as we listened when the pilot ran up each engine to near full power and checked the magneto switches on the way up. If the mag drop was beyond limits and there wasn't time to fix the fault, it might mean scrubbing the trip. But if all was well, then after the checks, the engines would be closed down and we would all get out of the aircraft for the final half-hour or so before we prepared for take-off. These were sometimes awkward periods. There was a feeling of 'wanting to get on with it'. The last cigarette would be smoked; conversations were nervous – sometimes almost forced; then the duty flight squadron commander would turn up in his van or car to check that all was well and to wish us luck. Then, as take-off time approached, we would all clamber aboard and go to our places. The skipper would check with those immortal words, 'All hatches closed'. The engines would be started up again and we would move out of our dispersal bays, on to the taxiways and join the line of other aircraft moving round to the start of the 'take-off runway'. Once there, we would wait for the 'green' flashed from the runway controller. The engines would be opened up – slowly at first to combat the Stirling's tendency to swing on take-off, roar down the runway, fingers crossed that we didn't lose an engine on take-off, then into the skies and away.

There was the thrill of returning to base; of seeing your airfield code letters flashing away below; of landing, taxiing round to your own dispersal bay, being guided in by the ground crew. They were always there, even at 4 o'clock in the morning. We answered their questions as the engines were closed down and we clambered out of the aircraft: 'Had a good trip? Did everything work OK? What did the target look like? Was the aircraft hit?'... and so on. There was a feeling of elation at being home again and in one piece. Then the crew bus would turn up and it was back to the briefing room for the intelligence de-briefing accompanied by excited chatter and sometimes congratulations on a job well done. All this was sometimes tempered by the news that one or more of our crews hadn't shown up yet.

We wondered and hoped. Maybe they'd landed somewhere else, short of fuel; or perhaps they'd ditched. Or maybe they'd lost an engine and were just late? We didn't want to believe that they were lost. Then it was down to the mess for breakfast; and then to bed. Sometimes, in the early mornings soon after dawn, the sun would be shining, the birds singing. The hedgerows were green and all was peaceful. Life seemed good. But we knew that perhaps the next night – or the one after that, we'd be doing it all over again.

Squadron Leader (later Group Captain) A.F. Wallace, OC B Flight, 620 Squadron, June 1943–September 1944

In 1943 Bomber Command returned to Hamburg in some strength and with a new weapon in its armoury. On 24/25 July 1943 791 bombers dropped over 2,200 tons of bombs on Hamburg. 'Window' was used for the first time and rendered the German radar system ineffective. The Hamburg Fire Department was overwhelmed and forced to seek outside assistance for the first time. 337 people lost their lives and 1,027 were injured. 14,000 people were made homeless. Damage amounted to the equivalent of £25,000,000. Firestorms devastated the city and fires were still burning twenty-four hours after the raid. On the nights of 27/28 and 29/30 July and 2/3 August, mass raids were again made on the city. In total, some 3,095 sorties were made and almost 9,000 tons of bombs were dropped. Over 42,000 people are thought to have been killed.

10 Squadron Halifax crew. Jim Sprackling is standing furthest left in the back row. (Sprackling)

On the 13th we bombed Aachen and on the 15th another long flog to Montbelliard in southern France close to the German border… Then a week with nothing but another practice formation flying exercise. We wondered if we were being trained to emulate the Americans and operate in daylight, but no, on the 26th we were detailed to attack Hamburg. This was the most effective Bomber Command attack yet. Hamburg was completely destroyed by a firestorm and our losses were possibly the lowest of the war. Not only was Hamburg almost a coastal target but it was also the first time 'Window' (bundles of metal strips) were used to counter the German radar defences. Paddy had to push the bundles down the flare chute, a bundle a minute. This was the first time that I had a seat, as they stored the packages on my platform. It was reassuring that from now onwards 2ft of tightly packed aluminium foil protected my backside. That finished July and on 2 August we went to Hamburg again but we could not get near the target because of the enormous thunderclouds caused by the heat of the inferno underneath. Bill tried to fly through the cloud but was caught by a vicious down current and we dropped from 22,000ft to 12,000ft. By the time we recovered, the navigator said that Kiel was dead ahead, so we dropped our bomb load on Kiel and turned for home, getting clear before the German Navy woke up.

Flight Sergeant B.J. 'Jim' Sprackling, Halifax II flight engineer, 10 Squadron

Never before had an aerial offensive against a single city been so carefully planned and perhaps this preparation was the greatest example of the fullest possible attention being paid to scientific RDF aids to ensure that the most effective strategy might be derived from their proper use. The C-in-C and Air Vice-Marshal Saundby were once more to display their advanced and progressive thinking by basing their entire plan of attack on the RDF that was available to the forces which were to be dispatched on four successive nights to destroy, on each occasion, one quarter of the city of Hamburg. Around the new *Gee* and *H2S* the form of the offensive was prepared in detail. For the defence of his forces, the C-in-C decided to utilise for the first time the highly secret strips of foil paper known as 'Window', which had been so cut that, when scattered in large quantities over defended areas, it would destroy completely the ability of the enemy locators to detect approaching aircraft.

By 24 July the stage was set. By 9.30 on that morning Hamburg was doomed and the operation, which went by the ominous code name of 'Gomorrah', was about to begin. As the last hours of that day were running out, a force of 740 Lancasters and Halifaxes were nosing their way through the darkness across the North Sea in an easterly direction. Navigators were busily checking their position at regular intervals with *Gee*, maintaining with absolute accuracy their exact and predetermined route to the target. Pilots were implicitly following the instructions of their navigators in the full knowledge that these emanated from accurate scientific devices, which were fundamentally incapable of giving anything but the correct answer.

With complete confidence they turned in towards the coast from their predetermined turning point which was a position exactly 15 miles north-east of Heligoland. The *Gee* set could not be wrong. They turned. Then, knowing that they would soon cross the coast in the neighbourhood of Cuxhaven, the navigators and bomb-aimers suddenly focused their attention on the *H2S* indicator. Slowly the clock-like finger of the time-base rotated round and round as they gazed into the cathode ray tube, waiting for the appearance of the coastline which they knew must inevitably display its presence in exact replica by a shimmering green trace, accurately distorted to bear a precise resemblance to the shape of the coast over which they were about to pass. Then at the bottom of the cathode ray tube the coastline appeared. Deliberately it slid up the tube until it passed the centre and slowly the tube became filled with a series of bright patches of light closely related to the shapes of the surrounding towns. To the right was a black snake-like ribbon of clear and easily identifiable definition. The River Elbe was deliberately unfolding itself as far as Hamburg, displaying with vagueness at first, but later with detailed clarity, the bright fingers of the dock area. As the city of Hamburg approached the centre of the tube it became more and more doomed.

Group Captain Dudley Saward OBE, Operation Gommorah, Hamburg raid, 24/25 July 1943. Some 791 aircraft – 347 Lancasters, 246 Halifaxes, 125 Stirlings and 73 Wellingtons, were dispatched. Twelve aircraft (1.5 per cent of the force) – four Halifaxes, four Lancasters, three Stirlings and one Wellington, were lost. During the Battle of Hamburg 24/25 July–3 August 1943, 'Window' saved about 100–130 potential Bomber Command losses

OUR BOMBS WIPED OUT 77 PER CENT OF HAMBURG – 5,000 ACRES TO COVENTRY'S 60
The Air Ministry last night issued facts, figures and pictures showing that 77 per cent of the built-up area of the once great port of Hamburg has been obliterated. An RAF photographic interpretation officer said: 'To all intents and purposes Hamburg lies in absolute ruins. This has been achieved for the loss of eighty-seven Allied aircraft. This mightiest blow in the history of air warfare was delivered in four nights and two days by the RAF and USAF.

In the city of 1,800,000 people between 5,000 and 6,000 acres were completely blocked out. The great raids were launched by Bomber Command on the nights of July 24–25, 27–28, 29–30 and August 2–3. US bombers made their raids in daylight on July 25 and 26.

50 TONS A MINUTE
In all, 11,000 tons of bombs were dropped on the port and what this means was explained by the RAF interpretation officer by comparisons with Coventry and the City of London. He said: 'Over Coventry the Luftwaffe used 400 aircraft in their biggest raid on the town, dropping 450 tons of bombs. The attack lasted nine hours, so that roughly 50 tons of bombs were dropped an hour, a little less than one ton a minute. In the last of the three big raids on Hamburg high explosives and fire bombs went down in a total weight

of 350 tons in 45 minutes; at the rate of more than 50 tons a minute." In other words, 50 times the intensity- and more than five times the size of the raid on Coventry was achieved in-this big attack on Hamburg.

SUBMARINES HIT

At Coventry not more than 60 acres were completely devastated. At Hamburg between 5,000 and 6,000 acres were blocked out.

In the City of London, following the raid in December 1940, there were 105 acres of built-up area destroyed by fire.

Not only have most of Hamburg's factories, buildings and houses in the city's centre ceased to exist, but the devastation extends to the dock area and widely to the east and west on both sides of the Aussen Alster. Two submarines in dock were damaged, seventeen merchant ships were sunk or damaged, the main passenger station and five suburban stations were damaged and two great power stations were destroyed.

Express *Air Reporter*

It appeared to me that every section of this huge city was on fire. An ugly pall of smoke was blowing to the south-west. It looked the way that one might imagine Hell to be.

1st Lieutenant John W. McClane Jr, B-24 Liberator navigator, 44th Bomb Group, during a US 8th Air Force daylight mission after the raids

The bells of hell go ting-a-ling-a-ling
For you but not for me;
And the little devils how they sing-a-ling-a-ling
For you but not for me.
Oh Death, where is thy sting-a-ling-a-ling
O Grave, thy victor-ee?
The bells of hell go ting-a-ling-a-ling
For you but not for me.

A wave of terror radiated from the suffering city and spread throughout Germany. Appalling details of the great fires were recounted and their glow could be seen for days from a distance of 120 miles. A stream of haggard, terrified refugees flowed into the neighbouring provinces. In every large town people said: 'What happened to Hamburg yesterday can happen to us tomorrow'. Berlin was evacuated with signs of panic. In spite of the strictest reticence in the official communiqués, the Terror of Hamburg spread rapidly to the remotest villages of the Reich.

Psychologically the war at that moment had perhaps reached its most critical point. Stalingrad had been worse, but Hamburg was not hundreds of miles away on the Volga, but on the Elbe, right in the heart of Germany. After Hamburg in the wide circle of the political and military command could be heard the words, 'The war is lost'.

Adolph Galland

SEVENTEEN

CHASTISE

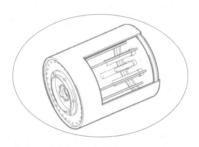

In the early hours of this morning a force of Lancasters of Bomber Command led by Wing Commander G.P Gibson DSO DFC attacked with mines the dams of the Ruhr Basin. Eight of the Lancasters are missing...

BBC news bulletin, 17 May 1943

The moon was full; everywhere its pleasant, watery haze spread over the peaceful English countryside, rendering it colourless. But there is not much colour in Lincolnshire, anyway. The city of Lincoln was silent – that city which so many bomber boys know so well, a city full of homely people – people who have got so used to the Air Force that they have begun almost to forget them. Lincoln with its great cathedral sticking up on a hill, a landmark for miles around. Little villages in the flat Fenland slept peacefully. Here nice simple folk live in their bastions on the East Anglian coast. The last farmer had long since gone to bed; the fire in the village pub had died down to an ember; the bar, which a few hours ago was full of noisy chattering people, was silent. There were no enemy aircraft about and the scene was peaceful. In fact, this sort of scene might not have changed for a hundred years or so. But this night was different – at least different for 133 men: 133 young fliers and I was one of those men. This was the big thing. This was it.

We were flying not very high, about 100ft, and not very far apart. I suppose to a layman it was a wonderful sight, these great powerful Lancasters in formation, flown by boys who knew their job. Below us, and also practically beside us, at 200mph flashed past trees, fields, church spires and England.

We were off on a journey for which we had long waited, a journey that had been carefully planned, carefully trained for, a journey for which was going to do a lot of good if it succeeded; and everything had been worked out so that it should succeed. We were off to the Dams.

'Flight Out', Enemy Coast Ahead, *Wing Commander Guy Gibson VC DSO* * *DFC* *.
Operation Chastise involved nineteen Lancasters of 617 Squadron who took off from Scampton to breach the Ruhr dams with 'bouncing bombs' invented by Dr Barnes Wallis. It was, as Wallis

'The city of Lincoln was silent – that city which so many bomber boys know so well, a city full of homely people – people who have got so used to the Air Force that they have begun almost to forget them. Lincoln with its great cathedral sticking up on a hill, a landmark for miles around. Little villages in the flat Fenland slept peacefully.' (Author)

'Then I looked again at the dam and at the water, while all around me the boys were doing the same. It was the most amazing sight. The whole valley was beginning to fill with fog from the steam of the gushing water… The floods raced on, carrying with them as they went – viaducts, railways, bridges and everything that stood in their path.' (René Millert via John Williams via Theo Boiten)

said, 'the most amazing feat the RAF ever had or ever could perform'. The massive Möhne, Eder and Sorpe Dams served the industrial Ruhr Basin and more than a dozen hydroelectric power plants relied on their waters. So did foundries, steelworks, chemical plants and other factories fuelling Germany's war effort. Winston Churchill had authorised the operation and he used it as a coup to seek greater support from the USA

Gibson was a straight-talking, no bullshit sort of bloke. He wouldn't ask you to do anything he had not first done himself. Because we had been flying so intensively we were scruffy, with unpressed suits and tarnished buttons, and when the Station CO saw us, all hell was let loose. He read us the riot act and told us to parade for a punishment march. Gibson told him, 'In that case, I'll be leading them'. That shut him up! Gibson made it clear we were there to do a job, not to play silly buggers. But the other two squadrons on the base took an intense dislike to us because we were allowed to violate all the rules of flying. We had been quarantined for six weeks, having no contact with civilians, no access to telephones and being unable to write letters. I'd been married for less than a year, but I couldn't tell my wife what I was up to. So speculation was rife. Some of us thought the targets were submarine and torpedo boat pens. It was a great surprise when we found out where we were going.
Ray Grayston, flight engineer in Australian Pilot Officer Les Knight's crew of N for Nan, *whose target was the Eder Dam. Of Knight, Grayston says, 'Les was remarkably quiet. He didn't smoke or drink, didn't go out with women, couldn't drive a car or even ride a bike. But he could fly a Lancaster! He was a brilliant pilot, even in the worst predicaments. I never heard him issue a harsh word, apart from telling us to shut up because we were all talking at the same time on the radiotelegraphy. Even though I was the flight engineer Les would let me fly the plane to get used to the controls. You never knew when you could be shot, so it was wise to have somebody to take over in an emergency. I did quite a few hours flying'*

Nearly all the flak had now stopped and the other boys came down from the hills to have a closer look to see what had been done. There was no doubt about it at all – the Möhne Dam had been breached and the gunners on top of the dam, except for one man, had all run for their lives towards the safety of solid ground; this remaining gunner was a brave man, but one of the boys quickly extinguished his flak with a burst of well-aimed tracer. Now it was all quiet, except for the roar of the water, which steamed and hissed its way from its 150ft head. Then we began to shout and scream and act like madmen over the R/T, for this was a tremendous sight, a sight which probably no man will ever see again.

Quickly I told Hutch to tap out the message, 'Nigger', to my station and when this was handed to the air officer commanding there was (I heard afterwards) great excitement in the operations room. The scientist jumped up and danced around the room.

Then I looked again at the dam and at the water, while all around me the boys were doing the same. It was the most amazing sight. The whole valley was beginning to fill with fog from the steam of the gushing water and down in the foggy valley we saw cars speeding along the roads in front of this great wave of water, which was chasing them and going faster than they could ever hope to go. I saw their headlights burning and I saw water overtake them, wave by wave and then the colour of the headlights underneath the water changing from light blue to green, from green to dark purple, until there was no longer anything except the water bouncing down in great waves. The floods raced on, carrying with them as they went – viaducts, railways, bridges and everything that stood in their path. Three miles beyond the dam the remains of Hoppy's aircraft were still burning gently, a dull red glow on the ground. Hoppy had been avenged.

Enemy Coast Ahead, *Wing Commander Guy Gibson VC DSO★ DFC★, 617 Squadron, describing the attack on the first target, the Möhne Dam. Gibson went in and sent his mine successfully bouncing up to the concrete wall, where it sank and exploded. The next two Lancasters missed. M-Mother, flown by Flight Lieutenant John V. 'Hoppy' Hopgood DFC★, was shot out of the sky and his mine exploded on the powerhouse on the other side of the dam. Flight Lieutenant Mick Martin DFC RAAF in P-Popsie got his mine away but the dam held. The fourth and fifth hits by Squadron Leader Melvyn 'Dinghy' Young DFC★ and Flight Lieutenant David J. H. Maltby finally breached the dam at 0056hrs. Then Gibson flew on to the Dam Busters' next target, the Eder Dam. Gibson, circling above, sent two Lancasters in ahead of N for Nan. The first was L-Love piloted by Flight Lieutenant Dave J. Shannon DFC RAAF, then Z for Zebra piloted by Squadron Leader Henry E. Maudslay DFC*

[Ray Grayston watched Shannon make five runs at the Eder Dam before eventually releasing his mine and] it was way off centre. Then Maudslay made his run and it was a disaster. His mine bounced over the dam wall and exploded in the valley below. Gibson called him up to ask him if he was all right and all he said was 'I think so' and those were the last words we heard from him. We think he flew on for a while before crashing or being shot down.

So then it was us, the last of the main wave of nine aircraft. We'd never practised anything like it. When we saw the location, we thought it was near impossible. The Germans were so certain no aircraft could attack it that they had not defended it with anti-aircraft batteries, which was the good news. The bad news was that the dam wall was at the head of a narrow, crooked reservoir in a steep, wooded valley with a sharp hill at either end and a peninsula jutting out in the middle. We would have to fly over a castle 1,000ft above the reservoir, drop down like a stone, fly above the water at no more than 60ft, hop over the peninsula, drop down again and release our mine, then climb like fury to miss the hill at the far end. I suppose we were lucky really. We did one dummy run and got it pretty well right. So we circled and came in again at about 800ft. As flight engineer, I was responsible for the air speed. I'd tumbled to the fact that if I chopped my engines right back and let them idle she would glide down to 60ft. That's what I did – with my fingers crossed that they'd open

Wings over the Derwent during the fiftieth anniversary of the Dams raid in May 1993. (Author)

up again. At 60ft I slammed the throttles forward and they did. The machine took a few moments to level off and seconds later we released the mine. Immediately afterwards we went into a blistering climb, with engines hammering up through the emergency gauge to get enough power to get out the other end. As we banked, we looked back and, by God, we'd been spot on, absolutely spot on. A huge column of water had been thrown up to about 1,000ft. We had hit bang in the middle of the dam and had blown a hole straight through it. The bottom came out, then the top fell away and that was it. There was great excitement among the crew about our success. We were all on a high for a few minutes. Gibson called up and said simply, 'OK fellas, that's your job done. No hanging about, you know. Make your way home.' That was easier said than done, of course, because the Germans had woken up to what we'd done and they were out to get us. And they did get a few.

Ray Grayston, flight engineer, N for Nan. The Eder Dam, the largest masonry dam in Germany – 1,310ft wide, 138ft high, 119ft thick at the base and 20ft thick at the top – opened up and 200 million cubic metres of water began to pour into the valley below. Describing the breach, Gibson wrote that it was 'as if a gigantic hand had pushed a hole through cardboard'. Banking below him, Les Knight reported a 'torrent of water causing a tidal wave almost 30ft high'. The crew of N for Nan watched in awe as car headlights in the path of the water turned from bright white to murky green to nothing. The remaining aircraft, still with mines aboard, went on to attack the Sorpe Dam. Though badly damaged they failed to breach its massive wall. However, the damage inflicted in the first two attacks proved the operation's success. The surge of water from the Möhne and Eder Dams knocked out power stations, damaged factories and cut water, gas and electricity supplies. As many as 1,300 civilians, including about 500 Ukrainian women slave labourers, died. Eight Lancasters were lost, fifty-three men were killed and three were captured. The Dam Busters proved that the war in Europe was being prosecuted dramatically well at a time most of President Roosevelt's advisers were committed to targeting Japan first. Two days after the operation, Churchill was given a standing ovation at the Trident Conference with Roosevelt in Washington. Gibson was awarded the Victoria Cross for his leadership on the raid. Later he was sent to America as an air attaché but he begged the Air Ministry to allow him to return to operations. On 19/20 September 1944 he flew from Woodhall Spa in a Mosquito of 627 Squadron and crashed at 2300hrs near Steenbergen, Holland, killing himself and his navigator, Squadron Leader J.B. Warwick (twenty-one other veterans of the Dams raid were also killed on ops)

'Gibson spotted Micky Martin with satisfaction. They had met at Buckingham palace when Gibson was getting his DSO and the King was pinning on the first of Martin's DFCs. Though he came from Sydney, Martin was in the RAF, slight but good looking, with a wild glint in his eyes and a monstrous moustache that ended raggedly out by his ears.' (Ron Bartley Collection)

Lancaster gate guardian at Scampton. (Author)

Above left: 'Les Munro was a New Zealander, tall, blue-chinned and solemn, a little older than the others. He was standing by the bar looking into space when Gibson located him. "Glad to see you Les", Gibson said. "I see you're setting a good example already, drinking a little and thinking a lot." Munro up-ended his pint and drained it. "No sir," he said, "thinking a little and drinking a lot."' Flight Lieutenant J. Les Munro RNZAF, pilot, W-William, on the Sorpe Dam raid, 16/1May 1943. (Author)

Above right: 'Towering above the rest was the blond head of a man who weighed nearly fifteen stone, with a pink face and pale blue eyes; good looking in a rugged way. Joe McCarthy, from Brooklyn, USA, former life-guard at Coney island, had joined the RAF before America came into the war.' Flight Lieutenant Joe C. McCarthy DFC RCAF, pilot, T-Tommy, on the Sorpe Dam raid, 16/17 May 1943. (Author)

W/C Guy Gibson DSO★ DFC★ (centre), when CO of 106 Squadron from 14 March 1942, with his two flight commanders, S/L/ John Searby (left) and S/L/ Peter Ward-Hunt DFC (right), at Syerston before leaving to form 617 Squadron. Behind is Gibson's Lancaster III ED593 ZN-Y Admiral Prune II which survived at least seventy-two ops and finished the war as a ground instruction airframe. In mid-March 1943, Gibson, having completed two bomber tours and one night-fighter tour, left to take commang of 617 Sqaudron. (IWM)

617 SQUADRON, RAF SCAMPTON, LINCOLNSHIRE, 5 GROUP
PRIMARY TARGETS: MÖHNE, EDER AND SORPE DAMS
SECONDARY TARGETS; SCHWEIM, ENNERPE AND DIEMI DAMS

Aircraft (Lancaster BIII)	Captain	Target	Remarks
ED864 B-Beer	Flight Lieutenant David Astell DFC	Möhne	Shot down en route to the dam
ED886 O-Orange	Flight Sergeant W.C. Townsend	Ennerpe	
ED906 J-Johnny	Flight Lieutenant David J.H. Maltby DFC	Möhne/Eder	(KIA 14/15 September 1943)
ED910 C-Charlie	Pilot Officer Warner Ottley	Lister	Lost en route to the dam
ED918 F-Freddy	Flight Sergeant Ken W. Brown RCAF	Sorpe	
ED923 T-Tommy	Flight Lieutenant Joe C. McCarthy DFC RCAF	Sorpe	
ED925 M-Mother	Flight Lieutenant John V. 'Hoppy' Hopgood DFC★	Möhne	Lost at the Möhne Dam
ED929 L-Love	Flight Lieutenant Dave J. Shannon DFC RAAF	Möhne/Eder	
ED934 K-King	Flight Sergeant Vernon W. Byers RCAF	Sorpe	Lost
ED937 Z-Zebra	Squadron Leader Henry E. Maudslay DFC	Möhne	Lost: blown up by the blast of his own bomb
ED865 S-Sugar	Pilot Officer Lewis J. Burpee DFM RCAF	Sorpe	Lost: killed by flak
ED887 A-Apple	Squadron Leader Melvyn 'Dinghy' Young DFC	Möhne/Eder	Shot down over the Dutch coast on return
ED909 P-Popsie	Flight Lieutenant Mick Martin DFC RAAF	Möhne	Returned after bombing Möhne
ED912 N-Nuts	Flight Lieutenant L.E.S. Knight RAAF	Möhne/Eder	(KIA 15 September 1943)
ED921 W-William	Flight Lieutenant J. Les Munro RNZAF	Sorpe	Damaged by flak over Vlieland on Dutch coast on the way in and forced to abort
ED924 Y-Yorker	Flight Sergeant Cyril T. Anderson	Sorpe	
ED927 E-Edward	Flight Lieutenant Robert N.G. Barlow DFC RAAF	Sorpe	Lost
ED932 G-George	Wing Commander Guy Gibson DSO DFC	Möhne/Eder	(KIA 19/20 September 1944). His crew on the Dams raid were all lost on 15 September 1943)
ED936 H-Harry	Pilot Officer Geoff Rice	Sorpe	Hit the sea before crossing enemy coast and aborted, flying home on two engines (KIA 20 December 1943)

EIGHTEEN
BLACK FRIDAY

Like the gentleman guns in a partridge shoot waiting for the coveys to sweep over them. The resulting
slaughter was much the same.

During my leave in Canada, Bomber Command suffered its worst defeat of the war. This
was the Nuremberg raid on the night of 30/31 March 1944, with the loss of more aircrew
than were lost in the entire Battle of Britain. Over 800 experienced aircrew were dead,
wounded or missing or prisoners of war. Bomber Command's maximum acceptable rate
of loss was considered to be 200 four-engined bombers with their seven-man crews a
month. Not much to look forward to on my return.
Pilot Officer J. Ralph Wood DFC CD RCAF

And I said to the boys, look it's on for young and old tonight. Just keep your eyes on
the sky because they started to fall within ten minutes of crossing the coast and from
then to the target the air was not only of good visibility but seemed to be bright. The
moon was really shining brightly although it wasn't a full moon… I was first back at
Waddington and Sir Ralph Cochrane called me up to the control tower. He said, 'How
did it go?'.
　I said, 'Jerry got a century before lunch today.'
　'He didn't quite – he got 95.'
*Squadron Leader Arthur William Doubleday DFC RAAF (later Wing Commander Doubleday
DSO DFC and CO of 61 Squadron), 'B' Flight CO, 467 Squadron RAAF in 5 Group at
Waddington. In total, 795 bombers were dispatched, and the formation was attacked just before the
bombers reached the Belgian border. The attacks lasted for the next hour, and eighty-two bombers
were lost en route to and near the target. In all, sixty-four Lancasters and thirty-one Halifaxes
(11.9 per cent of the force dispatched) were lost. Another twelve crashed on return, fifty-nine
were badly damaged and 745 aircrew were missing. It was the biggest Bomber Command loss
of the Second World War – a total casualty rate of 20.8 per cent*

Instead of the bomber stream being 5 miles wide it was more like 50. Some had already been shot down and, before I reached the far side of the stream, they were being shot down on my left. Masses of 'Window' were being tossed out of the bombers, which also jammed our radar. We tried three times, but each time came up below a bomber, the rear gunner spotting us the third time, his tracer coming uncomfortably close whilst his pilot did a corkscrew. It was hopeless; we were doing more harm than good. Ahead bombers were being shot down one after another, some going all the way down in flames, some blowing up in the air, the rest blowing up as they hit the ground. I counted forty-four shot down on this leg to Nürnburg. What was happening behind I could only guess... I was inwardly raging at the incompetence of the top brass at Bomber Command.

Flight Lieutenant R.G. 'Tim' Woodman, Mosquito pilot, 169 Squadron, 100 Group Bomber Support

Jack worked swiftly to calculate winds, which were then transmitted back to Group by the WOP, Jock Michie, who had to risk breaking the radio silence that all bombers observed. At Group the winds from all sources were averaged out and re-transmitted back to the bomber stream in the half hourly 'group broadcast'. The windfinders complained that Group were far too conservative and always played safe with the averages. Jack was still disgruntled about the last Berlin raid when he had found winds of well over 100 knots due to freak weather conditions (since known as 'jetstream'). Group would not accept them, which badly upset the planned time over the target. The intercom crackled again, 'Nav to pilot. Group has done it again, Johnny. They are still using the forecast winds, which will put everybody north of track.'

Unwelcome proof of this came from both gunners who had been reporting unusually large numbers of 'scarecrow flares', mostly off to the port quarter and quite a way behind. 'Scarecrow flares' had been first mentioned at briefing some weeks earlier with the explanation that the Germans were sending this impressive firework up to 20,000ft to look like exploding aircraft and lower our morale. We hardened cynics were pretty sure that they were exploding aircraft but, knowing nothing of the night-fighters using upward-firing tracerless cannon, we could not understand why there were not the usual exchange of tracer in the normal 'curve of pursuit'. What the gunners were reporting were the deaths of over fifty bombers. This was the night that the German controllers got their calculations right and ignored a spoof attack in north Germany, deciding that the bomber stream would use a favourite flak gap just south of Cologne to penetrate into the hinterland and maybe turn left to Leipzig or Berlin. Me 110 and Ju 88 squadrons had been pulled in from the north and south to orbit fighter beacons 'Ida' and 'Otto' near Bonn and Frankfurt. They could hardly believe it when they found the bomber stream flying *en masse* between the two beacons and into their waiting arms, like the gentleman guns in a partridge shoot waiting for the coveys to sweep over them. The resulting slaughter was much the same.

In the perfect conditions it was easy to follow the bomber stream and the aces among them managed to shoot down six or seven apiece before they had to break off and refuel. We, the lucky ones at the front end, had managed to slip through the deadly gap before the wolves gathered and we ploughed on towards turning point C where we made a right-handed turn almost due south towards Nürnberg 76 miles away. Normally, a steep turn like this would throw off many fighters, but conditions tonight so favoured them that they were able to follow round the corner and shoot down another thirty bombers...

John Chadderton DFC, pilot, Lancaster E-Easy, 44 Squadron, whose crew were on their twenty-third operation

Halifax on fire. Some thirty-one Halifaxes were lost on the Nuemberg raid. (IWM)

We were flying as 'windfinders' as usual. As we flew south of Cologne at about 26,000ft, Len Whitehead, the mid-upper gunner, and I began reporting aircraft going down. Sid got a bit fed up with logging them after a while and told us that as there were so many they must be 'scarecrows'. As we began approaching the target area a Lancaster flew close alongside us. It was upside down and blazing like a comet. I asked Sid to come and look at this 'scarecrow'. We tried to turn away from it but it seemed to follow us. Then it slowly dipped and exploded.

As we approached Nürnberg we were horrified to see the great spread of the target area. Most aircraft were turning and bombing too soon. We saw the last of the PFF aircraft going down with TIs pouring out of it… We continued turning on to the target but by the time we arrived all the markers had gone out. We began to circle. Sandy Lyons, the bomb aimer, thought he saw either a railway station or yards and so we bombed that and left the target area. We continued to log aircraft going down as we flew along the 'Long Leg'.

Sergeant Leslie Cromarty DFM, rear gunner, Lancaster Royal Pontoon *of 61 Squadron*

NINETEEN
LINGO

Aircrew spoke a rare lingo of their own

Dear Boys of the RAF,

I have just seen that the RAF flyers have a life-saving jacket they call a 'Mae West', because it bulges in all the right places. Well, I consider it a swell honour to have such great guys wrapped up in you, know what I mean?

Yes, it's kind of a nice thought to be flying all over with brave men… even if I'm only there by proxy in the form of a life-saving jacket, or a life-saving jacket in my form.

I always thought that the best way to hold a man was in your arms – but I guess when you're up in the air a plane is safer. You've got to keep everything under control.

Yeah, the jacket idea is all right and I can't imagine anything better than to bring you boys of the RAF soft and happy landings. But what I'd like to know about that life-saving jacket is – has it got dangerous curves and soft shapely shoulders.

You've heard of Helen of Troy, the dame with the face that launched a thousand ships… why not a shape that will stop thousands of tanks?

If I do get in the dictionary – where you say you want to put me – how will they describe me? As a warm and clinging life-saving garment worn by aviators? Or an aviator's jacket that supplies the woman's touch while the boys are flying around nights? How would you describe me, boys?

I've been in *Who's Who* and I know what's what, but it'll be the first time I ever made the dictionary.

Sin-sationally,
Mae West, January 1942

When I joined Ninety-Eight Squadron
In late May of nineteen forty-four
Strange words were used in conversation
Puzzling words I had not heard before.

A 'Sprog' was what they at first called me
Meaning that on an Op I had never flown
'Flak' was the term used for anti-aircraft fire
Aircrew spoke a rare lingo of their own.

'Flak Valley', I learned was the Ruhr Valley
Where many bombers had been mortally hit
With 'Ack-Ack' guns it was heavily defended
The flak was so thick you could taxi on it.

'No Ball' targets were the V-1 launch sites
From where was launched a pilotless plane
'Doodle Bug' or 'Flying Bomb' we called them
A new weapon that brought death and pain.

'Bogie' was a strange, unidentified aircraft
Given location was by an hour on the clock
'High' or 'Low' meant above or below you
I was now learning the way aircrew talk.

'Prang' meant a good hit on your target
A wheels-up landing on water was to 'Ditch'
'Abortive' was when you abandoned a mission
New words that would my learning enrich.

'Mae West' was your inflatable life jacket
Keeping you afloat if 'Downed In The Drink'
That is if you escaped from your aircraft
Before under the water it would quickly sink.

Soon I would learn this strange language
The unique vocabulary spoken by just a few
Jargon without meaning to all the outsiders
But it is the lingo of a bomber's aircrew.

'Aircrew Lingo', Sergeant George 'Ole' Olson RCAF, air gunner

As far as possible, crews used to like to stick to their 'own' aircraft. It was a bit of a thing really: we tended to be superstitious. What about the gremlins? We hated carrying passengers, especially padres. Most of us felt close enough to God without having them on board to cramp our styles!

Squadron Leader (later Group Captain) A.F. Wallace. OC B Flight, 620 Squadron June 1943–September 1944. A gremlin is a mythical mischievous creature invented by the RAF, to whom is attributed the blame for anything that goes wrong in the air or on the ground. There are different sorts of gremlins skilled in different sorts and grades of evil. The origin of the term is obscure, but has been stated variously to go back as far as the Royal Naval Air

(Punch)

"And pray, what might 'Nil excretum Taurus' mean."

". . . and this is the undercarriage control."

"Whaddya mean — Back a bit?!"

"Calling C for Charlie. Calling C for Charlie. All right — sulk if you want to."

Service, to have some connection with the RAF in Russia and the Kremlin, and to have come from India, where, it is alleged, in the early 1920s an officer was opening a bottle of Fremlin's Ale when the overheated gas blew out the cork, taking him by surprise. Meaning to say, 'A goblin has jumped out of my Fremlin's', he spoonerised and said, 'A gremlin has jumped out of my Foblin's'. In his book It's a Piece of Cake!: RAF Slang Made Easy *(Sylvan Press, around 1942), Squadron Leader C.H. Ward-Jackson adds, Officers and airmen who are on the right side of the gremlins are thought very highly of by station commanders but are objects of suspicion among their fellows.'*

The meteorology reports were very important to the success of our operations. The met section, at times, left a lot to be desired. We called the meteorology information 'met gen', which usually turned out to be one of the following: 'Pukka gen', meaning 'good information', or 'duff gen', meaning 'bad information'.

Pilot Officer J. Ralph Wood, Whitley navigator, 102 Squadron

Press on regardless – never mind the weather
Press on regardless – it's a piece of cake
Press on regardless – we'll all press on together
'Cos you're bound to see the Dummer or the Steinhuder Lake.

(Tune: 'Poor Joey')

First the port outer went. 'What do we do skipper?' the crew said.
I said: 'Press on regardless.'
Then the port inner went. 'What the **** do we do now skipper?' they said.
I said: 'Say after me the Lord's Prayer.'

Bomber pilot

A quickening of interest, a sort of tensed leaning forward to hear better, among the pilots, who a few minutes earlier had been listening abstractedly to the planning details, greeted the intelligence officer's commencement of the current summary of the location and weight of the flak, searchlight and night-fighter defences of Germany as it was likely to affect us.

There was, it seemed, nothing to worry about.

'Should be a piece of cake, chaps', he said, smiling at the cynical grunts and mirthless snorts of laughter from the old hands.

Geoff Taylor, RAAF, pilot, Z–Zebra

No Ball targets were the V-1 launch sites. (IWM)

TWENTY
SHOOTING A LINE

I'll shoot 'em down sir, I'll shoot 'em down, sir,
I'll shoot 'em down if they don't shoot at me.
Then we'll go to the Ops Room and shoot a horrid line, sir,
And then we'll all get the DFC.

A Hun bomber, chased over the wilds of North Wales, caught fire. The crew bailed out. One of them, a man of 6ft, with the face of a boxer, landed in a field near a lonely farm whose only occupant was a young farm worker. The lad immediately jumped into action, seized the nearest weapon to hand, which happened to be a pitchfork and strode out, the whole 48in of him, to meet the enemy from the sky. *'Rho dy ddwylo i fyny, yr hen ddiafol'* ('Put up your hands, you old devil'), he challenged in Welsh and made a stab with the pitchfork. The Nazi put up his hands. 'Me no speak English', he protested. The 4ft defender of Wales glowered at him and made another stab with the pitchfork. 'Me no speak English, neither', he replied indignantly.
    Laugh With the RAF

'It's disgraceful', said the dear old lady indignantly, 'permitting all this gambling in the RAF and causing the poor young fellows to run into debt.'
'What do you mean, Auntie?' enquired her nephew in surprise.
'Why, these sweeps the RAF are having every day', persisted Auntie, pointing to a newspaper. 'The Irish Sweep was bad enough, but daily sweeps are far worse. No wonder Mr Churchill said that never did so many owe so much to so few!'
    'Sweeps', Laugh with the RAF

There was a story going around about a Whitley crew becoming lost and running out of fuel. The pilot set the automatic pilot and told his crew to bail out. This they did, with the exception of the tail gunner, whose intercom had become disconnected and he failed to hear the order. A short time later the aircraft made a remarkably good landing on a sloping hill in Scotland. The tail gunner, upon vacating his turret, commented loudly on the pilot's smooth landing. You could almost see him passing out when he discovered he was the only occupant of the aircraft.

Pilot Officer J. Ralph Wood DFC CD RCAF

The Luftwaffe now rates Mosquitoes on night attacks so high that when a Nazi pilot shoots one down he is allowed to count it as two.

British newspaper column

" That makes us quits for the damn great hole they made in my garden."

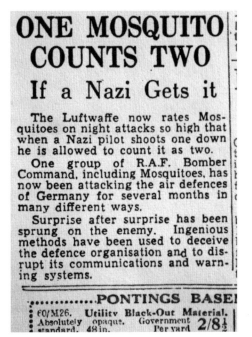

ONE MOSQUITO COUNTS TWO
If a Nazi Gets it

The Luftwaffe now rates Mosquitoes on night attacks so high that when a Nazi pilot shoots one down he is allowed to count it as two.

One group of R.A.F. Bomber Command, including Mosquitoes, has now been attacking the air defences of Germany for several months in many different ways.

Surprise after surprise has been sprung on the enemy. Ingenious methods have been used to deceive the defence organisation and to disrupt its communications and warning systems.

·············PONTINGS BASE
FO/M26. Utility Black-Out Material.
Absolutely opaque. Government standard. 48 in. Per yard **2/8½**

Above right: *It didn't!*

Strange events are unfolding within the German Reich. It is only gradually and with little certainty yet, that we can build up a picture of those events. On a recent evening, Herr Von Dickerblne, a local party official, observed a handsome Jersey cow descending by parachute over a farm near Essen. He watched this event with some interest, when suddenly his suspicions were aroused by observing that the cow had a wireless aerial stretched between its horns. By the time he had returned to the scene with 400 members of the Gestapo, the sagacious cow had mingled with the other cattle on the farm and the matter for the time being was dismissed.

Next morning, the farmer's daughter, Fraulein Hammerkiavier, was going the rounds with her milking stool and pail when a strange thing happened. One of the cows showed signs of extreme embarrassment when she tried to approach it. She had hardly set down her stool when the cow mounted a tandem bicycle, which had been concealed in the hedge, and made off like a mad thing.

[Reynolds News

Dear Mum,
   I'm sorry to hear Willie's got measles and that Uncle George fell down
stairs but didn't hurt himself much. . . .

During the next night a considerable force of Allied specialised troops entered Germany by swimming up certain rivers from the sea. They burnt their water-wings and disappeared into the woods. It would not be politic to disclose full details of the way in which the Jersey cow is directing the operations of this force!

Since that fateful invasion, the German leaders have had little peace of mind. Not a German professor but has had his spectacles broken by an unseen hand. Many important buildings have been fitted with wheels during the night and pushed across the frontier into France. In almost every German public park the rowing boats have been mysteriously scuttled while the park was shut. Rude words have been scrawled on the Führer's blotting pad. And Goering's boots have been filled with treacle.

'*The Rampole-Frogworthy Plan*' *by Squirt,* Laugh with the RAF

'I dived to sea level.'
'I sat on his tail.'
'He was a sitting bird.'
'I gave him a short sharp burst.'
'The rear gunner slumped back.'
'The gas-works seemed to come up and hit me in the eye.'
'The whole place was left burning. I saw the flames thousands of miles away.'

'*Modesty on the Ether*', Flight

'You could almost hear the tracer sizzling as it went past.'
'I've flown a Beaufighter at nought feet on instruments.'
'We do our air tests on ops.'
'We've been doing our ops so fast that I've lost count!'
'I'm always glad to go on ops; it takes my mind off the war.'
'I remember one night, I was shooting-up road signs...'

(Punch)

"... and light but accurate flak."

"I wasn't sure whether it was one of theirs or one of ours, so I only gave it a short burst."

"... and then with a final twenty-minute burst, I more or less dismantles the entire aircraft."

"We went down to a few inches."

'You may cuss the Tiger Moth, while you're blowing off the froth.' (DH)

[The Aeroplane

" —All the way from Hamburg on one engine."

'Why *I* must buy everyone else a drink every time *I* shoot down a wretched Hun, is something I can never understand.'

David Langdon, *Punch*

Navigator: 'Did you hit the drogue?'
Pilot: 'No, I left it this time. I shot so many away on the gunnery course, they're getting a bit short.'
'We've never been known to come back unserviceable unless the 'plane's practically in two pieces.'
'When things get rough I light my lighter, throw it out and get a pinpoint.'
'The only time I get to sleep is when I'm on ops.'
Pilot on his low-flying prowess: 'I used to cut the grass for my wife when we lived out.'
   From the Line Book

Pilot to ground crew: 'I could not drop my bombs over the target.' After the ground crew had listed all the possible reasons except for lateral thinking, the pilot answered: 'I'll tell you all why. We were upside down.'
   Anon

The Cadet on his first solo had engine trouble and was forced to land his Tiger Moth in a field. He was followed a little later by his instructor overhead, who, seeing his predicament in the tiny field, thought: 'If he can land in that small field, so can I.'
   The instructor brought the Tiger in but made a hash of it and crashed in a heap of tangled wreckage. Extricating himself with as much aplomb as he could muster, he said to the onrushing cadet: 'How on earth did you get your Tiger Moth into this field?'
The cadet replied: 'Through that gate over there sir!'
   Anon

Our job – 681 Spits and 684 Mossies – was to give notice of any Jap reinforcing after Slim's 14th 'Forgotten Army' had foiled the Jap invasion of India and was following them across the Yomas into the plains of northern Burma. We did this by photographing every town, every tin-pot port, every 'drome, roads and every inch of the railway system. We could keep track of every railway wagon the Japs had. If the Japs mislaid one we could have told them where it was. We had a line shoot. The old stations had toilets at each end of the platform, so we said, 'The Jap stationmasters can't go to the crapper without our knowing.'
   M. Howland RAAF, 684 Squadron pilot

'Reminds me of the time I sank the *Tirpitz*', comments a Spitfire pilot.
'Just one pass, of course, old boy.'
POW commenting on a sketch in the Volkischer Beobachter *and* Allgemeine Zeitung *of a Fw 190 at low level, strafing a British battleship*

TWENTY-ONE
BLESS 'EM ALL

There's many a troopship just leaving Bombay,
Bound for old Blighty's shore
Heavily laden with time expired men
Bound for the land they adore
There's many an airman just finished his time,
And many a twerp signing on
They'll get no promotion
This side of the ocean
So cheer up my lad, Bless 'em all.

The C-in-C, a Lancaster pilot, took the left-hand seat of the Sunderland and a young sergeant pilot took the right-hand seat. The C-in-C took off from Calshot water and headed inland. He approached the runway of an airfield, dropped the flaps, throttled back and then, much to the relief of the sergeant (who, conscious of his rank, had remained tight-lipped throughout the descent), was relieved to see the C-in-C open up the throttles and set course for Calshot, whereupon he alighted. When the Sunderland had stopped, the C-in-C said: 'I bet I had you worried, sergeant? Well, son, I'm full of tricks.'

With that he opened the door and stepped out!

Anon

I flew a tour on Halifaxes in 102 Squadron in 1942/3. During this time a donkey was tethered in a remote part of the airfield – it was alleged that the CO was unaware of its existence. Where it came from I do not know. The donkey was 'looked after' by several members of ground crew and aircrew. There was plenty of grazing for it but they kept it supplied with tit bits from cookhouse and NAAFI. Sadly, one morning word got around that the donkey had died during the night. The problem now arose of how to dispose of it.

'I'll shoot 'em down sir, I'll shoot 'em down, sir, / I'll shoot 'em down if they don't shoot at me. / Then we'll go to the Ops Room and shoot a horrid line, sir, / And then we'll all get the DFC.' (Gordon 'Reg' Thackeray Collection)

'The long and the short and the tall.' (S/L Bob Davies)

'Faster, boys—its the only bit of shade we may see for weeks.'

Fitz, *Punch*

'Now pilots are highly trained people / and wings are not easily won… / But without the work of the maintenance man / our pilots would march with a gun…' (Tim Woodman Collection)

Opposite below: *'When the Sunderland had stopped, the C-in-C said: "I bet I had you worried Sergeant? Well, son, I'm full of tricks." (Ashley Annis Collection)*

Right: *'Where are they now, those young men of all nations / Who flew though they knew not what might lie ahead, / And those who returned with their mission accomplished / And next night would beat up the Saracen's Head?' (IWM)*

'Flight Sergeant said: "Go and give 'em a hand in the cookhouse." Trouble is I don't know the first thing about cooking.'

David Langdon, *Punch*

Below: *'During this time a donkey was tethered in a remote part of the airfield – it was alleged that the CO was unaware of its existence. Where it came from I do not know…' (Dave Smith Collection)*

It was finally decided that one of the crews would that night take an unusual additional payload and dispose of it over Germany. But which crew would do the deed? A hastily arranged draw took place, involving crewmembers who had been 'looking after' the donkey. Ours was the 'unlucky' crew that drew the short straw. Our skipper 'understandably' was not very happy about the situation. He said he did not even want to know it was on board. With much heaving and pushing the navigator and engineer dispatched the donkey out of the crew door on the port side of the aircraft as soon as we were over German territory. One wonders what were the thoughts and comments of those on the receiving end, 16,000ft below.

Drop The Dead Donkey, John Anderson Hurst

TWENTY-TWO
TYPES

Vain type –	Undoes five buttons where one would do.
Excitable type –	Pants twisted, can't find the hole, tears pants in temper.
Sociable type –	Joins friends in piss whether he wants one or not – says it costs nothing.
Timid type –	Can't piss if anyone is watching, pretends he has pissed and sneaks back later.
Indifferent type –	Urinal being occupied, pisses in sink.
Clever type –	Pisses without holding his tool, shows off by adjusting necktie at same time.
Frivolous type –	Plays the stream up, down and across. Tries to piss on flies as they pass.
Absent-minded type –	Opens vest, takes out tie and pisses himself.
Disgruntled type –	Stands for a while, grunts, farts and walks out muttering.
Personality type –	Tells jokes while pissing, shakes drop off his tool with a flourish.
Sneaky type –	Drops silent fart whilst pissing, sniffs and looks at bloke next to him.
Sloppy type –	Pisses down his trousers into his shoes and walks out with flyhole open and adjusts.
Learned type –	Reads books or papers whilst pissing.
Childish type –	Looks down at the bottom of the urinal while pissing to watch the bubbles.
Strong type –	Bangs tool on side of urinal to knock the drops off.

TWENTY-THREE
GROUND CREWS

To the men who turned the spanner, to the men who pulled the wrench,
To the men who did refuelling with the octane in heavy stench,
To the 'genius' with radar, to the man who fired the gun,
To the services crews in freezing cold when working was not fun,
To those who brought the bombs along and loaded them aboard,
To the artist of the mascot, be it Pluto or a broad,
To the cooks who cooked the dinner, though not always Cordon Bleu,
To the girl who brought the break truck (and what you thought of her?),
To those who spread the bullshit from their office in the warm,
To those who crewed the ambulance in case you came to harm;
For each and every flyer owes a debt he cannot pay
To those who worked upon the ground and sent him on his way.

'Cheers (A Flyer's Toast)', Jasper Miles

For lack of a bolt the engine was lost,
For want of an engine the bomber was lost,
For want of a bomber the crew were lost,
For want of the crew the battle was lost,
For want of the battle our freedom was lost,
And all for the want of a bolt.

They were the backbone without whose expertise no operations would have been possible. They worked all hours and in all weathers to ensure that our aircraft were serviceable. And on many occasions when we carried out two or three ops in a day they were always on duty to refuel, bomb-up and re-arm the guns and patch up the odd flak damage. Very rarely did they grumble and on the occasions when they did we fully sympathised with

'They were the backbone without whose expertise no operations would have been possible. They worked all hours and in all weathers to ensure that our aircraft were serviceable.' (Ken Lowes via Theo Boiten)

them. Their 'Chiefy' was an older man with years of service and encouraged his lads in every possible way. On the occasional 'stand down' we would take them out to one of the local pubs, which they enjoyed and we most certainly appreciated their interest in us and our aircraft, which they considered to be their aircraft. Although our closest association was with our ground crews, we also remember with gratitude the WAAF drivers who took us to our aircraft. We remember the parachute packers, the cooks who provided excellent meals at some very odd hours and, of course, many other trades too numerous to mention. Our successes were due to team effort and *esprit de corps*.

John Bateman, Boston gunner

> Now pilots are highly trained people
> and wings are not easily won...
> But without the work of the maintenance man
> our pilots would march with a gun...
> So when you see the mighty aircraft
> as they mark their way through the air
> The grease stained man with the wrench in his hand
> is the man who put them there.

Anon

RAAF and RAF ground crew working on a Mosquito's Merlin engine. (Ken Lowes via Theo Boiten)

It seemed quite a long time after we had arrived before the kite was spotted silhouetted against a sky that was breaking down. It looked like a giant lizard on tall front legs. As we pulled closer to it we could see damage to the fuselage. We dismounted and surrounded the kite but found no crew. I did notice that the front turret was at some 45 degrees and that there was a figure still inside. I shouted to tell Chiefy what I had seen and was ordered into the aircraft to find out what was going on. I clambered up to the front. I could see the turret doors were damaged. Running back to the fuselage doors I shouted out my findings. As there had been no movement from the figure in the turret I assumed that the gunner was dead.

After a short discussion it was decided that the only way the gunner's body could be moved was by breaking the outside perspex of the gun turret. As this was some 15ft or so from the ground a trestle was required. I was told to stay with the kite whilst the rest moved off in search of some help. After they disappeared I became apprehensive and, lighting a cigarette, I started to walk around the kite. Somehow my eyes became riveted on the gun turret and in the dawn light I fancied that the figure moved now and again. 'How much longer will they be fetching the equipment', I thought? I felt very lonely stuck there with a bloody great kite and a dead man in its nose. I wondered if he was the guy who was sick just before take off.

In the distance I could now hear the noise of vehicles and approaching me was the Hillman Minx towing a mobile trestle with a mobile 'Coles' crane following. As they got closer I felt much more at ease until a voice shouted out, 'Get the fire axe from out of the kite.' Once again I entered the fuselage and peered at the partly turned turret with some horror. Grabbing the axe I quickly got outside and was then told to climb the already positioned trestle and smash the perspex away. In a dream I reached the outside of the turret only to get a closer look at the victim who was unrecognisable because his flying helmet and intercom were still over his face. There was blood spattered all over the perspex as I started carefully to crack it. Suddenly the axe was wrenched out of my hand by the orderly who was now by my side, knocking hell out of the turret. He shouted, 'You can't hurt the bugger now.'

Feeling disgusted I climbed down the trestle to be met by Chiefy. I told him what had happened and he told me to stand aside – much to my relief. By now I believe the others had gone to help and found myself next to the medical officer and Chiefy who were looking up and giving orders. I spent most of the time gazing at the ground.

Orders were given for the mobile crane to move in. For a while there seemed to be some commotion then the crane driver was given the order 'take it up'. Within seconds shouts of, 'he's coming in half', echoed across the racecourse. With his hands cupped to his mouth, the medical officer told them to go ahead. Looking up in horror I could see half a body hanging on the crane and slowly being lowered to the ground. 'God almighty', I thought, 'poor bugger'. Catching a glimpse of what looked like a large kit bag being held by others the top half of the corpse was gently lowered in. By now I felt quite sick and moved away. I did not watch the rest of the operation but was jolted to my senses by Chiefy calling me to get aboard the Hillman truck and away we made back to camp.

AC1 Jack Bennett, flight mechanic and fitter, 214 Squadron at Stradishall, late August to early September 1942

'To those who brought the bombs along and loaded them aboard, / To the artist of the mascot, be it Pluto or a broad...' (CONAM)

To the Ground Crews
Four times seven hundred Merlins
Throbbing through the inky night.
Seven times seven hundred airmen
Setting course and gaining height.
Over Norfolk, over Suffolk,
Over Lincoln's beauteous spires,
Over England we are massing
Bent on lighting freedom's fires.

Not a spark plug is misfiring,
Not a single mag drop there,
Two six fifty revs are spinning
Coarse pitched props through England's air.
Ground crews, resting in your billets,
Or relaxing in your mess,
It's the outcome of your labour
Setting course from Orfordness.

Come the dawn, we'll be returning -
If we're lucky to survive!
Tired and weary – bent and battered,
Only glad that we're alive.
Then, around us you will gather,
Shaking heads in disbelief;
What has happened to your aircraft
Overwhelms your heart with grief.

But, staunch brothers, you will rally.
Fitters, Riggers – Armourers too,
There's another raid a-building,
You know it depends on you.
Set the gantry, fetch the spanner,
Work through burning sun, or rain,
By tonight you'll have those Merlins
Setting out to fight again.

When they come to write the story
Of those bitter years of wars,
It's our deeds they will remember,
And they'll tell our tale – not yours.
Be you WAAF, or be you Airman,
Sergeant, Corporal, LAC,
It's YOUR skill and your endeavour
Helped to keep our England free.

Ken Grantham, 35 Squadron

We liked to have our own ground crews. The sergeant-in-charge of the crew was usually a 'Fitter One' – always a veritable fund of knowledge and experience. He knew all there was to know about the aircraft; at least, he always said he did – and we believed him! Then

'We feel a strong bond/And feel very fond/Of air crew past by/Who've all lov'd to fly/Through the clouds, blue skies and beyond.' (Counter Attack, being handed over to the RAF by NAAFI canteen assistant Nora Margaret Fish.) (RAF Swanton Morley)

there was the flight mechanic, the rigger, the electrician, the radio-man, the armourer; if there were problems with the radar, then the technician had to be sent for – there weren't enough of them to have one per crew! They were all 'our people', part of 'our team'. We knew that if they did their jobs properly then there was a better chance of operational success and personal survival. It was vital that the engines kept turning and that our equipment kept working. The ground crews would help us through the pre-flight checks and the run-up of the engines. We would check that the pitot-head cover was off, that the undercarriage was OK, that the bomb-doors could be opened and closed and that the bomb-load was secure. We would check the flying surfaces; the rudder, the elevators and the flaps; that the chocks were in position for the final engine-run-up; and, inside the aircraft, all our equipment, the turrets and the rest were OK. There was the Form 700 to be signed and handed back to the sergeant in charge of the crew.

Squadron Leader (later Group Captain) A.F. Wallace. OC B Flight, 620 Squadron, June 1943–September 1944

When two 'planes collided and went up in flames, the fire crew ran out of foam and came back to the stores for a further supply. Sergeant Booty, a Norwich man, demanded a voucher. He was lucky to survive! I had a run-in with the engineering officer [EO], who rang when I was alone in the stores one day. He wanted to know how many rear tyres we had for our Blenheim aircraft. Now we were out. The aircraft at Attlebridge were running on a concrete runway (it was later tarred, had sawdust rolled into it and then sprayed green camouflage). The rear wheels did not run true, so every time a 'plane landed they became u/s. I told the engineering officer that I didn't think we had any. He said I wasn't paid to

*Armourers and other ground
crew working on a Spitfire.
(IWM)*

'Yes, I think that $\frac{3}{16}$ nut on the starboard outer's prop spinner's okay now, Corp.'
David Langdon, 1945

think. Crash went the phone at the other end. Minutes later the EO arrived, bawled for the
key to the rubber store and off we went. Of course there were no tyres to be seen. I told him
I had sent a dispatch rider to Horsham St Faith, West Raynham and Marham to collect a few
until we could get a supply from a MU [Maintenance Unit]. Without a word he went.

On another occasion I was asked, 'Where are the Wellington bombers?'

I said we hadn't got any, but the Air Ministry was adamant – they wanted to know if
they were still serviceable. Then the penny dropped. They were the plywood dummies in
a field along the Norwich road, which had been put there as decoys!

One day we ordered six airscrews from 25 MU for our Bostons. A few days later I got
a 'phone call from Dereham asking for transport from the station. Six aircrews, eighteen
flyers, had turned up! As a result in future all requests for 'Airscrews' were changed to
'Propellers'!

Corporal A.E. Orford

TWENTY-FOUR

RANKS OF THE ROYAL AIR FORCE

Air Marshal

Can leap tall buildings with a single bound,
More powerful than a steam train,
Faster than a speeding bullet,
Walks on water,
Gives policy to God.

Air Commodore

Can leap tall buildings with a running start,
More powerful than a diesel engine,
Just as fast as a speeding bullet,
Walks on water if sea is calm,
Discusses policy with God.

Group Captain

Leaps short buildings with a single bound,
More powerful than a tank engine,
Can occasionally keep up with a speeding bullet,
Walks on water in small lakes,
Talks with God.

"Transplant. It was originally old Freddie Bigginshaw-Hill's before he pranged!"

Wing Commander

Leaps short buildings with a running start,
Is almost as powerful as a tank engine,
Is able to avoid a speeding bullet,
Walks on water in indoor swimming pools,
Talks to God if special request granted.

Squadron Leader

Can just clear a small hut,
Loses tug-of-war with tank engine,
Can deflect a speeding bullet,
Swims well,
Is occasionally addressed by God.

Flight Lieutenant
Demolishes chimney when leaping small huts,
Is run over by steam trains,
Can handle a gun,
Dog-paddles adequately,
Talks to animals.

Flying Officer
Runs into buildings,
Recognises steam trains two times out of three,
Is not issued with guns,
Can stay afloat with a Mae West,
Talks to walls.

Pilot Officer
Falls over doorsteps,
Says: 'I see no trains',
Trusted only with water pistols,
Stays on dry land,
Mumbles to himself.

Warrant Officer
Lifts tall buildings and walks under them,
Kicks steam trains off tracks,
Catches bullets in his teeth,
Freezes water with a single glance,
Because he is GOD.

TWENTY-FIVE
P-POPSIE

How is the Met., sir, how is the Met., sir,
How is the Met.? – it looks very dud to me.
Let's scrub it out, sir, let's scrub it out, sir,
'Cos I've got a date fixed with my popsie.

When we weren't on ops, York was our oyster. We'd go in by bus and repair to one of our two haunts, Betty's Dive Bar or, if we were in contemplative mood, The Half Moon. Here, Harry Moore, the landlord, was a great friend to any aircrew. It was said that he would cash a cheque for £5 for any aircrew officer. He claimed he had never had one bounce. He was either extremely lucky or a real gentleman. His greatest feat as far as Morty and I were concerned was that, by some alchemy known only to himself, he could conjure up a Pimms without the bottled mixture, always in short supply. When in contemplative mood, Pimms was our drink.

The Half Moon was the resort of the more senior and affluent aircrew. Willie Tait and Chesh had been known to frequent it when they were at Linton together. The story has it that on one occasion they had imbibed rather well and were driving home in Willie's old Bentley. As a companion in the rear seat they carried George Foster, the ill-fated 78 gunnery leader. Just for fun, George gave a fighter warning, 'Enemy fighter starboard bow. Turn to port, turn to port, Go'. Whether continuing the fun, or following a natural reaction, Willie gave the steering wheel a wrench to the left. The Bentley left the road and came to rest in the ditch, front against a tree. There was little damage, except to Chesh's shoulder. He suffered from a broken collarbone and was rather quiet for a few days.

Every modest town near a group of RAF bases had its aircrew pub. The Saracens Head in Lincoln, The Kings Head in Darlington, the Crown in Scarborough, were all ones I used, but for me, Betty's was the most memorable. Under tearooms, the Dive Bar was home to hundreds of aircrew from the ten or so airfields around York. There we foregathered to talk about flying, to forget about ops and our lost friends, above all to seek the solace of the girls that offered friendship and fun. Its mirrored walls record the names of hundreds of aircrew patrons scratched on their surface. For many, it was their last frivolous act and last evidence of their existence before dying over Germany. Although no longer a bar, some parts of that wall, inscribed with those memories of departed aircrew, remain today, generously preserved by the proprietors.

On non-flying nights, straight off the bus from Linton, we would head for Betty's for the early evening drinks. Later we would retire, sometimes accompanied, sometimes not, to the De Gray Rooms, the local dance establishment. Located in an old Georgian house in the centre of the city, its spacious accommodation offered a large and gracious ballroom, with a tea and sandwich bar below. Drinks were not served in the De Gray Rooms. Bert Keech, manager, bandleader, doorman, all one in his ample frame and his gracious wife, ran it on quite strict lines. You had to check in before nine and obtain a pass-out to return, necessary to prevent an influx of drunks when the bars closed.

Here there gathered all the nice young ladies of the town. If we arrived unaccompanied, we never left in the same state. As usual Morty and I sought the good dancers, of which there were quite a few. We also tried to pick the beauties but these were much sought after and we were still new boys. Visiting the bar before attending the dance, we were often left with little choice but the wallflowers.

'Late activity on the airfield would see the huge petrol bowsers moving from one aircraft to the next and long trailers hauling their bomb loads from the bomb-dump to dispersal points with gangs of armourers waiting to winch them into the aircraft bomb-bays...' (Via Mike Bailey)

'It is difficult to describe but for five or six hours you entered a different world in which you were completely cut off from your normal life. On landing back at base you suddenly switched back to real life – the next op.' (Stan Reed via Theo Boiten)

To avoid this fate, we decided to go early, not just to obtain our pass-out for return after ten, but to review the talent available. We arrogantly decided who would, or would not, be acceptable partners at the end of the evening. Our remarks would be along the lines, Not that one in blue. She's too fat to hold on to', 'Forget the one in red with the big teeth' and so on. Returning later, the one in blue and the one in red would be the only ones left. Still, as we remarked, they all looked beautiful after a few whiskies and beauty, after all, is in the eye of the beholder.

As we became regulars, the opposition fell away and we found regular 'popsies'. We generously spread our favours among four or five, frequently changing girlfriends, when one took a fancy to the other's 'popsy.' In RAF terms, all girlfriends were 'popsies'. A term in no way pejorative.

Ron Read, Halifax pilot, 78 Squadron. Flight Lieutenant E.G. 'Morty' Mortenson, Ron Read's long-standing friend from their training days was KIA on 16/17 April 1943 when his Halifax was shot down by enemy fighters on the raid on the disastrous Skoda armaments factory at Pilsen.

Frankie is here and he's brought both his 'popsies,'
And George and Joe and Bill and all the rest.
Some of the WAAF have got a special permit
And show themselves uncommonly well-dressed –
Sheena in sunny blue, Davida in emerald,

And Vera in a gown of lace and black.
Oh! eves of Waterloo and shades of Thackeray,
What of the morning's Scharnhorst low-attack?
Swing the hot numbers! Swing and lilt and laughter,
And let there be no crowding at the bar,
Before another night has drooped from sunset,
Some of our comrades will have travelled far!
Start up a song now! Let it be a good one –
'There's no promotion, this side…' Oh! we know
That's just an old one… 'Hi-jigger-jigger mush-mush.'
Raise up your voices, chaps and let it go!

Rustle of skirt and silk, rustle of footsteps,
Rhythm of foot and form that glide, out, in –
Hot up those saxophones, wake up that drummer,
Bring out your crooners, then, stir up the din!
And even those familiar walls have brightened,
Because of youth and all its coloured tones,
Should we remember yesteryears have echoed
Less to our laughter, oftener to moans?

Frank with his 'popsies', Sheena with a boyfriend,
Billy and George and Jack and all your crew,
Who steps unseen beside your arm and beckons,
And seeks an introduction, new to you?
These were here first! They will remain long after,
When all the lights are gone and no sound comes
Of your gay voices and the shrilling fiddles
Are packed and parcelled with the silent drums.

These are the ones I knew, who have forgathered
For their brief hour, returning to this place
Where once they, too, had moments of great laughter,
Before they met the Hunter, face to face.
Step not aside, no graveyard draught arises,
No chilly air is blowing to stir your dress!
Like you, these, too, once lifted high their glasses,
Nor found their cups too brimmed with bitterness!

'Mess Dance', Flight Lieutenant Anthony Richardson RAFVR, 1941

TWENTY-SIX

WHY WERE THEY BORN SO BEAUTIFUL?

Why were they born so beautiful?
Why were they born at all?
They're no bloody use to anyone
No bloody use at all.

Bedale, the squadron village, was a couple of miles distant and was a great place for relaxation. It boasted eight pubs, which, during off-duty periods, could mean a drink at each. I think the favourite was the Green Dragon, which had a cross-eyed barmaid named Kathy who played darts for her knickers or your underpants! One or two, but very few, airmen had Kathy's knickers displayed on the bedroom wall. I think she had acquired a job lot, as they were all the same, emblazoned with traffic-light motifs in the appropriate places.
  Basil Craske, Whitley pilot, 10 Squadron

We were introduced to English food, English pubs and English girls – in that order. The pubs were happy new experiences for Canadians used to the dingy taverns of home where one was made to feel uncomfortable, if not immoral. They were the Englishman's gracious way of living. The food was plain, palatable and rationed. The girls were friendly and good company. One thing I liked very much about English girls was that they seemed to use English so correctly and so naturally it was a pleasure to listen to them. It almost didn't matter too much about the words; the sound of them was what counted...
  Pilot Officer J. Ralph Wood DFC CD RCAF

Oh! Mary, this Waaf is a wonderful life,
Sure you might get a job as an officer's wife.

There are plenty of airwomen digging for gold,
At least, when I asked 'em, it's what I was told.
So I soon took a hand in this digging, y'ken,
And I tried very hard to attract all the men,
I saluted quite smartly by winking one eye,
But ignored all the airmen unless they could fly.

A young Flight Lieutenant was the cause of my fall,
So handsome, attractive and heavenly tall,
Took me for a ride in his little MG,
When something went wrong with the engine, y'see.
We were running on Pool and 100 octane,
Though I shouted quite loudly no help could obtain.
He'd twenty EAs to his credit already,
So one little Waaf couldn't make him unsteady.

And now on my story I will not enlarge,
Sufficient to say how I got my discharge.

'Oh! Mary, This WAAF' (Tune: 'The Mountains of Mourne')

As an officer I had the services of a batman, or, should I say, batwoman, as it was the WAAF who had taken over the batman's duties, freeing him for heavier duties. She would come around in the morning to 'knock you up' (awaken you) with a cup of tea. This usually got you up in a hurry, especially if you had been on the beer the night before. Besides my instructional duties, I had two other jobs during my stay at Abingdon. One was to act as guard over two RAF officers who were under house arrest. They had just recently returned from the Middle East and their crime was getting caught in the station chapel, making love to a couple of WAAFs.
  Pilot Officer J. Ralph Wood DFC CD RCAF

The lipstick he felt in his pocket,
Was Fern's – and he threw it away,
Anne's stocking he found and it followed;
And so did the hairpin from May,
Nell's garter came out of his suitcase
And through the window was tossed;
While Mabel's brassiere and step-ins
Were dropped in the river they crossed.
The vanity case was of silver;
He wrapped and addressed it to Grace,
Then cast in the aisle beside him
Pearl's handkerchief bordered with lace.
He wasn't destroying mementos
He had valued for half of his life;
He was just an Air force officer
Going home on leave to his wife.

'Taking Inventory'

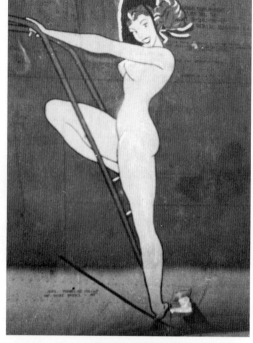

Above: 'Angels One-Five' at Duxford. (Author)

Right: 'Why were they born so beautiful?' (Stanley Burgess Collection)

'We became quite close to our intelligence staff as they debriefed us on return. Pam Finch, a smart, sympathetic WAAF officer, was most popular. Short but well proportioned, her elfin face was surrounded by jet-black hair. Her voice and posture indicated a good girl's school background but all that breeding couldn't hide a slightly predatory air when she looked squarely into the eyes of the officer she was debriefing...' (RAF)

The squadron padre was a jolly soul and one day he looked at the beautiful, voluptuous female painted on the side of V-Virgin and declared: 'She's far too broad in the hips for a virgin!'

Fred Wingham, pilot of Wellington X V-Victor (later re-christened V-Virgin*), 420 Squadron*

My pal tells me he took his WAAF friend out on a star-lit night and proposed to her. She accepted him. I bet she did: in a twinkling.

Laugh With the RAF

> My mistress is the sky,
> She calls forever "Fly".
> Often she treated me shamefully –
> Tried putting me to the core
> Yet still I cry for more
> And yearn for her embrace,
> Her clear and open face
> Above the cloud and rain
> O let me fly again.
>
> My Mistress, *Jasper Miles*

Many WAAFs on this station. They wear battledress in transport section and those of comparable rank eat in our mess. This isn't a man's army anymore... Interrogation after the trip is always a pleasant time. It is carried out in the warm, brightly-lighted mess while we are eating. WAAFs move about serving food; all our own officers are around and usually a number from the Air Ministry look on; much laughter, many inquiries among the crews about incidents en route. There is much kidding. If you didn't land promptly in your turn, the whole scene a complete contrast to that of half an hour ago when most of us were stacked on the circuit listening to the others and the WAAF in the control tower, cursing like troopers if any stooge didn't land on first try.

Sergeant Robert S. Raymond, an American Lancaster pilot, flew a tour in RAF Bomber Command and after two-and-a-half years in the RAF, was returned to the USAAF in early 1944

You could drink all the beer you wanted on a station or at the village pubs and there were always plenty of WAAFs for company.

Piece of Cake, *Geoff Taylor, RAAF Lancaster pilot*

One of our duties was to guard Hockley's Hotel, the 'Waafery' as it was called. It housed the WAAFs who managed the paperwork behind the scenes and was presided over by the Queen Bee, the chief WAAF officer on the unit...

One Man's War, *Johnnie Clark*

> Where now is the girl with the Golden Voice?
> who called us out of the air,
> who stacked us up and sent us round,
> and set us upon the stair.
> T'was orbit angels one, or two,
> or at angels three or four,
> whilst those who lagged in the bomber stream
> had to wait an hour or more.

When her voice came through the dark of night,
it told us we were home,
what mattered then the enemy sky,
lit by the searchlight cone.
Who cared for the fighters' zipping guns,
or the splintering flash of flak,
when the girl in the tower called to us,
we were safely back.
I never met that Golden Voice
who sat in the tower below,
in my mind's eye I pictured her
lit by the lamplight glow.
One night as a blond, with bright blue eyes
and a skin of peach like hue,
another night as a dark brunette
whose radiance filled my view.

Where now is the girl with the Golden Voice?
if I the truth do tell,
she keeps a corner of my heart,
I hope life treats her well.
Sometimes I sit and ponder if,
with all the passing years,
she too recalls my weary voice,
as I remember hers.

'Golden Voices', Kenneth Grantham, 35 Squadron

Night traffic is controlled by radio telephony and the voice best known to every pilot is the pleasant, staccato soprano of a WAAF named Yvonne, who answers all our calls, gives us instruction, brings us in according to priority, stacks us up on the circuit when visitors intrude and never forgets where we are. She gives us advice in emergencies, always in the same even tone; few have ever met her. She sits behind the big glass windows of the dark watch tower overlooking the field each night and from the tone of her voice, I believe she likes her job. Certainly she is efficient at it.
Sergeant Robert S. Raymond

A WAAF is neither a bit of stuff, a bag of tricks, a fisher of men, a lady of leisure, a blessed Madonna, a Dresden ornament, a useful kitchen crock, an intriguing Circe, a scheming Delilah, a deceptive Eve, or a paragon of virtue. Nor is she that product of Air Ministry, a cross between a tomboy and a Gremlin, known as an Air-woman. She is a natural woman; and therefore she is an unknown quantity composed of all those adverse elements in greater or lesser degree and skilfully blended by the Great Creator to make up one unique *objet d'art...*
The Tropic Times, 1944

I made a number of friends at Swinderby, like the WAAFs in the various stores, the parachute stores in particular, a place visited every time we flew. All parachutes were returned there after each flight for checking and storing, being re-issued as and when required. The pace of our training was such that, apart from a few quiet moments with the ladies and the occasional visit to Lincoln, it was a case of all work and very little play!

Right: *B-Babe. (CONAM)*

Below: *Sleepy Gal. (CONAM)*

"—approaching the target, showers of—er—stuff came up—we jinked like—er—anything, which completely—er—er—messed up our bombing run—we turned and dropped the whole bl—inking load through a hole in the flak!"

Above left: *A WAAF. (Gordon Kinsey)*

One of the favourite places for spending a while with a favourite girl was in the boiler house on our accommodation site. It was nice and warm; the boiler man left a seat there with just enough space on it for two. By now I had friends among the girls serving with the WAAF and I found that with care I could make it to the boiler house before any of my colleagues. They also found it a warm place for spending an hour or so cuddling and kissing out of sight and, I hope, away from prying eyes.

Sergeant Roland A. Hammersley DFM, 57 Squadron Lancaster gunner

Pre-war, Jock worked for Montague Burtons tailors. He was a Scot with a bizarre sense of humour. He considered that anything on camp that was left alone or unattended could be 'borrowed' or 'moved'. Apparently he was having an affair with an attractive lady school ma'am in Tyler, Texas. He was certainly besotted with her. About forty-eight hours before we were to depart for New York, Jock vanished. So did one of the Stearmans from the line. They were all fully fuelled. I learned later that he had cranked up the kite on his own, had taken off and flown to Tyler, where he landed in a small field straight into the arms of his lady love. The Stearman could not be flown out of the field. It was too small! It had to be disassembled and hauled out. Some months later, while I was in a camp hospital near Blackpool, Jock looked me up. He was eventually picked up by the local police and handed over to the RAF MPs, brought back, found guilty of going AWOL and got one month inside. He then remustered. I have never seen or heard of him since.

L. James Freeman, cadet pilot, 1 BFTS, Terrell, Texas

The average bomber station was devoid of news. We seldom saw a newspaper and occasionally heard the BBC news if we happened to be in the mess when the wireless was on. I was on leave in August 1943 and so happened to meet a young female in whom I was interested. We didn't talk about what we'd do when the war was over; it was never going to end. We lived for the next leave in six weeks' time – we had double leave because flying was considered to be more dangerous than staying on the ground. Oh yes, they gave us an extra bob a day as well – flying pay, not 'danger money', as the more daring participants would have it.

Geoff Parnell, air gunner

Nelly was a Titian-haired WAAF. Mainly, I wanted to see her about collecting the crew's flying rations, which were our due when we were operating. Made up of chocolate, boiled sweets, chewing gum and canned tomato juice, most of it, except for the gum and tomato juice, found its way to the kids in the households of our English crewmembers.

Waiting for the arrival of the bar sergeant to issue the rations, I made a date with Nelly for the following night. 'I'll meet you at the Blue Boy in the village at seven', I said. Nelly looked at me with a pair of quizzical blue eyes. 'Don't be late', she said. We left it at that.

Geoff Taylor, RAAF, Lancaster pilot

I remember hearing the bombers leave and counting them coming in over the field early next day. Sometimes we lost a lot of friends and you could see WAAFs red-eyed from weeping for one special boy. A terrible loss of human life, but you had to carry on with what had to be done.

Daphne Smith

'The aircrew bus, invariably driven by a pretty WAAF, would arrive to take us back to the operations block for debriefing by the Intelligence staff who had probably been sitting around for hours awaiting our return.' (IWM)

'There was a feeling of elation at being home again and in one piece. Then the crew bus would turn up and it was back to the briefing room for the intelligence de-briefing accompanied by excited chatter and sometimes congratulations on a job well done. All this was sometimes tempered by the news that one or more of our crews hadn't shown up yet.' (Tom Cushing Collection)

Was advised that if we came down in the desert and were rescued by Arabs, the women would act as sort of servants, but on no account should we thank them or even smile at them.

M. Howland RAAF, pilot

March 12th 1943 dawned at Linton-on-Ouse like any other day on an operational airfield of RAF Bomber Command. Kay, our mysterious WAAF batwoman, tapped gently on the door and slid quickly into the room, placing cups of tea beside our beds. She was out again before we were awake. She was an enigma to my wireless operator roommate Flying Officer Bill Ramsey and myself. A lovely redhead with a pale, delicate complexion whose WAAF uniform failed to hide the fullness of her figure, nor could her Air Force issue lisle stockings disguise the shapeliness of her legs. As full-blooded young aircrew, Bill and I thought it only a matter of time before we were on good talking terms with her, if nothing else. Kay had other ideas and every day slipped in and out of our room with averted eyes, rather like an escaped nun. Not that I knew many nuns, escaped or otherwise. They were far too rare a breed to be entertained by wartime aircrew but just about the only breed that wasn't. Kay's major mystery was the intriguing 'USA' flash she wore on her shoulders. What was an American girl doing in the RAF? And, from the few occasions she did speak, her accent was of Northern England. Her daily appearance was always a titillating start to the harsher facts of the day to come but alas, the answer to our enigma was never revealed. Our relationship with her remained confined to day-to-day greetings, nothing else...

I had my favourite little WAAF driver, 'Blondie' to the squadron. Short, curly blond hair, sparkling blue eyes and a broad Glaswegian accent. The rest of her was enveloped in battle dress. Her sharp Glaswegian humour made her stand out from the other drivers. I managed, as usual, to grab a seat in the cab beside her and her Glaswegian chatter kept me occupied until we reached the aircraft.

We became quite close to our intelligence staff as they debriefed us on return. Pam Finch, a smart, sympathetic WAAF officer, was most popular. Short but well proportioned, her elfin face was surrounded by jet-black hair. Her voice and posture indicated a good girl's school background but all that breeding couldn't hide a slightly predatory air when she looked squarely into the eyes of the officer she was debriefing. She was a favourite of my crew and fortunately I was one of her favourite pilots. The crew was quick to notice this as soon as Pam discreetly arranged for us to jump the queue. As we walked into the briefing room to find several other crews waiting, Pam rounded off the debriefing she was engaged in, just in time to call us to her desk. She almost always managed to do this. Aware of our feelings, she usually accepted our brief statements without probing too much for detailed expansion. Consequently, we said that it was a good 'prang' on the target. We had seen a fighter, though we couldn't see the type. The defences were heavier than last time; otherwise it was pretty well a normal Ruhr trip. I was always under pressure from the crew to take Pam out. Unfortunately, I felt she was a little too high-class and genteel for our rollicking evenings. We were good friends and that's how I liked it.

Ron Read, Halifax pilot, 78 Squadron

In September 1944 I was stationed at 89 MU, Barton Mills, Suffolk. The main function of the base was to provide technical RAF personnel concerned with the enlarging and upgrading of the airfield at Lakenheath and other bomber bases in the area. Our camp was divided into two separate parts – the work and administrative area, and the domestic site – and was located about 4 miles south-east of the Royal Air Force Bomber Command airfield in Mildenhall.

Our quarters, in what was affectionately known as 'The Waafery', were located on the domestic site and were situated about ½ mile away from the station headquarters in which I worked as a clerk in the Orderly room. Mildenhall at the time was home to Lancasters of 15 and 622 Squadrons and occasionally to Stirlings of 149 Squadron, completing their last weeks of operational flying in the role of a heavy bomber.

Most mornings we would assemble at 7.50 a.m. and march as a squad of fourteen or twenty WAAFs to the main camp area under the supervision of an NCO. Our route took us under the approach of the main runway at Mildenhall. Sometimes we would look up at the bombers as they descended to land, each one of us with our own thoughts, as the battle-scarred aircraft covered the last miles before touching down with their precious cargo of aircrew, often having endured ten or more hours on a night raid over enemy occupied territory or right to the heart of Hitler's well defended Nazi Germany, constantly under attack in one form or another.

One morning, none of us could hide our concern and apprehension as we heard an aircraft approaching much lower than normal, obscured from sight by the woodland that bordered our route, with its engines screaming as they were forced to their maximum to keep the machine airborne. As the aircraft came into view just above the trees, we could see it was struggling to maintain height, wallowing as it clung to flight. Only two of its four engines were working and one of these was streaming oil and smoke. Its fuselage and wings were badly scarred, with large pieces of metal flapping and banging against the framework in the slipstream. Part of the tail and the rear gun turret was non-existent and the starboard under-carriage leg hung grotesquely at an angle, like a broken limb. The clarity of the crisp, clear September morning somehow intensified each second, with the aircraft sharply defined against the blue, cloudless sky, allowing the memory to register each moment as it unfolded before us.

Our marching lost its rhythm and we shuffled along for a short distance until we came to a standstill, as our thoughts – each in our own way – willed the aircraft with simple but profound prayer to continue flying for the last few miles and to land safely with its crew, having come this far to reach its home base. Our eyes were for those few indelible moments transfixed on the machine as it passed over our heads and out of sight and, as it did so, in a clear, calm but positive voice of command, our NCO simply said: 'Pray for them. Just pray.'

There was not a girl whose head did not drop in pleading, heartfelt prayer.

Our marching regained its discipline and we continued towards station headquarters, waiting for the dull, ominous thud in the distance that precedes the explosion of a crashing aircraft, with the tell-tale pall of black smoke rising skywards – but it did not come. There was just silence. There was little conversation between us and but one thought in our minds: could our prayers have been answered?

For all her firmness our sergeant was not insensitive to our feelings and eventually made contact with a colleague in air traffic control at Mildenhall. The pilot had put the aircraft down on the edge of the airfield and although the Lancaster would never fly again, he and his crew were safe. Some of the crew were wounded when they had come under attack and the rear gunner was missing, but we knew that the simple prayers of a group of fourteen young WAAFs had been answered. We would probably never meet the crew in person, but we felt we had played our part in saving their lives.

An Indelible Moment in Time: A WAAF Remembers, Joyce E. McConnell (née Leading Aircraftswoman Joyce Bayes)

I met Colin Finch at a dance I think. I was engaged to Colin for only one day as it turned out. I was phoned to say that there had been an accident at the aerodrome and perhaps I shouldn't come back that night. I wanted to come back. I had no idea at that time. I was fearful inside but I thought he had been injured. When I got back to the station I thought: 'Well it can't be so bad, there can't be anything so terrible', because I heard the sound of music and jazz, dancing and hilarity. I went in and was taken aside by a friend, a WAAF officer, who told me that Colin had in fact been killed… It was immediately horrifying to me because this terrible jarring between personal sorrow and hearing that music, which absolutely jarred. But on the other hand, I had learnt earlier that this had to go on and after I had gone to my room and released some of the emotion that I felt, I realised of course it had to be. If one went into mourning or stopped life going on in the normal way on the station, you would have had no morale at all. It was the same in London and all the bombed cities. You couldn't just go into deep mourning because this tragedy had happened because personal tragedies were happening all the time.

Jan Birch WAAF, who later married another airman, Brian Reid

He always phoned me when he came back. I waited and waited and the whole place emptied. I sat down and, looking at my watch, I thought I'd wait a few more moments. There was no call. I suddenly thought, I've just got to go back now. I had a cold, empty feeling. If you have been through something when you've worried and then things haven't gone badly, you then talk your self into something like, 'Don't be stupid, you know, it's just a small thing that's happened – he couldn't ring'. As I got outside an older WAAF officer, Section Officer Moneypenny, a funny character, but very warm hearted and very kind to me, said: 'Oh Jan, would you cycle over to the MO. He wants to see you'. Afterwards I realised that those friends of mine and most people on the station could not really face telling me. I felt so sorry for them afterwards. They had been a part of that marriage. I went into Doc Rogers. He said, 'Jan, I've got to prepare you for something. Brian and the crew didn't return'. 'I felt cold inside. I couldn't cry. I couldn't do anything. I think said: 'Oh no, but it isn't possible, it wouldn't happen twice'. I remember cycling down this lane, getting off my bike and going into the woods and being surrounded by beauty and solitude, which wasn't sad in a way because amongst all the grass under the trees were these wood anemones, just a white cloud of delicate things blowing in the wind. I thought, 'Well it isn't all in vain. Whatever's happened, whatever has gone wrong, life does go on. Brian would feel that. Colin would feel that. The other boys I knew would feel that'. It wasn't the sudden solution to all my problems but it remained as a comfort.

Jan Birch WAAF

TWENTY-SEVEN
2ND TAF

We're flying binding Bostons
At 250 binding feet,
Doing night intruders
Just to see who we might meet.
And when the daylight dawns again
And when we can take a peek,
We find we re made our landfall
Up the Clacton binding Creek.

In the summer of 1943, 2 Group was transferred from Bomber Command to the newly formed 2nd TAF. On D-Day the RAF flew a total of 5,656 sorties with only very light losses. The breakout from the beachheads and the advance across France and the Low Countries was assisted by thousands of sorties by Spitfires, Tempests, Typhoons and Mustangs, which were called upon whenever resistance was encountered. The RAF's contribution to the Allied Expeditionary Air Force was the 2nd Tactical Air Force, which by 1945 consisted of four groups with a total of eighty-one squadrons. Units of the 2nd TAF began to move to forward airfields in France just two weeks after D-Day and by the end of the war many squadrons were based on abandoned Luftwaffe airfields in Germany itself.

Gestapo spies among our forces
Investigate subversive sources
Whereby Teutons sensing spring
Feel the urge to have their fling.

Wilhelmstrasse finds of late
A tendency to masturbate,
And with their natural superfluity

'When I joined Ninety-Eight Squadron/In late May of nineteen forty-four/Strange words were used in conversation/Puzzling words I had not heard before…' (Via Paul McCue)

The air and ground crew of N-Nuts 'Avt rvmpere avt stercvs facere' (the nearest that one of the squadron's Latin scholars could get to a well-known service expression) of 88 Squadron at Hartford Bridge in late 1944. From left to right: A.F.W. Valle-Jones; Mike Henry DFC; Wing Commander (later AVM) Ian J. Spencer (CB DFC) with 'Butch' and Flying Officer G.E. Ploughman. Below the Latin inscription are two rows of foaming beer mugs instead of the usual little yellow bombs denoting the number of sorties completed and above them is the fierce portrait of 'Butch' with tin helmet and holding a bomb. (Mike Henry via Roy Brookes)

Of good Germanic ingenuity
Seek a suitable diversion
To put an end to this perversion.

A Flying Brothel is the thing
To ease the urgencies of spring
For then each soldier dissolute
May have his airborne prostitute.
Berlin was scoured and Dresden, too
To find sufficient trollops who
Could give the joys of copulation
Yet be *au fait* with aviation.

At last the scheme has reached fruition
Our troops are in top line condition,
And through their *ersatz* food may cloy
They can still have their strength through joy.

'The Flying Brothel', by a captain ALO (Army Liaison Officer) at the end of a talk to 2nd TAF crews on his experience with 1 TAF, summer 1943

Once the Camel made them dance
O'er the fields of Northern France
As its forebears called the tune
So (with knobs on) does Typhoon.

(On D-Day, no fewer than sixteen squadrons of 2nd TAF were equipped with Hawker Typhoon fighter-bombers)

Typhoon.

TWENTY-EIGHT
AMERICA HERE WE COME

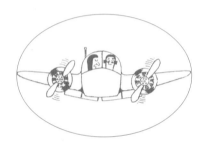

Yes, I trained out in the States, out in Arizona, mates,
In a place that was as hot as Satan's kitchen.

In addition to training schools in the UK, which trained over 88,000 aircrew, a large number of schools were set up overseas under the British Commonwealth Air Training Plan. Canada became the main centre for training, where a total of 137,000 aircrew were trained. The other Commonwealth countries also made a major contribution: Australia trained 27,000, New Zealand trained 5,000, South Africa trained 25,000 and Rhodesia trained 10,000, with other schools being set up in the USA, which produced a further 14,000 aircrew.

   Chris Hobson, senior librarian, RAF Staff College, Bracknell, writing in 1995

Perhaps the first thing we noticed after gazing with awe at the Stearman aircraft on 'the line' was the names of some of the flying instructors – Goethe, Schmidt, Burkhalter, Fitze, Haut and Schellenberger.

   Reg Everson, who arrived at Darr Aero Tech, Albany, Georgia on 2 October 1941 and who later flew Mosquitoes in Europe. During its existence, 2,000 British cadets passed through Darr. When the Arnold Scheme finished in February 1943, with Class 43-D, the thirteen classes had produced some 4,500 RAF pilots from an intake of 7,500 RAF entrants

Les Jones climbed to 4,000ft and began his aerobatics in the Stearman. He did not notice a strong wind blowing him north. When he was ready to return to base he was lost. He looked for a space to land and finally put down on a small landing strip near Rockwall. Some Texans in Stetsons, chaps and wearing revolvers, came over and said, 'Hi y'all. Where you from son?'

   After a brief explanation and directions from the Texans, Les said, 'Thanks a lot. I'll get off then'.

No!–I was'nt low flying sir!– it was
a very very tall cactus !!

'Not before you pay the landing fee', said the Texans.
'Landing fee?' said Les. 'How much?'
'$25 American, son', said the Texan.
The outcome was that Les walked some way to a 'phone and called base. Eventually, two instructors flew out in a Stearman, paid the fee and Les flew back.

L. James Freeman, cadet pilot, 1 BFTS, Terrell, Texas

After Tiger Moths, which are of course a lot lighter, I had some difficulty in landing the Stearman. In my opinion, flying a Stearman properly was more difficult than a Harvard. It was more 'seat of the pants' stuff. It was a very tough, robust aircraft and, despite a few problems, I did enjoy it!

Paul Ballance, who completed seventy hours on Stearmans at 1 BFTS, Terrell, Texas

> You may cuss the Tiger Moth, while you're blowing off the froth
>   From your tankard of good honest English beer, man,
> But they put me through my paces in the great wide open spaces
>   When they trained me on the AT and the Stearman.
> Yes, I trained out in the States, out in Arizona, mates,
>   In a place that was as hot as Satan's kitchen,
> And it did no good to fret when you fairly dropped with sweat;
>   'Cause they only tell you: 'Brother, quit your bitching!'

David Livingstone-Spence (Course 25), 4 BFTS, Mesa, Arizona

189

In all, about 2,200 cadets passed through Terrell. After return to the UK Nos 4 and 7 Courses suffered particularly badly on operations. Flight Sergeant Arthur Louis Aaron from No.6 Course was awarded a posthumous Victoria Cross for his act of courage while a pilot of a Stirling in 218 Squadron, Bomber Command, which made a night attack on Turin, Italy, on 12 August 1943.

As I was approaching to land I could see another Stearman behind me on the crosswind leg… I looked up and back for the other Stearman. All I saw was a propeller somewhere over my tail and two wheels heading my way. I ducked my head low and heard (and felt) a crunch. Those wheels had gone into my upper wing on either side of the fuel tank. At the same instant a fairing strip at the joint of wing and fuel tank zinged like a spring somewhere above my head. At that moment the other 'plane was virtually superimposed on mine. Fortunately, there was a fairly good wind blowing. The other cadet knew exactly what had happened, gave her full throttle and dragged her off. As his tail passed over it also struck my top plane, but he went on to do a normal landing. In a concerned state I hurried over to the dispatch area. Someone said, 'If I wuz you I'd get a gun and shoot the sonofabitch!'.

The cadet was washed out immediately and sent to Trenton, Canada, where they remustered cadets to other aircrew trades.

Where this cadet's fate was not deserved, another's was. Careless taxiing remained a curse in the RAF throughout the war. In this instance a cadet taxiing his Stearman back to the flight line headed directly for the wing of the last parked one and proceeded to chew his way through almost half the starboard wings.

Victor Deboni, 1 BFTS, Terrell. More than 7,000 pilots were produced for the RAF at seven British Flying Training Schools in the USA

One of the most vivid memories is my first solo in the Stearman. I was having a particularly bad morning doing circuits and bumps with my primary instructor, Ray Shelton – a nice but emotional man who played a violin in his spare time! I had done about five hours on the Stearman and cadets were given an elimination test at seven hours if they had not gone solo. So I took the bull by the horns and suggested that I had a go on my own! Ray Shelton stood up in the front cockpit, threw his helmet on the ground and said,

'You f****** sonofabitch, you will break your goddamned neck'.

I calmly replied, 'No I won't'.

Without further ado, he threw his parachute out of the cockpit and sloped off, muttering 'sonofabitch'. I got on with the job and managed to get up and down, just avoiding two ground loops. The remainder of my course went very well, including the Advanced on AT-6s (Harvards). I think that my subsequent career in aviation and the 'exceptional' assessments in my log books justify Ray Shelton's decision.

Brian Trubshaw CBE, MVQ FRAeS, 4 BFTS, Mesa, Arizona (later Concorde test pilot)

In the dim light of the February morning we saw our transport. It was a ship called the *Empress of Scotland*. We were told it had been named the *Empress of Japan* but for patriotic reasons had been renamed. The sleeping accommodation consisted of chicken-wire bunks in tiers of six, while down in the bowels were slung hammocks and palliasses were on the floor. Sardines in a tin had more room. Still, what the hell, it was only for a week or two. The three of us, stupidly as it turned out, grabbed three of the lowest bunks in the six-tier layers. Since we were going to make the crossing without escort, as the incessant 'Tannoy' informed us, we could only take our boots off at night when we bedded down and we should use our life jackets as pillows. We were served two meals a day in a dining room, which could accommodate only a small number of those on board. For the first

"That's the second time this week he's taken the boundary fence on take-off!!"

JSG DEACON 16/7/44

twenty-four hours we ate, then joined the queue, which circled the deck, to receive our second meal. It passed the time and kept us away from the Crown and Anchor boards, which the crew operated, illegally, in every sheltered corner.

Once out into the Atlantic we ran into some of the worst weather the Atlantic could produce in February. The result was that the queues melted away from the dining room, as only the strongest stomachs were unaffected by sea-sickness and could face food. The three of us didn't mind the weather. We enjoyed leisurely meals served in a heaving dining room while the majority lay on their bunks, moaning and puking. There were buckets set aside for the express use of these poor people. The cry of 'Puke bucket, quick!' echoed at regular intervals around the decks, usually followed by shouts of 'Too late', with the unfortunate recipient on a lower bunk stumbling away to clean off the mess gratuitously deposited on him. We, the occupants of the first tier of bunks, received more than our fair share. The stench was appalling.

On the morning of the second day we were sitting having a leisurely breakfast of bacon and eggs. I was surprised to be asked if I wanted six eggs or two with the bacon. Riches beyond the dreams of avarice, I thought, but I settled for two. I didn't want to spoil the newly baked white bread and unlimited butter, which accompanied it. We were eating bread and butter like cake. It had been years since we had experienced anything like it, also the black cherry jam which was dotted around the table…

The next evening we bought our way into the 'bowel's bar' as we called it. The beer tasted abysmal and the old lags looked at us with some amusement.

'So you're twenty-one years old', said one, looking owlishly down his specs at me.

'There are two of us', I replied.

'That's a bit of a coincidence isn't it? Had a lot of love and kisses from your mums and sweethearts?'

'Have we hell,' I responded, 'but we'll have a real party when we reach Halifax in Nova Scotia.'

'Halifax?' queried the old boy with the spectacles. 'You'll have to swim there from New York. If all goes well we're docking there on Saturday. Don't spread it around, though. Let's say it's my present to the two of you on your birthday – confidential like.' He closed his eyes conspiratorially.

'New York!' we echoed and promptly bought him another beer. It was a place of skyscrapers, fast cars and even faster women, we had been told.

'Don't get too excited about it,' continued the sailor, 'you won't be allowed off the ship. You'll see it from the dockside only. Some of your mates have vanished on previous trips.'

At the time I didn't know what caused it, but our birthday drink came to an abrupt end. Dick felt violently sick, a feeling which soon reached its culmination in the lavatory alongside the bar. Andrew and I took him back to the minstrels' gallery – the orchestra stalls as we called them (where a pre-war orchestra had entertained the diners) – taking the precaution of picking up a puke bucket as we went. Andrew and I reckoned the dreaded seasickness had hit Dick a bit later than most of the others.

The rest of the trip was uneventful. We ran out of the storm and reached New York, as the bespectacled old sailor had said, late on Saturday afternoon. Seasickness had run its course and on the last couple of days the dining room had begun to fill up again. Even the cadet, who it was assumed had fallen overboard, was found groaning in one of the life-belt cages. How long he had been there was not known. He was cleaned up, then put in the sick bay. Dick, who had remained off colour, picked up a bit and joined in the cheering as the ship passed the Statue of Liberty and docked at Pier 54 on Manhattan Island. We had noticed that, although the ship had travelled 3,000-odd miles on its own, the US Navy, complete with aircraft cover, had appeared only on the last 50 miles of our journey.

The lights started to come on in the skyscrapers. The cars running along Riverside Drive began to switch on their lights and the whole lot, mingling with the red and green navigation lights of the ships on the river, gave the place a look of fairyland. Coming from three years of blacked-out Britain we gazed in awe at the spectacle. New York – so near and yet so far. We were held on the ship. No one, not even if his mother or wife was on the quayside, was allowed to step off the ship. It was understandable. Several hundred cadets plus repatriated Canadians, Australians and New Zealanders would have required an army of military police to round them up. We just lined the rails of the ship and gazed at the lights. It was Andrew who diverted our thoughts: 'Now I know why it's called "the city that never sleeps"'. He was pointing to the flotsam that swirled around the ship's hull. It consisted mainly of used contraceptives.

Johnnie Clark, en route from England to air observer schools in Canada, prior to becoming a Mosquito navigator

'Three of us set out on a couple of weeks leave, in our serge uniforms and white armbands, to hitch-hike to Niagara, Buffalo, Schenectady and New York City. It was so easy. The Americans had not long been in the war and we were unusual people. The hospitality of everyone we met was overwhelming. I remember we met up with a bunch of young girls in Buffalo: they took us back to one of their homes for a transatlantic party. One of the fathers was a senior Buffalo policeman and another worked in the Fire Department. On leaving Buffalo to head further east into New York State, the Fire Department drove us to the City limits and the accompanying Police car stopped the first suitable vehicle going to Schenectady. Service, indeed. Schenectady, the home of the General Electric Company, was remarkable (then) for orange street lamps. I had never seen the like before. In New York, after half a dozen more generous and inquisitive responders to our thumbs, we put up at the YMCA and saw everything and did everything we could in the time. Particularly memorable for its welcome and camaraderie was Jack Dempsey's Bar on Broadway: New Yorkers queued up to buy us drinks. The whole trip was magic. But it had to come to an end and we hitched back up to Canada. Packing kit bags, we were soon on a train which took us the reverse way back to New Brunswick since Moncton had the honour of being the focal point both into and out of the Canadian Training organisation.

Pilot Officer (later Air Vice Marshal CBE DFC AFC) Jack Furner, who passed out as a navigator at 33 ANS (Air Navigation School) at Mount Hope in Canada in July 1942

TWENTY-NINE
A YANK IN THE RAF

D–Dog seemed like a black bug on a white sheet. The flak began coming up…

That was bad. We lost fifty-two on that raid. Went in at 12,000ft, got hit and damn near fell to pieces. Went down to 2,000ft and sort of stumbled home at about 90mph. Don't really know how we got home. All my crew were English. We used to have some pretty wild arguments about the States staying out of the war. After that night over Bremen we argued but we never really got mad any more. Going through something like that brings you pretty close.

Sergeant Harris B. Goldberg, born in Boston, USA, who trained as an air gunner in the RCAF and in October 1941 had arrived in Scotland. He and his crew of a Wellington flew the 1/2 June 1942 'Millennium' raid on Essen and the 25/26 June 1942 raid on Bremen, which was attacked by 1,006 aircraft, 102 of which were Wellingtons borrowed from Coastal Command, and 272 were from the OTUs. Forty-nine aircraft failed to return. After flying 273 operational hours in the RAF and surviving a crash in a 'Wimpy' in the Sinai Desert in November 1942, he transferred to the 8th Air Force

Went to Essen last night. Briefing is always a pretty grim business when that target is announced. Price, Warrant Officer, said, 'You faint and I'll carry you out.' We took a second pilot, a new boy on the squadron, to give him some experience. It was his first operational flight and he was still shaking after we landed. My boys are absolutely steady and normal under fire now, although we had never seen so many searchlights nor so great a barrage as over the Ruhr. It still represents to me a marvellously beautiful picture, especially on such a night with a few scattered clouds and the moon in its second quarter.

The sky was steel blue and everywhere below there was the restless criss-cross pattern of long white beams, the bright pinpoints of the bursting heavy flak shells at our level, leaving big, dark smoke puffs that are often mistaken for balloons by the uninitiated observer, the long strings of red tracers from the light flak guns being hosed up like liquid corkscrews, the brilliant flares that hang interminably between heaven and earth and never seem to move, the photo flashes exploding near the ground with a piercing blue-white light, then the long strings of incendiaries being laid out in geometrical patterns among the buildings and the great red mushroom explosions of the 4,000-pounders. It is destruction on a colossal scale and terrifying in its concentration and intensity.

We carried a 4,000-pounder and more than 1,000 incendiaries. It was the shortest trip we've ever made. We're usually among the last to return to base, because both Griffiths and I believe in saving our engines. He's a miser with petrol, quite rightly, and his most famous remark was in crossing the Alps when I asked for more power to gain height. He opened the throttles about half an inch and said, 'There, that's all you can have'. His knowledge of our engines, due to long experience, is amazing for a young man of nineteen years. One of our engines overheated badly at more than half-throttle, so that it wasn't much help. He and I talked over the possibilities and procedures in such cases by cutting other crew members off the intercom; otherwise they'll have too much to think about. The air temperature was -30°C and the North Sea is pretty cold at this season.

Sergeant Robert S. Raymond, pilot of a Lancaster of 44 Squadron, describing the raid on Essen, 13/14 January 1943

Boz, the bomb-aimer crackled through on the intercom: 'There's a battle going on on the starboard beam'. We couldn't see the aircraft but we could see the jets of red tracer being exchanged. Suddenly there was a burst of yellow flame and Jock remarked, 'That's a fighter going down – note the position'. The whole thing was interesting but remote. Dave the navigator, who was sitting back with his maps charts and compasses said: 'The attack ought to begin in exactly two minutes'. We were still over the clouds. But suddenly those dirty grey clouds turned white. We were over the outer searchlight defences – the clouds below us were white and we were black. *D-Dog* seemed like a black bug on a white sheet. The flak began coming up, but none of it close. We were still a long way from Berlin. I didn't realise just how far.

Jock observed, 'There's a kite on fire dead ahead'. It was a great golden, slow-moving meteor slanting towards the earth. By this time we were about 30 miles from our target area in Berlin. That 30 miles was the longest flight I have ever made. Dead on time Boz, the bomb-aimer, reported, 'Target indicators going down'. The same moment the sky ahead was lit up by brilliant yellow flares. Off to starboard another kite went down in flames. The flares were sprouting all over the sky – reds and greens and yellows; and we were flying straight for the centre of the fireworks. *D-Dog* seemed to be standing still, the four propellers thrashing the air. But we didn't seem to be closing in. The cloud had cleared and off to starboard a Lanc was caught by at least fourteen searchlight beams. We could see him twist and turn and finally break out. But still the whole thing had a quality of unreality about it. No one seemed to be shooting at us, but it was getting lighter all the time. Suddenly a tremendous big blob of yellow light appeared dead ahead, another to the right and another to the left. We were flying straight for them.

Jack pointed out to me the dummy fires and flares to right and left, but we kept going in. Dead ahead there was a whole chain of red flares looking like stoplights. Another Lanc coned on our starboard beam; the lights seemed to be supporting it. Again we could see those little bubbles of coloured lead driving at it from two sides. The German fighters were at him.

And then, with no warning at all, *D for Dog* was filled with an unhealthy white light; I was standing just behind Jock and could see the seams of the wings. His quiet Scots voice beat into my ears, 'Steady, lads – we've been coned'. His slender body lifted half out of the seat as he jammed the control column forward and to the left. We were going down.

Ed Murrow.

Jock was wearing woolen gloves with the fingers cut off. I could see his fingernails turn white as he gripped the wheel. And then I was on my knees, flat on the deck, for he had whipped the *Dog* back into a climbing turn. The knees should have been strong enough to support me, but they weren't and the stomach seemed in some danger of letting me down, too. I picked myself up and looked out again. It seemed that one big searchlight, instead of being 20,000ft below, was mounted right on the wingtip.

D for Dog was corkscrewing. As we rolled down on the other side I began to see what was happening to Berlin.

The clouds were gone and the sticks of incendiaries from the preceding waves made the place look like a badly laid-out city with the street lights on. The small incendiaries were going down like a fistful of white rice thrown on a piece of black velvet. As Jock hauled the *Dog* up again I was thrown to the other side of the cockpit and there below were more incendiaries glowing white and then turning red. The cookies – the 4,000lb high explosives – were bursting below, like great sunflowers gone mad. And then as we started down, still held in the lights, I remember that the *Dog* still had one of those cookies and a whole basket of incendiaries in his belly and the lights still held us. And I was very frightened…

Berlin was a kind of orchestrated hell – a terrible symphony of light and flame. It isn't a pleasant kind of warfare. The men doing it speak of it as a job. Yesterday afternoon, when the tapes were stretched out on the big map all the way to Berlin and back again, a young pilot with old eyes said to me, 'I see we're working again tonight'. That's the frame of mind in which the job is being done. The job isn't pleasant – it's terribly tiring – men die in the sky while others are roasted alive in their cellars. Berlin last night wasn't a pretty sight. In about thirty-five minutes it was hit with about three times the amount of stuff that ever came down on London in a nightlong blitz. This is a calculated, remorseless campaign of destruction. Right now the mechanics are probably working on *D-Dog*, getting him ready to fly again.

> *Condensed account of the bombing raid on Berlin on 2/3 December 1943, extracted from Edward R. Murrow's CBS radio broadcast, 3 December 1943. Lancaster D–Dog of 619 Squadron RAAF at Woodhall Spa, flown by Wing Commander William 'Jock' Abercromby DFC★, was one of 458 aircraft that took part. A month later and now with 83 Squadron, 8 (Pathfinder Force) Group, Abercromby was killed on the night of 1/2 January 1944 when his Lancaster FTR from an operation to bomb Berlin. Murrow, head of CBS European Bureau in London, had become well known for broadcasts during the Blitz, and his broadcasts were collected in 'This Is London' (1941). He continued to report on war from Europe and North Africa throughout the Second World War. A heavy smoker, Murrow died on 22 April 1965 aged fifty-seven*

Inspected a Liberator [at Thorney Island RAF Coastal Command station] and think it a piece of junk compared to our planes. So much space in it wasted, so many details retained from commercial types and such cheap material used that I would never feel safe in one. Give me a wing area and horsepower and forget the rest.

> *American Lancaster pilot, Sergeant Robert S. Raymond*

Oddentification.

Whistle, whistle, little bomb,
How I wonder where you're from.
Up above the world so high
There's a Fortress in the sky.

THIRTY

DOMINIONS

Where are the Aussies, the sports and the cobbers...
Where are the fliers from Canada's prairies...
Where are the Kiwis who left all the sunshine.

About half of my companions posted here with me are from New Zealand and Canada and among the latter are a half dozen of my countrymen. All of them are unanimous in their dislike of this country. To them the bread tastes like sawdust; they can't get a 'cuppa cawfee'; the tea is usually unsweetened; no candy, fruit, or milk, only boiled vegetables; few cigarettes; and they are always hungry... Many of the Canadians and other Dominions personnel other than pilots have a hard lot on this station. I'm ordinarily hardhearted about the misfortunes of others but I am unfavorably impressed by the manner of RAF officers toward the Colonials, especially the air gunners and wireless operators. Some are rather tough, but they should be treated more considerately... Every Canadian I've met dislikes the officers of the RAF. I believe it is due to that fact that the officers cannot conceive of anyone's talking in the breezy staccato manner that is the Canadians' natural mode of expression and being equal to the officers in intelligence and efficiency. That rule applies to the English, for all but the well-educated classes speak with an accent and act in every way as inferior beings, but the rule certainly does not apply to the Dominion personnel over here. I'm wondering what's going to happen on some of the long flights. The Canadian aircrewmen get along fine with English sergeants and other Colonials but they are as flint and steel to RAF officers.
Sergeant Robert S. Raymond

Oh, I have slipped the surly bonds of Earth,
And danced the skies on laughter-silvered wings:
Sunward I've climbed and joined the tumbling mirth
Of sun-split clouds – and done a hundred things
You have not dreamed of – wheeled and soared and swung
High in the sunlit silence. Hov'ring there,

'Where are the Aussies, the sports and the cobbers... Where are the fliers from Canada's prairies...' (RAF)

I've chased the shouting wind along and flung
My eager craft through footless halls of air.
Up, up the long delirious, burning blue
I've topped the wind-swept heights with easy grace,
Where never lark, or even eagle flew;
And while with silent lifting mind I've trod
The high untrespassed sanctity of Space,
Put out my hand, and touched the face of God.

'High Flight', John Gillespie Magee RCAF

Flight Sergeant Mick Christensen, the skipper was... a tall, strongly built Australian, with very much the look of a Viking (his surname, Christensen, indicated Viking ancestry) and a natural leader. The crew was fairly typical of those in Bomber Command. Although we were in a Royal Australian Air Force squadron, the pilot was the only Australian in the crew. I was the only officer. Mick was a flight sergeant and the remainder were all sergeants. This made no difference. We seven were firm friends with tremendous mutual trust and respect and rank or position had no part in our approach to the job. This was highly desirable, of course, in the making of an efficient bomber crew. As an officer, I felt lucky to have one or two privileges that the others did not get and to make up for this I tried to do a few extra chores around the aircraft, before or after a trip. We all felt ourselves lucky to be on this particular squadron as we found that Australians were a wonderful race with whom to go to war. They had little time for anyone who pulled rank or position and basic discipline was good, but it was a discipline coming from natural leaders with a team keen to get on with the job. As RAF chaps found, an Aussie could call a man 'a

Above: 'Their bomber… Had a kangaroo painted on its side/And carried them…/To their targets far and wide.' (Jack Hamilton 463 Squadron RAAF Collection via Theo Boiten)

Right: 'High Flight' was composed by P/O John Gillespie Magee Jr, an American serving with the RCAF. He was born in Shanghai, China in 1922, the son of missionary parents, Reverend and Mrs John Gillespie Magee. His father was an American and his mother was originally a British citizen. He came to the US in 1939 and earned a scholarship to Yale but in September 1940 he enlisted in the RCAF and graduated as a pilot. He was sent to England in July 1941 and posted to the 412 'Falcon' Squadron RCAF at Digby. There he flew the Spitfire IIa on fighter sweeps over France and air defence over England. In September 1941 Magee flew a high-altitude test flight in a Spitfire V. As he orbited and climbed upward, he was struck with the inspiration of a poem, 'To touch the face of God'. He wrote to his parents enclosing a verse, which 'started at 30,000 ft and was finished soon after I landed'. He wrote 'High Flight' on the back of the letter. On 11 December 1941 Magee was killed when the Spitfire V he was flying collided with a trainer aircraft. He was nineteen years old. 'High Flight' was included it in an exhibition of poems called 'Faith and Freedom' in February 1942. After that it was widely copied and distributed. John's younger brother, David B. Magee, joined the USAAC and trained as a bombardier on B-24 Liberators. John Magee is buried at Scopwick. (Author)

The crew was fairly typical of those in Bomber Command. Although we were in a Royal Australian Air Force squadron, the pilot was the only Australian in the crew. Australians were a wonderful race with whom to go to war. They had little time for anyone who pulled rank or position and basic discipline was good, but it was a discipline coming from natural leaders with a team keen to get on with the job. As RAF chaps found, an Aussie could call a man "a Pommy bastard" and make it sound an absolute term of endearment!' (G/C John Crotch)

Pommy bastard' and make it sound an absolute term of endearment! On the other hand, any officer who started to put on airs and graces – very few did – merited the derogatory description: 'He's gone Pommy.'

> Pilot Officer R.H. 'Chad' Chadwick, Lancaster navigator, 460 Squadron RAAF, RAF Binbrook

Three Canadian airmen, sleeping in a tent in one of the English training areas last summer, were rudely awakened by a terrific crash not far away.

'What was that – thunder or bombs?' asked one.

'Bombs', was the laconic answer.

'Thank heaven for that!' chimed in the third, 'I thought we were going to have more rain.'

> 'The Lesser Evil', Laugh with the RAF

In the main, we were all very young, the vast bulk of us being in the eighteen to twenty-three age group. There were one or two old men among us: Jock Hannah and F.C. MacDonald were in their late thirties; Butcher, the recently commissioned engineer officer, was also in his thirties; and, exceptionally, the Squadron Adjutant, a Canadian, was in his forties. But they were the exceptions. To a man all were volunteers. All were pretty fit; all were bright, intelligent people; all of us were trying to do a difficult job to the best of our ability – yet often with a sense of foreboding. We were a mixed bag. Probably for the first time in our young lives, we found ourselves working alongside people from

'It was no wonder that aircrew were the favourites of the young girls, lonely wives and widows.' (Mike Cleary via Paul Lincoln)

all over the place. They were fine young men. Our numbers included chaps from New Zealand, Australia, West Indies, Canada, Argentina; from Scotland, Ireland and Wales.

Squadron Leader (later Group Captain) A.F. Wallace. OC B Flight, 620 Squadron June 1943–September 1944

While on operations I took advantage, several times, of the Nuffield Leave Scheme. The Foundation paid for your accommodation at many nice hotels in England. This usually included breakfast. On one occasion I stayed at the Queen's Hotel in Torquay. On my first evening there I struck up an acquaintance with an Aussie and a New Zealander. They were just finishing their week's leave. They offered to show me all the best drinking spots in Torquay. To celebrate their final night, they persuaded me to join them in a 'down-under' drink. It was a pint of stout with some lemon juice to alleviate the heavy taste of stout. I found it enjoyable and drank it all night. The next morning I woke up with a dandy hangover. When the little lady came around with the morning cup of tea, my hand was shaking so bad I couldn't hold the cup. The little lady commiserated with me, thinking, I believe, that I was suffering from some kind of operational 'shakes'.

Flight Sergeant Jack Woodrow, Canadian Wellington observer, 425 Squadron RCAF

I was to operate and complete my first tour in 4 Group, Bomber Command. At this time we were all on loan to the RAF as the RCAF Bomber Command had not yet been established. Later, when it became active as 6 Group, some of the Canadians transferred

Above: 'How can we thank the men who crossed the great Atlantic, deep and wide, / And left their New World far behind / To fight for freedom at our side?' (Via S. Fochuk)

Right: 'Besides members from every county in Great Britain and Northern Ireland, there were Australians, Canadians, New Zealanders, a South African, a tea planter from Ceylon and a sugar planter from Jamaica.' (Ted Johnson DFC Collection)

to the Canadian squadrons. Several others and myself preferred to stay with the RAF. We got along fine with the Limeys and, besides, we thought that where we were on loan, we might get away with a little more murder and less discipline…

One of my compatriots from Moncton, a navigator, missed Great Britain altogether when returning from a raid. He landed in southern Ireland, which was neutral and remained there in internment for the rest of the war, enjoying good food and drink while his pay and promotion continued. I still haven't decided whether he was a stupid navigator or a smart operator. Making a good landfall on the English coast on our homeward journey boosted the navigator's morale. By a good landfall I mean approaching the coast and hitting it just about where you were supposed to – right on track. I recall my pilot asking occasionally, 'Where are we?'. I'd shove a map or a chart in front of him, pointing wildly to any spot over the North Sea or Germany, depending on the occasion. This having satisfied him, I returned to my plotting table to work out our actual position undisturbed.

Pilot Officer J. Ralph Wood DFC CD RCAF

For some peculiar reason seemingly inherent in the Lancaster's system I always got too hot, Jock at his navigator's desk a few feet behind me seemed to be perpetually frozen, and Joe, sitting at his radio just forward of the main spar, seemed to roast. Don, prowling restlessly back and forth at his flight engineer's panel, rarely seemed to use his jump-seat alongside me and appeared to be oblivious to the temperature. Smithy, lying bundled by his bombsight and panels in the cold transparency of the nose, was a Canadian and therefore didn't count, for if he complained about the cold he was promptly told to go back to the frozen north.

Geoff Taylor, RAAF, Lancaster pilot

Their bomber, called *Walaroo Warrior*
Had a kangaroo painted on its side
And carried them on many missions
To their targets far and wide.

Now the crew of the *Walaroo Warrior*
One Canadian and Australians three
Were experts in every position
The best bomber's crew you'll ever see.

Bomber's Crew, 29 July 1944, Sergeant George 'Ole' Olson RCAF, B–25 Mitchell air gunner, 98 Squadron

'You've been posted', he said. We looked rather crestfallen. 'Cheer up. I've been asked to supply two crews for a new squadron that is starting up at Bourn, just along the road from here, nearer Cambridge.' He doodled with a pencil on the blotting pad in front of him. 'Well, it's not a new squadron – No.162. It was Coastal Command before, I think, and they were flying Hudsons. Now it's being reconstituted as a Pathfinder Mosquito Squadron. I've been told to supply two crews to help it along. I was warned that they didn't want any rubbish, so it's quite a compliment to you both.'

'Yeah,' added his navigator, 'they don't want kangaroos that can't jump. You're good press-on types with lots of ops left in you.'

'It's a bit of a shoestring airfield compared with here,' broke in the flight commander, 'but you'll get used to it. By the way, I've recommended you both for commissions.'

He looked at me. I was trying to assimilate the information thrown at us so suddenly. 'Tell me, Sergeant, why were you not commissioned direct from your navigation school? Your records are good.'

I glanced at him, then at his Australian navigator, who was still gnawing on the burnt match.

'D-Dog *seemed like a black bug on a white sheet. The flak began coming up…' (Jack Hamilton, 463 Squadron RAAF Collection via Theo Boiten)*

'Thereby hangs a tale', and I recounted how one of our instructors had been an Australian; how he had marched into the lecture room one day; how he had asked us, looking pointedly at Andrew and me, what the bloody hell was a University Air Squadron and why should their members be made officers in preference to others? He evidently thought we were from the privileged classes in Britain. He said we could expect no privileges from him. The outcome was inevitable. Both Andrew and I became sergeants after the course.

'Doing a bit of Pommie-bashing was he?' said the Aussie from his corner on the seat. 'Some of our boys are like that. They carry a chip on their shoulders.'

More like a tree-trunk, I thought, but answered: 'Yes, sir, I suppose so.'

'It states here,' said the flight commander, 'that you should be – and I quote – "promoted in the field".'

'Thank you, sir.'

As if to change the subject he continued: 'There's a good pub near Bourn airfield called the Gibbet Arms. Perhaps your Australian instructor's ancestors should have been strung up on the gibbet rather than sent to the other end of the earth.'

'That's quite a thought sir.'

We hung around the mess and presented ourselves in the crew room at 6 o'clock where we met the rest of the squadron. The CO looked as if he had just left the upper sixth form. His display of gongs disproved that. Our flight commander, on the other hand, wouldn't have looked out of place in a comfortable chair by the fireside wearing a pair of slippers. He must have seen thirty or thirty-five summers – aged by our standards. The rest of the bunch seemed to be a cross section of the Commonwealth and the Colonies. Besides members from every county in Great Britain and Northern Ireland, there were Australians, Canadians, New Zealanders, a South African, a tea planter from Ceylon and a sugar planter from Jamaica. There was even a Czech. How he arrived in the squadron only he knew. We were going to meld into a new squadron. All of us had flown on ops before. It was satisfying to know that Bill and I were no longer sprogs but had several trips under our belts.

After a lot of introductions, talk of building up *esprit de corps* and technical details about the aircraft, the CO suggested that the best thing to do was to head for the Caxton Gibbet, have a few jars and meet each other informally. He added that there was transport waiting at the door. The suggestion of beer at the Gibbet was greeted with acclaim by all the crews.

One Man's War, *Pilot Officer Johnnie Clark, Mosquito navigator, on his posting, along with his pilot, Bill Henley, from 571 Squadron to 162 Squadron*

THIRTY-ONE
MOSSIES

Mossies they don't worry me,
Mossies they don't worry me,
If you get jumped by a One-nine-O,
I'll show you how to get free.
Keep cool and collected,
Keep calm and sedate,
Don't let your British blood boil.
Don't hesitate
Just go right through the gate,
And drown the poor bastard in oil!

The pilot and navigator sat side by side in this 'Wooden Wonder', or 'Termite's Delight', as it was sometimes called. The pilots had a steel plate under their seats to protect them. Navigators had an extra sheet of plywood. We all had a nagging fear that our jewels might be shot off. The moral seemed to be that pilots make better fathers.
Pilot Officer J. Ralph Wood DFC CD RCAF, 692 Squadron Mosquito navigator. De Havilland Mosquitoes served in a multitude of roles including night-fighting, bombing, pathfinding and photographic reconnaissance

'Lofty' Fletcher, a giant of a fellow, Sergeant Richard C. Fletcher, aged thirty-one, of Enfield, Middlesex, told me about the afternoon raid.

I did not know until Saturday morning. When my pilot called across to me I was having a hand of solo with the other aircrews. The pilot said: 'We are to be briefed shortly.' I said to myself, 'Ah well, this is just another one.'

But when we turned up for the briefing we got a slight shock on hearing we were bound for Berlin.

"Come out of the road—you'll get run over."

Sunday Express, Mar. 5th, 1944

The planes behaved like bucking broncos in the fierce wind. We, too, expected to get some opposition as we crossed the enemy coast, but nothing happened. We were told of another place where we might also get some sign of disapproval. When we got there the Huns did give us a squirt or two, but they were hopelessly inaccurate.

Just as we got to Berlin the cloud ran out. There below was the German city. I said: 'God bless my soul, there it is' and went forward and started unloading our contribution to the German festivities.

I can tell you the bombs we used are pretty powerful. I did not see them burst, but I know the enormous damage they can do. I hope the Huns felt them good and hard.

Our bombs went down at dead on 1600 hrs – 4 p.m., when Goebbels was about to speak. Berlin was still and dead. I saw no flak. We all felt that the Germans had put up a poor show in defence.

Daily Express *press report of the first daylight raid, by Mosquitoes of 105 and 109 Squadrons,on Berlin, Saturday 30 January 1943. The first raid, by three Mosquitoes of 105 Squadron, was made mid-morning, at the exact time that Goering was due to speak. The second raid, by three Mosquitoes of 109 Squadron, was made in the afternoon, at the time Goebbels was due to speak*

Her name was Grace; she was one of the best,
But that was the night I gave her the test.
I looked at her with joy and delight
For she was mine and mine for the night.
She looked so pretty, so sweet and slim,

And the night was dark, the light was dim.
I was so excited my heart missed a beat
For I knew that night I was in for a treat!
I had seen her stripped, I had seen her bare,
I felt her round and felt her everywhere,
But that was the night I liked the best,
And if you wait I'll tell you the rest.
I got inside her, she screamed with joy.
For this was her first night out with a boy.
I got up high and quick as I could,
I handled her well for she was good.
I turned her over upon her side,
Then on her back – that was all tried:
I pushed it forward; I pulled it back,
Then I let it go, until I thought she would crack.
She was one great thrill the best in the land,
The twin-engined MOSQUITO of Bomber Command.

'Grace', Sergeant Harry Tagg, 1655 Mosquito Training Unit, RAF Marham, April 1943 (via Daphne Light, ex-Marham WAAF)

A month at the Mosquito Training Unit and we headed for our new station, 692 Squadron RAF Graveley near Cambridge in eastern England. We shared this station with 35 (Pathfinder) Squadron, which was flying Lancasters. A friendly rivalry existed between these two squadrons, especially when we were both frequenting the same local pub or the officers' mess. While our Mosquitoes roamed the German skies in all kinds of weather, the heavies (mostly Lancasters and Hallybags) were more particular about when they went aloft. We took special delight in provoking the gentlemen who flew the heavies in the pubs we both frequented by singing our song – 'We Fly Alone' – our rewritten lyric of the juke-box favourite 'I'll Walk Alone'.

Pilot Officer J. Ralph Wood DFC CD RCAF, 692 Squadron, 8 Group (PFF) Mosquito navigator

We fly alone, when all the heavies
Are grounded and dining
692 will be climbing.
We still press on.

One unusual return from enemy territory and most satisfying included a dive beginning at the French coast from 32,000ft to 10,000ft, reached at Southwold on the English coast. This 88-mile journey was completed in eleven minutes, which was fast, even for a Mosquito. With our cookie (4,000lb bomb) gone, our two 50-gal drop tanks discarded and our fuel load pretty well depleted, it wasn't too hard to ccomplish this feat.

Pilot Officer J. Ralph Wood DFC CD RCAF Mosquito navigator, 692 Squadron, 8 Group Light Night Striking Force

24 August. Well, I have been flying in a Mossie at last. They are wizard aircraft and Phil is a very good pilot. There isn't a lot of room after a Lane though. Yesterday afternoon we did two hours stooging around. This morning we did a cross-country, which took us out over the Isle of Man and the north of England. It was wizard up at 25,000ft; at one time

Mosquito gave 1½ ring deflection and opened fire with a four second burst at 600ft range. Strikes were seen all along the top of the mainplane leading to a large explosion in the fuselage which as quickly well on fire. The e/a was now definitely established to be a Me 110. E/a turned over on its back and passed underneath Mosquito and was followed down to 3,000ft range on AI then blip disappeared.' (IWM)

Above: *'Flying solitary operations over heavily defended enemy territory in unarmed, wooden aircraft, I suppose, needs special qualities.' (IWM)*

Opposite above: *This tranquil scene will quickly change/Soon they will enter night fighter range.' (Ken Lowes via Theo Boiten)*

Opposite below: *'I have been flying in a Mossie at last. They are wizard aircraft.' (Flight Lieutenant 'Hank' Cooper DSO DFC Collection)*

"WHAT!! YOU FORGOT TO BRING THE GLUE ?!!"

(L.R. Dick)

we could see England, Wales, Scotland and Ireland. After flying we had the rest of the day off, but as it has rained ever since it wasn't much good. What lousy weather! Anyone would think it was November instead of August.

Derek Smith, Mosquito navigator, 692 Squadron, 8 Group Light Night Striking Force

> Single engine? Keep on turning!
> 'Tis our gratitude you're earning,
> For we nearly 'copped our lot'
> And our undercart is shot.
> Dear old Mossie? Wooden steed?
> One more mile is all we need!

'Almost Home', Jasper Miles

Flying Spitfires was the thrill of my life – there was nothing like it. However, the Mosquito came a close second and I was lucky to be flying what I consider to be the top two 'planes of the war. At Benson in 541 Squadron, in the Photographic Reconnaissance Wing, I completed forty-four sorties on specially modified unarmed Spitfires. Later I joined 544 Squadron flying PR Mosquitoes and did twenty-six additional sorties for a total of seventy operational flights. PR was a very interesting job. We knew in advance of many occurrences, i.e. the Dams raids, V2 rockets etc. It was also one of the few jobs where one had the opportunity for independent action. We operated singly and although we were briefed for definite targets, how and when we got there was largely up to us. We also had authority to divert to photograph any convoys, or other unusual targets spotted. We covered the whole of Europe in daylight from Norway to Gibraltar and inland as far as Danzig and Vienna.

Flight Lieutenant John R. Myles RCAF, 544 Squadron PRU Mosquito IX pilot

Above: *Loading a 4,000lb 'Cookie' bomb into a Mosquito. (IWM)*

Right: *'I did not know until Saturday morning. When my pilot called across to me I was having a hand of solo with the other aircrews. The pilot said: "We are to be briefed shortly." I said to myself: "Ah well, this is just another one." But when we turned up for the briefing we got a slight shock on hearing we were bound for Berlin…' (RAF Marham)*

Flying solitary operations over heavily defended enemy territory in unarmed, wooden aircraft, I suppose, needs special qualities. Having once watched a huge formation of Fortresses flying into and through heavy flak without budging, apart from the ones that were hit, I think PRU suited Frank and me. Like everyone else of any experience in PRU we had our moments and I think all of them reveal the cool calculation, coupled with the ability to make lightning decisions that made Frank the magnificent pilot he was and saved our lives quite a lot.

Not too many RAF crews have taken photographs of both sides of the superb German battleship *Tirpitz*. After the bomber boys had put a Blockbuster down its funnel, it was a piece of cake for us to get some almost sentimental sea-level pictures of the upturned hull and pootle back to sun-soaked Sumburgh.

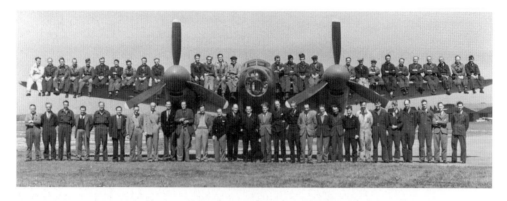

Geoffrey de Havilland: 'We believe we can produce a twin-engined bomber which would have a performance so outstanding that little defensive equipment would be needed. This would employ the well-tried out method of construction used in the Comet and Albatross and being of wood or composite construction would not encroach on the labour and material used in expanding the RAF. It is especially suited to really high speeds because all surfaces are smooth, free from rivets, overlapped plates and undulations and it also lends itself to very rapid and subsequent production.'

We gentled up the coast and started to sneak into the many fjords past the Lofotens until we came to Alten. There it was, 42,000 tonnes of *Tirpitz*, looking oddly menacing and peaceful at the same time. A bit of desultory flak (we were at an uncomfortable 8,000ft under the cloud, in an essentially high-level kite) down the fjord, persuaded Frank to steep turn on to a short photographic run on the ship. Almost immediately there was a huge explosion, maps, Q codes, escape kits, Horlicks tablets, hopes and fears flew wildly around the cabin and I remember thinking, 'God, these Germans are bloody good'. They weren't. The top of the cabin had just flown off into the fjord. We had no sunshine roof – no look out. Anxiously we checked that we were OK, then noted with surprised relief that so was the kite apart from the top.

We did the run, Frank calmly keeping me paying attention, then set off for a very long, chilly, anxious, noisy, frustrating 1,000-mile, four-hour trip back in a damaged aircraft, with a vast question mark over landing conditions. A petrol switch and – what I was to find a lot later – the fact that nobody would talk to us on W/T or R/T because all the codes, which changed frequently, had gone out the top into the oggin of Alten Fjord. I put some outrageous priorities on my W/T requests for courses to steer and aerodromes to land at. I think I once told them our squadron, aircraft number and service numbers in order to establish who we were, but to no avail.

We discussed feathering one engine as the fuel situation was getting desperate (in our crippled condition we had to keep away from the enemy and having to fly at 15,000 because of the fuel position, was just about our most vulnerable height). The sea, what we could see of it through generally 10/10, looked unusually calm for the North Sea, suggesting that the light winds I had found on the way up, had, crucially, not changed much. At long, long last, we saw a gap in the cloud just after ETA, dived anxiously through it and saw land. Soon it became Wick, the most northerly mainland drome there and with all fuel gauges reading zero, Frank made the most treasured landing of all (it would have been a good one to me with fifteen bounces, but it was not at all like that). By the time we got back to Leuchars for a debriefing and a much appreciated operational meal (one revered egg), the bar had closed.

We had spent nine hours twenty-five minutes in the air that day, with Frank's careful course keeping and cosseting of the engines a vital factor in our survival and in getting some useful gen.
    Eric Hill DFC DFM, navigator, PRU 544 Squadron, talking about Flight Lieutenant (later Group Captain) F.L. Dodd DSO DFC AFC

'While our Mosquitoes roamed the German skies in all kinds of weather, the heavies (mostly Lancasters and Hallybags) were more particular about when they went aloft.' (IWM)

'The Mosquito completed its turn to show me my contact directly ahead at a distance of two miles but well below our own altitude of 15,000ft. On this occasion I was really going to have to apply myself. The target ahead was weaving steadily about to right and left, added to which it was a question of reducing our height whilst trying to follow spasmodic twists and turns and close the distance respectfully between us. After ten minutes Graham obtained a visual thanks to the clean brilliance of the white moon on an aircraft flying at least 1,500ft ahead of us… Finally, it turned once more, this time out of the glare altogether, and we were able to close without more ado right in to firing range. We opened fire at once in two short bursts. Large pieces flew off and passed uncomfortably close above our heads just as they had with the 110 up at Hamburg and this time-both engines burst into flames simultaneously.' S/L Graham Rice, pilot, and F/O Jimmy Rogerson, radar operator, of 141 Squadron, night of 27/28 June 1944.

THIRTY-TWO

SPOOFING

As I was walking up the stair
I met a man who wasn't there.
He wasn't there again today.
I wish, I wish he'd stay away.

Hugh Mearns (1875–1965)

On 23 November 1943 100 Group (Special Duties – later Bomber Support) was formed under the command of Air Commodore (later Air Vice-Marshal) E.B. Addison to bring together existing Radio Countermeasures (RCM) and Electronic Intelligence (Flint) operations and help significantly to reduce Bomber Command aircrew casualties. Stirlings, Wellingtons, Halifaxes, Liberators and Fortresses variously equipped with thirty-two different types of RCM, in conjunction with ground RCM equipment, made feint attacks on the enemy heartland, while Mosquitoes gave direct support to night bombing and other operations by attacking enemy night-fighters in the air and over his bases. It was a clandestine war of move and counter-move in which first one side, then the other, attempted to render the opposition's radar and homers ineffective before new counter-measures re-established ascendancy again.

Operations were of two distinct types. In the first, two or three of our aircraft would accompany the main bomber stream and then circle above the target; the special operators used their transmitters – in particular 'Jostle' – to jam the German radar defences while the Lancasters and Halifaxes unloaded their bombs. Then everyone headed for home. Our friends in 214 Squadron seemed to do more of these target operations than 223 Squadron. My own crew did a small number of these but the majority of our operations were of the second type, the 'Window Spoofs'. The object of these 'Window' raids was to confuse the enemy as to the intended target. There was a radar screen created by other aircraft

Air and ground crews of 192 Squadron at Foulsham, Norfolk. (CONAM)

'No summer walks, no Christmas trees, no pretty girls for me, / I've got the chop, I've had it, my nightly ops are done, / Yet in a hundred years from now, / I'll still be twenty-one.' (CONAM)

Above: *Crew of* B–Bambi, *192 Squadron. (Jack Short)*

Opposite above: *'It took us a long time before we spotted the bomber and we attacked it no less than six times before we were able to shoot it down. At once when the bomber exploded the jamming of the SN-2 ended.' Oblt Hermann Leube Staffelkapitän 4/NJG3 describing his shooting down of Fortress BII of 214 Squadron on 24 May 1944; F/O Allan J.N. Hockley RAAF and Sgt Raymond G.V. Simpson, his mid-upper gunner were KIA. The other seven in the crew survived. (Gerhard Heilig via CONAM)*

Opposite below: *'To the men who turned the spanner, to the men who pulled the wrench,/To the men who did refuelling with the octane in heavy stench…' (CONAM)*

patrolling in a line roughly north to south over the North Sea and France. A group of us, perhaps eight aircraft, would emerge through this screen scattering 'Window' to give the impression to the German radar operators that a large bomber force was heading for say, Hamburg. Then, when the Germans were concentrating their night-fighters in that area, the real bomber force would appear through the screen and bomb a totally different target, perhaps Düsseldorf.

After several nights, when the Germans had become used to regarding the first group of aircraft as a dummy raid, the drill was reversed. The genuine bombers would appear first and with luck be ignored by the German defences, who would instead concentrate on the second bunch, which was of course our 'Window Spoof'. So we rang the changes, sometimes going in first, sometimes last, in an attempt to cause maximum confusion to the enemy, dissipation of his resources and reduction in our own bomber losses.

Sergeant Don Prutton, B-24 flight engineer, 214 Squadron

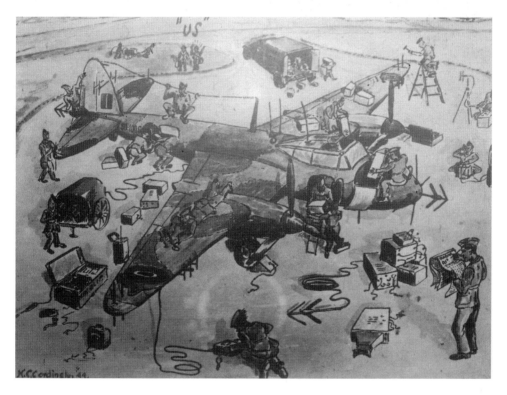

There was no shortage of night-fighter aircraft. From the middle of 1944 onwards we could even speak of a surplus. The decrease of the German night-fighter successes in this period was mainly due to interference, shortage of fuel and the activities of 100 Group. The task of this specialist unit was to mislead our fighters and to befog our conception of the air situation by clever deceptive manoeuvres. This specialist unit finally solved its task so well that it was hardly ever absent from any of the British night operations and it can claim to have set really difficult problems for the German night-fighter command. The British increased their raids at the end of 1944 from month to month, with decreasing losses.

Adolf Galland

THIRTY-THREE
THE BIG CITY

Tonight you are going to the Big City. You will have the opportunity to light a fire in the belly of the enemy that will burn his black heart out.

Air Marshal Sir Arthur Harris, C-in-C, Bomber Command. Thirty-five major attacks were made on Berlin and other German towns during the Battle of Berlin from mid-1943–March 1944. There were 20,224 sorties, 9,111 of which were to the Big City. From these sorties (14,652 by Lancasters), 1,047 aircraft failed to return and 1,682 received varying degrees of damage

Op No.8 on 7 September was to Berlin. Berlin in a Whitley? I didn't believe it! Well, ten hours later as we were being debriefed at interrogation, I felt quite elated. We had actually bombed the capital of Germany but the trip wasn't that pleasant. I thought about that goddamn 'Butcher Harris' (Bert) Butcher was the deserved nickname of the RAF chief of Bomber Command. He didn't give a damn how many men he lost as long as he was pounding the shit out of the Germans. He was just as willing to sacrifice Englishmen as Canadians.

Berlin, 7 September 1941, Pilot Officer J. Ralph Wood RCAF, Whitley navigator, 102 Squadron, Topcliffe

In mid-March 1941 I was crewed up with a new flight commander [Squadron Leader David Torrens] who had flown fighters in the Battle of Britain for what was then the longest trip in the RAF repertoire – Berlin. The trip was to take the clumsy, overladen Wellington nearly five hours just to get there and in those days each machine followed the other at intervals of about five minutes. The theory presumably was that the German civilians would be scared out of their wits by the thought that the RAF had unlimited supplies of heavy bombers. In fact there were eighty aircraft [thirty-six of them Wellingtons] from several stations on 9/10 April 1941. At 5 o'clock in the afternoon of 9 April we entered the briefing room and sat down. At the end of the room was a large map, covered with a curtain. The briefing officer dramatically pulled the curtain aside

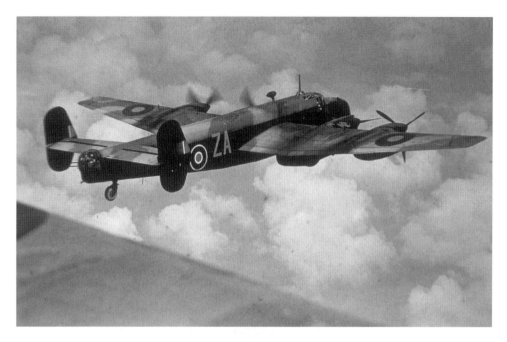

Halifax of 10 Squadron. (Via Jim Sprackling)

and we were startled to see a red ribbon that seemed to go on forever! It meant a four-and-a-half-hour trip to Berlin. The RAF hadn't been to the Big City since the previous September. We all thought, 'Jesus Christ! Why me?'.

After briefing finished we ate our flying supper in the mess. It was rather poor fare, usually corned beef and chips, bread pudding and tea. Everyone was in a high state of nervousness and excited hysteria, although no one showed any sign of despondency. We were quite well trained and highly motivated. It was really dark, cold and clear. A bomber's moon shone overhead. I climbed into the astrodome area and stowed my parachute. Our pilots wore theirs in flight. As we taxied out and lined up on the new tarmac runway I gripped the astrodome hatch clips, in case I needed to get out quickly, as I always did. We were away first. Torrens thundered down the runway (our bomb load was small because of the need for extra fuel). With flaps full on we climbed slowly into the sky above Waterbeach. I climbed into the front turret immediately (enemy fighters might already be about).

Grinding away slowly we headed for Southwold, our point of departure. Nearing the coast of Holland I exclaimed, 'Enemy coast ahead!'. There were a few shots, then all was quiet again. The captain talked quietly to us, telling us to keep our eyes peeled. As usual on any night raid, the first sign of enemy activity as our Wellington crossed the Dutch coast was a burst of flak from the ground, fired it seemed with the intention of letting the RAF know that the defenders were alert. There followed a nerve-wracking three hours during which very little anti-aircraft fire was encountered. Instead, as the lone bomber edged its way towards Berlin at about 120mph, it was passed in silence from one searchlight to the next and at any moment an attack by night-fighters was expected. We made it to the capital where an entirely different experience was in store for us.

Field Marshal Goering had only recently announced that the RAF would never get through to Berlin and, because a few had, he was determined to claw down every one in future. Goering was able to concentrate as much heavy flak as he wished – some said

1,000 guns – and from less than 15,000ft, which was as high as most laden Wellingtons could fly, that looked plenty. And to make his task easier, we were going over one at a time. Down below, Lake Wannsee shone in the moonlight. Buildings, or imagined buildings, appeared in the Berlin suburbs below. One of my tasks when over the target was to report heavy flak bursts on the ground to enable the pilot to take evasive action in the time it took the shells to lift themselves up to our level. For a while this ploy worked and our bombs went down, hitting the opera house we were later told.

We could actually smell flak. The Germans were very good gunners. Then it happened. There was a loud explosion in one of the two engines and the war was nearly over for us. *M for Mother* could not maintain height and, though it succeeded in flying out of the heavy barrage, was down to 1,000ft within half an hour. Near Hanover it was time to jump and I thought the war was over for me. But it had merely changed and a new phase was about to begin – the psychological one against our German captors. That was to last four years and is another story.

Sergeant Alfred Jenner, WOP/AG (front gunner), Wellington IC R-Robert, 99 Squadron, Berlin, 9/10 April 1941, his thirteenth and last op. R-Robert was one of three Wellingtons which failed to return, and a Stirling and a Whitley were also lost

We can wreck Berlin from end to end if the USAAF will come in on it. It will cost between 400–500 aircraft. It will cost Germany the war.
Air Marshal Sir Arthur Harris

March 1943 came in with a roar, when on the 1st we were briefed for Berlin – 'the Big City' as we knew it. It was a feared target and there was no doubt it would be defended fiercely. Cheshire was going and Jock Hill, his wireless operator, was going to Berlin for the fourteenth time. Jock, a good friend of mine, was determined to make a full tour of thirty trips to Berlin if he could. He was the Signals Leader of 76 and could choose his trips. They were always the difficult ones. He had made several to Berlin with Cheshire on their first tour.

I had, for my last few trips, given up trying to get our Halifax, *C-Charlie*, up to our briefed bombing height. She was dreadfully slow on the climb and wallowed like a waterlogged boat at maximum altitude. I always became impatient and levelled off a couple of thousand feet below the stipulated height. This gave me more time on the run-in and a steadier platform over the target. It also made me look rather daring, always bombing at a lower height than most, although I didn't realise that at the time. These tactics were not at all popular with my crew, who believed, probably correctly, that every inch of height should be taken. They insisted that going to 'the Big City' I should climb all the way up to our bombing height of 20,000ft. I felt perhaps this time they had something and promised to do so.

Setting off before dusk, it was dark when we got to the North German coast. The plan was to fly north along the coast across Schleswig Holstein and turn south somewhere east of Hamburg to indicate that we might be going for one of several targets, Kiel, Hamburg, or Rostock. We would pass them closely before making a last minute turn south to Berlin. Over Germany the winds were all over the place and we were soon well off track. We flew over Kiel by mistake and got a very hot reception. It even woke Taff up from his job of monitoring and jamming German R/T transmissions by using tinsel. All aircraft carried a microphone in an engine nacelle. When he heard any German broadcast, the wireless operator pressed his key and the noise of the engine was transmitted on the German fighter frequency to distort any instructions. As we bounced about the sky, Taff, while listening out, had been reading his musical magazine, *The Melody Maker*. Seeing the title of a popular melody of the day, he came up on intercom: 'Hey Skip, it says here that

"Anywhere on Earth is Heaven"'.

'You're bloody right Taff,' I replied through my teeth, hanging on to the shaking control column, 'and I wish like Hell we were anywhere on earth now'.

We ploughed on to the Big City, me hauling and coaxing old *C-Charlie* higher than she'd ever been before. Finally I told them we were at last at 20,000ft. There were muted cheers all round. When we reached Berlin the Pathfinders, affected by the fickle winds, were late, so we had to stooge around. After a while some fires and flares appeared ahead and Harry led us to them. We were quite close to them, when Mac said that there were other flares going down behind us. I looked around over my shoulder. No doubt about these, they were the real ones and the ones we were chasing were dummies well east of the target. Now I had to go back against the stream of incoming aircraft. There were over 300. As I turned I saw a few more aircraft doing the same. Making my turn fairly sharp, *Charlie* lost a bit of height. By now there were aircraft all around us, going in all directions. It was bloody dicey. Wanting to get over the target, drop the bombs and get out as soon as possible, I pushed the nose down to speed things up. We soon had a good view of the correct marker flares but I now had to go the full distance back across the target among the heavy flak and against the oncoming stream before turning once more on to the correct heading. By the time we'd done that I was down to 17,500ft for the bombing run. Once more I hadn't managed to bomb from the full height. However, the crew weren't complaining now; they wanted to get it all over with and get out just as quickly as I did.

It was hot over Berlin all right. We saw several Halifaxes coned in searchlights. One was Bertie Neal, who returned with a great picture of just searchlight glare. Roger Coverly actually spun in his efforts to avoid them but managed to pull out below 20,000ft. Having dropped our bombs in the approved fashion and spent ten long seconds waiting for our photo flash to go off, I turned for home at just about the correct position. At least we thought it was. Harry claimed another pinpoint, a junction of river and railway, just where they should have been. If we really knew where we were then, it was to be the last time for three more hours.

As we headed back over Germany we saw flak coming up at aircraft in almost every direction. Normally, the location of flak and searchlights was a good aid to navigation but this time they seemed to be everywhere. I was pretty sure that the flak ahead was the Ruhr. I noted two aircraft, at least, go down in flames. It was coming up in such quantity that there must have been a lot of aircraft ahead of us in the same predicament. I took some small consolation from this and pressed on. Fortunately, I had held height after we left Berlin and we were still at 15,000ft. I wasn't crossing the Ruhr lower. We ploughed our way through the flak, getting bounced about in the process and eventually, thirty minutes later, came out the other side. Ahead lay the coastline but we were headed for yet another concentration of flak. I flew north of most of it but we were hit just as we passed out to sea. It wasn't bad, but noisy, as a lot of shrapnel rattled our tail.

Back at Linton awaiting our turn to land, a Halifax came flying along over the runway shooting off red Verey flares. We made way for him immediately. It was Roger Coverly, literally coming back from his spin. All his radios and electrics were out and he had to make a landing without any communications. He made it OK, the final happening of an eventful night. Counting the cost next day, we found that of the force of 302 aircraft setting out, seventeen were lost: a nasty 5½ per cent. Six of them were Halifaxes. 76 Squadron lost two crews, both of whom had been with us since December. In 78 our luck still held, but it was a frail thread, as we were to find out.

Flying Officer Ron Read, pilot, 78 Squadron, Berlin, 1/2 March 1943, who later that same month was promoted flight lieutenant and appointed deputy flight commander. All told, 302 aircraft raided the Big City and seventeen bombers were lost

We had been there two nights before and Harris was determined to get in another raid on the Big City before the light evenings. The weather forecast at briefing was ghastly and our station Met. officers unofficially predicted a certain 'scrub'. Came take-off time and the weather was on the deck with heavy rain from the occlusion running N to S over Yorkshire to Lincolnshire. Cloud as solid up to 15,000ft with severe icing predicted.

Take off was put back and we knew there had to be a 'scrub'. The weather persisted and take off was again put back. But Harris would not cancel and eventually we took off. The occlusion tailed back over Yorkshire and almost as soon as we took off we were in cloud as set course over the North Sea. We had the oldest, clapped out Halifax on the squadron – Q-Queenie – quite notorious for its lack of climbing ability and poor ceiling. We flogged our way upwards through the occlusion and at 15,000ft we were still in cloud and were unable to climb another foot. Our climb had been so slow we had taken the whole of the North Sea to reach this height. Now straight and level and still in cloud, we found ourselves with iced-up windscreen and turrets and a maximum IAS of 135 knots.

At this point we must have been somewhere near Flensburg for we suddenly became the object of some heavy AA fire. Even the Germans didn't seem to believe an aircraft could be flying so slow since most of the bursts seemed to be ahead of us. With everyone operating 'blind' because of the icing, discretion now had to be the better part of valour. We dropped our bombs hoping against hope that they might give the German gunners earache but more in the hope of getting a bit more speed from the lightened aircraft.

Thankfully, we turned for home and managed to re-cross the occlusion without incurring any further icing. As we reached the end of the runway we had to feather the starboard outer as the oil pressure dropped off the clock. Arriving at dispersal we got out and walked around the aircraft where one of the ground staff was getting rather excited. A steady flow of glycol was being shed by both inner engines. From one of the wing bomb bays two 4lb incendiaries were protruding with the other eighty-eight lying loose in the bomb-bay doors. The IFF aerial had disappeared. Had we gone on to Berlin it seems certain that we would either have run out of engines, had a wing on fire, or in the last resort, have been shot down by Fighter Command. Sometimes it was easier to fight the Germans.

And Then There was the Weather, *Sergeant Tom Wingham DFC, bomb aimer, Halifax II, 102 Squadron, tenth op, 29/30 March 1943, Berlin. Twenty-one aircraft were lost*

23 August 1943 saw us making our first assault against Berlin – always considered to be the 'big one'. It meant a long trip over heavily defended enemy territory and the defences were savage in the protection of the great city, which the Nazis had sworn would never be subjected to air bombardment. What a long way I had come since those dark days in 1940 when there appeared to be no salvation from the gloom. Here we were attacking the German capital in strength and talking more and more of an invasion of Europe. This was my fifty-seventh operation. Could I survive to see that sixtieth operation? It did seem to be inviting the inevitable with each further raid, so many crews had not even reached double figures and with so many more aircraft involved, losses mounted so that the likelihood of aircrews surviving twelve raids was still minimal. Apart from the heavy flak and searchlight activity, the flight was uneventful, far less frightening than any trip to the Ruhr and after bombing from 18,000ft we were back at base in six hours thirty-five minutes.

Warrant Officer Eddie Wheeler, WOP/AG, 97 Squadron, Bourn, Cambridgeshire, Berlin raid, 23/24 August 1943

Over 800 kites went, all four-engined. Not much trouble on the way there. The visibility was good so we could watch the attack as it developed. In six short minutes of the raid the place was glowing with fires and enormous flashes were lighting up the ground. Searchlights and flak not very intense, but bags of fighters. Making our final run-up on to a marker we were suddenly attacked from very close range by a Dornier. She scored several hits on our kite but Len and John kept their heads and brought her down. Once in flames, the Dornier was picked up and finished off by searchlights and flak. Bombed dead central on a marker and got out like bats out of hell. Counted six of our kites going down in flames in the short time we were over the target. Over the target there was a plane circling around the whole time with one of the Pathfinder laddies making a continual running commentary telling us where to bomb and cheering like mad whenever we scored a hit. This fellow is called the Master of Ceremonies. They use him on all the big raids. On the way back we got quite considerably off track crossing the Baltic. There were doubts about us even reaching England. Also, one engine packed up for a while. We threw out quite a lot of things though – my guns, ammo etc. – and just made Coltishall with eighty gallons. We were flying about eight hours forty. Damn tired.

Flight Sergeant Arthur 'Spud' Taylor, Stirling observer, M for Mother, 90 Squadron, Wratting Common, Berlin raid, 23/24 August 1943. 727 aircraft were dispatched on this raid, which saw Bomber Command's greatest loss of aircraft in one night so far in the war. Fifty-six aircraft were lost. M for Mother was left at RAF Coltishall, its tailplane and rudder full of holes

In those fifty awful minutes on Monday night the RAF's bombs turned the whole of the centre of Berlin into a honeycomb of ruin. Street after street was blasted and devastated by fire.

The facts about the welter of destruction, on which Himmler had clapped an iron censorship, came out tonight. Travellers told them: but they must be nameless, because of official warnings to all people who now leave Germany that if they give the slightest information away in neutral countries they will be punished.

Today, they say as wrecked buildings still blazed, Himmler ordered that all foreign workers should be moved from their barracks in the city to the outskirts. This was said to be a 'safety measure', but it is not their safety he was considering, but that of the valuable goods scattered about the ruins, among which looters are busy. For many nights, say my informants. Berliners had been sitting in their blacked-out homes, waiting, listening. Then, when just before midnight on Monday the sirens moaned their overture to the raid, everything happened at once. Within five minutes of the time the people first heard the throb of our Lancasters there were scores of fires already getting their grip on the city. Zoo station hit

And the high explosives came down so that you couldn't count any thuds, but could hear only a roar and feel a rocking of the earth that was like the end of the world.

Newspaper report on the Berlin raid of 23/24 August 1943

We turned towards the north-east and headed for the 'Big City'. The TIs went down on time and I noticed another bunch on my left. Potsdam was being marked for the Main Force of 'heavies'. They were operating much lower than we, the Mosquitoes were. Then the searchlights came into play. First the bluish ones, operating singly and radar-controlled, wandered haphazardly, or so it seemed. Suddenly, one of them darted sideways and caught a Lanc in its beam. The Lanc dived and wriggled left and right, but hadn't a hope as twenty or thirty other searchlights immediately lit the sky around it. It was caught in a wigwam of light. Then the sparks of flak began to burst around the aircraft. Some of the flak shells must have hit the starboard wing, for within a minute flames were rolling over the wing and the Lanc started to spin round and down ever so slowly, I thought. I heard myself yelling into the microphone which was clamped to my face: 'Bail out, you stupid bastards. You haven't a hope. Don't you know you're on fire?'

As if they had heard me, the silk parachutes began to appear in the searchlight beams. I started to count them – one, two, three – then no more. Four hadn't made it. As if to underline the whole affair which was unfolding, the aircraft seemed to disintegrate as it went down. The three parachutes hung like stationary mushrooms in the cone of light. Just then there was a flash and what looked like an explosion. Two aircraft must have collided in mid-air. There would be no parachutes coming out of that, I reckoned.

As we were running up to the target a bunch of searchlights caught us. It had been sheer good luck on their part that they did so, since all the pale blue ones were latching on to the Main Force on our right. I was completely blinded by the light and couldn't see the TIs, far less bomb on them: 'I've overshot the TIs – we'll have to go round again,' I said into my mike, adding automatically, 'bomb doors closed.'

'Oh, bloody hell,' replied the somewhat strained voice of Bill, 'which way do you want me to turn the damned thing?'

It was the first and only time I had ever heard him swear. After a moment's thought I replied: 'Make it a wide right turn. All the others will be making a left turn after dropping their loads. We don't want to run into any of them.' Bumping into another aircraft's slipstream was no fun either, as I had found out over Hannover when night-fighters had attacked us. Our right turn seemed to fox the searchlights. Presumably, they had anticipated we would be making a left turn, heading for home. Anyway, we lost them and were shrouded in darkness again.

I resolved to concentrate on the markers and ignore what was going on around me. This I found rather hard to do; it was difficult to tell which were bombs bursting and which were aircraft either on fire or blowing up. It seemed to me that Dante had underestimated his description of Hell. I went through the patter on our second run-in, dropped the TIs, waited for the photographs, then headed for the Cromer beacon and home.

'Sorry about the run-in to the target. I couldn't see a thing; the searchlight blinded me', I said rather lamely.

'Not to worry Johnnie, we're still in one piece. It was a good idea of yours to make a right turn – it caught the Jerries on the wrong foot.'

I didn't explain to him that I had been thinking more of the aircraft following us than of the German defences.

We landed safely. Bill, following the laid-down instructions, opened the bomb doors at dispersal before cutting the engines. I was doing my usual – having a pee and spitting out the wad of chewing gum which had kept my mouth moist during the trip – when an armourer of the ground staff approached me.

'I say Sergeant, come and see this. It looks a bit queer to me.'

'Nothing wrong I hope?' We ducked into the empty bomb bay together.

'Do you know where you collected that?' He pointed to the whole side of a flak shell embedded in one of the main spars.

'Over the "Big City" I suppose', I answered.

Bill had joined us and was looking curiously at the splinter. 'I never felt a thing hit us during the whole trip. It must have gone through the bomb doors or the fuselage. Isn't there a hole somewhere?'

'That's what's making me wonder. There's not a mark on the outer skin of the aircraft at all,' replied the armourer.

I looked at Bill and found him gazing at me. 'Are you thinking what I'm thinking?'

I shrugged. 'I don't know, but I reckon we could only have collected it after I'd dropped the bomb and before you'd closed the bomb doors – a matter of seconds.'

'That's what I thought,' said Bill, 'thank God the bomb had gone.'

We turned to the armourer, who was looking as if he had seen a couple of ghosts. 'Yes, a matter of seconds – the difference between the quick and the dead.'

At the debriefing my Canadian oppo said: 'I hear you went round the target twice tonight?'

'That's right. I liked the look of the place', I answered, dryly.

One Man's War, *Sergeant Johnnie Clark, Warrant Officer Bill Henley, RNZAF's Mosquito navigator, 571 Squadron, Berlin, November 1944*

On New Year's Eve 1944 it was the long slog to Berlin again. We were airborne just before 1800hrs. I tried to ignore the searchlights and box barrage flak over the target, concentrating on my charts illuminated by the small navigation light which stretched over them. We dropped our bombs, got our photographs and headed for home. I turned the oxygen up; it perked me up quite a bit. While we were emptying our bladders at the edge of the dispersal pan after landing, Bill remarked: 'That was our thirteenth trip.'

'Oh was it? Superstitious are you?'

'No, I just thought you'd like to know.'

One Man's War, *Sergeant Johnnie Clark, navigator, 162 Squadron, January 1945. Of the fifty-one ops he and his pilot Bill Henley did, fifteen were to the Big City. Both received the DFC. Just after the end of the war Bill Henley was killed flying as a passenger in a Dakota returning from Malta*

Back at home I have a mountain of work to deal with. But I can now get on with it very quickly and energetically since I have got a real burden off my chest. In the evening we have the regulation Mosquito raid: the cursed Englishmen are over Berlin nearly every night and deprive one of the few hours' sleep which one needs more than ever these days.

'The Cursed Englishmen are over Berlin', *the* Goebbels Diaries, *27 February 1945*

Lanc being bombed up for a raid on the Big City.

THIRTY-FOUR
BRYLCREEM BOYS

It was no wonder that aircrew were the favourites of the young girls, lonely wives and widows…

In many ways, bomber aircrews were the spoiled babies of the Armed Forces. Apart from liberal leaves, we were given all sorts of delicacies. We had fresh oranges and orange juice, when these were unobtainable anywhere. On every operation, we were given a real fried egg and bacon before we went and another when we got back. During the pre take-off meal, Morty always solemnly exhibited his macabre sense of humour, by stating aloud, 'The condemned men ate a hearty breakfast'. This cheerful statement normally accompanied the notice of execution of a murderer. We all ignored him and chewed on. On each trip we were given one or two chocolate bars and a generous ration of chewing gum, to keep the saliva flowing when on oxygen at 20,000ft. We had extra cigarette rations. Ultraviolet lamps were provided for our use; if we tried we could appear tanned and healthy even if we weren't. It was no wonder that aircrew were the favourites of the young girls, lonely wives and widows of surrounding districts. But it was rather like fattening turkeys for Christmas: they didn't call him 'Butch' Harris for nothing.

Ron Read. On 16/17 April 1943 Flight Lieutenant E.G. 'Morty' Mortenson's Halifax was brought down by the combined fire of two German fighters on the raid on Pilsen and it crashed near Trier. Morty and a sergeant were killed. Five of the seven crew were made POW

This is a very good station in all respects. Good food in the sergeants mess and I am lodged in married quarters, have my own bath and a fireplace if we care to use it.
Sergeant Robert S. Raymond

16 August. I have moved over to Wyton so I thought I had better give you the gen. This is a peacetime mess and absolutely wizard. There are two of us to a room about the size of a large office and as my pilot is not coming over until tomorrow or Friday

"They met exactly two years ago on a float in the Channel."

[1945]

I have it to myself at the moment. It has two chests of drawers, a built-in wardrobe, two chairs, tables and reading lamps. The food is terrific; tonight for dinner we had soup, a choice of rabbit or cold meat and salad, plum pie, stewed plums, trifle or rice and plums and cheese and biscuits. We are waited on at table and the messing is only a shilling a day.

Derek Smith, Mosquito navigator, 692 Squadron, 8 Group, in a letter home, 1944

We led strange lives, residing in reasonably comfortable civilised surroundings. This was especially true at Dishforth, which was a permanent RAF station. We had lots of free time when we weren't required to fly. The nearest town to Dishforth was Boroughbridge. We would visit the neighbouring pubs and maybe a little further afield to go to dance halls. There were lots of nice-looking girls. We also spent a lot of time in the mess. The food on the squadron was good. The only complaint would be the Brussels sprouts. They must have grown in profusion in England because there never seemed to be a shortage. We got so many that it was quite a few years after the war before I could eat one again. Many stations had four meals a day. Tea was roughly from 3.30 to 4.30 and supper from 7 to 8. As a sergeant I was billeted in a two-bedroom permanent married quarters row house with three other senior NCOs. We slept one in each bedroom and two in the living room. All eating and entertaining was done in the sergeants mess.

Flight Sergeant Jack Woodrow, 425 Squadron, Dishforth, Yorkshire, 7 October 1942–4 June 1943

We usually slept until the last minute, then made a mad dash for the mess before the doors closed. Most of us had this timed pretty well, so well that I decided to upset the pattern by piling as many bicycles as possible on top of the latrine building. Of course, a great many missed their breakfast that morning, including the CO, whose bicycle was also included.

With a gut load of sergeants mess garbage stuck in my crop, I'd hop on my bicycle and pedal into Abingdon for a few beers to wash it down. The mess food was usually mutton and more mutton, kidneys, curried rice and, of course, Brussels sprouts. The latter were a kind of miniature cabbage, eaten boiled. At our mess the cook must have boiled them and re-boiled them until they emerged a sickly green gob. My RAF friend who often ate with me used to mutter, '13-8, 13-8, 13-8' whenever we had these Brussels sprouts as a vegetable. My curiosity got the better of me and I asked him what he meant by this expression. He said, 'When I'm served this mess I just have to express my displeasure, but it's not swearing, it's taken from the Bible. Hebrew, 13th Chapter, 8th Verse: "Jesus Christ, the same yesterday and today and forever"'.

I agreed that we had been getting this vegetable just about every day and turned my attention to the ever-present trifle with repellent custard. Small wonder that we looked forward to a snack in the village where we had the big choice of Welsh rarebit (cheese on toast), beans on toast, or fish paste on toast. One night I was enjoying a special dinner treat of chicken stew until someone mentioned that it was rabbit stew. But even that was a treat. Some nights at our debriefing my pilot and I would use up the rum ration of those who preferred their coffee without this additional fortification. This on top of our own ration had the effect of making everything seem great. The only difficulty was bicycling from the ops room to our barracks without going in the ditch. Our real treat was the flying breakfast of bacon and eggs back at the base and our discussions of the attack with the other crews on the raid. I used to think they used this as bait to get us to fly. Once in a while we would bicycle around the countryside, looking for farmers to sell us some eggs. We would then have the cook at our mess prepare them for a snack at night after visiting the pub. The eggs kept getting a little tougher and eventually we realised that the farmers were passing off duck eggs on us.

Pilot Officer J. Ralph Wood DFC CD RCAF

The RAF used to have eggs and bacon for breakfast. All we got were beans on the second sitting. We had this corporal in our company who could imitate the air raid warning whistle. Sometimes he would stand in the main doors of the mess and whistle. All the RAF people would come running out and dash into the air raid shelters. Then we would go in and eat their breakfast for them. As we left the mess he would give the 'All Clear'!

David Woodhouse, 70th Suffolk Yeomanry

A Brylcreem bottle lying in undergrowth on an airfield fifty years after the war. (Pete Howard)

'Forty odd years ago they were known as the "Brylcreem Boys".'

D. G. K.

We are the Air-Sea Rescue, no effing use are we;
The only times you'll find us are breakfast, dinner and tea.
And when we sight a dinghy, we cry with all our might:
'Per Ardua ad Astra – up you, Jack, we're all right.

"—Won't keep you a minute. The Skipper's sea-sick."

I spent the next night drinking beer in the Caxton Gibbet with the rest of the squadron who weren't flying that night. I liked squadron life, I reflected. There was no discipline sergeant barking at you. Provided you turned up for briefing on time, bombed the target and came back in one piece you were left to get on with it.

One Man's War, *Pilot Officer Johnnie Clark, navigator, 162 Squadron*

When I was commissioned as a Pilot Officer, off came the Sergeant's stripes and on went a thin blue bar on each shoulder strap. It meant goodbye to the sergeants mess and over to the luxury of the officers mess and a new way of life. A room all to myself with a nice WAAF batwoman to clean my room and shoes etc. and a cup of tea when I was called in the morning. No money was allowed in the bar. All drinks were booked and paid for at the end of the month. No more pay parades, a bank account and a nice lump sum every month from Cox and King, the RAF pay agents. Also, a lump sum to buy a tailored uniform and greatcoat etc.

When we had another six-day break I went off to London to buy my No.1 uniform and cap. Most of the West End tailors were keeping going by supplying officers' uniforms. Gieves, Moss Bros and Austin Reed supplied the Air Force. I had been told that Austin Reed were a bit cheaper than the other two if cash was paid, so that is where I went. I was a standard size and a uniform was found that needed little alteration, which I could pick up the next day, which I purchased. I could no longer stay at my old haunt, the Union Jack Club at Waterloo, but was directed to the Junior Officers Club or Wings Club, in Grosvenor Place. Some wealthy house owner had turned their house over for the duration of the war for the use of junior officers on leave in London, very handy for the West End theatres and the stations of Victoria and Waterloo. I collected my uniform the next day and then took Ethel home to meet Mum and Dad and the tribe. She had never been on a farm and Mum didn't appear to approve of a city girl, but she couldn't complain, she had worked in London in the First World War and came from Taunton herself. She considered herself definitely upper middle class. Nevertheless, she did her best. It was to be Ethel's only visit. About three months later she went down with TB, which was rife in London in 1943–44 and in three weeks was dead. I didn't go to London again until the whole crew went in the last week of April 1944.

Later I was posted to 4 Group HQ to become a staff officer. I soon found that this was a temporary posting to learn the job. It had been decided to form a new Group, to be called 7 Group, and put all the Heavy Conversion units in to one Group and there were to be two flight engineer staff officers, one to look after the Lancasters and the other for the Halifaxes. I was to have the Halifax post. In the meantime I had to get used to a very different life. The HQ, which was located at Heslington Hall (now York University), was crawling with wing commanders; men like Hank Iveson and Jerry Warner, who had made two or more tours. My mentor was Eddie Edwards who had been badly burnt at some time. And another new experience: civilian digs. I was billeted with Mr and Mrs W. who had a nice detached house in Heslington Lane, which connects the Hall to Fulford and then to York. Besides being a very nice house, Mrs W. had two daughters – Dee, who was eighteen and had just left school and was going to Cambridge to train as a teacher, and Eff, who was twenty and worked as a civil service secretary. It wasn't long before the ice was broken and, when she found out that I liked dancing, it was off to the De Grey Rooms, the upmarket dance hall in York. The posting at 4 Group HQ went very quickly. When the posting to Grantham came it was agreed that I would come back to York at weekends and it wasn't very long before we started getting serious. An engagement was discussed but Eff's father was a bit old fashioned and we could get engaged after her twenty-first birthday on 29 March but we were not to get married till after the war was over. There were a lot of young widows round York and he didn't want his daughter to be one.

Flight Lieutenant Jim Sprackling

One of the good things about operating with the RAF was the knowledge that when you got back from an operational sortie there was a bed for you to sleep in with sheets. There was food on plates; there were glasses to drink from. I remember contrasting these things with our friends and colleagues serving in the desert; in the jungles of the Far East; or perhaps at sea almost anywhere in the world. When we went into the mess dining room, there was a glass of milk for the aircrew. I always felt slightly embarrassed because there was none for the ground crews on whom we were all so dependent.

Squadron Leader (later Group Captain) A.F. Wallace. OC B Flight, 620 Squadron, June 1943–September 1944

Brylcreem, a contraceptive and one's extra dollars,
Clean underclothing, shifts and collars;
A checklist for leave in America
Of an RAF man, training in Canada
One could take only a few dollars I understand!
More of which were regarded as contraband
And as this amount restricted one a lot
Airmen packed their Brylcreem pot
Containing cash within a condom, knotted,
And for quite a time this ruse went unspotted
Until someone got suspicious and said
"Why should bald airman carry Brylcreem for his head?"
Then delving, pulled the contents out
Which was how 'Brylcreem Boys' came about
I wonder? Would 'Durex Boys' have sounded better?
Or was no name on that French Letter?

'Brylcreem Boys' (The True History), Jasper Miles

THIRTY-FIVE

HIGH COCKALORUM

Where are the Kiwis who left all the sunshine
For bleak windy airfields and fenland and dyke,
Playing wild Mess games like high cockalorum,
And knocking the hell out of Hitler's Third Reich?

Occasionally a 'scrub' just before take-off happened because of weather deterioration and intelligence information pointing to the operation being too risky. Then mayhem would break out in the messes. All the crews were wound up and many had taken Benzedrine, which was issued to crews who felt they needed pepping up and of course no one had any intention of going to bed. They drank everything that was available in the bars, which was considerable. Aircrew had a monthly whisky ration drawn on the first of the month, so if any crews were missing during the month their ration was drunk by the survivors. New crews had their ration issued on arrival. The main entertainment was singing bawdy songs and playing various mess games. High Cockalorum was one of these. Two teams, one of which would get down in a line to the end wall forming a vaulting horse, the other team would vault, one at a time, the object being to collapse the horse or pitch one of the riders on to the floor. This could be achieved by a well-timed wiggle when the jumper was airborne. If all the jumpers got on the horse and the horse didn't collapse the horse won. There were usually two or three casualties.

Pilot Officer Jim Sprackling

In the course of our fifty-three operational ops together I got to know Frank Leslie Dodd pretty well. The first thing I noticed about him was his calm, quiet, almost sleepy exterior and the second was that it covered a steely, inflexible determination to get things as right as he could possibly make them. The third was his modesty: 'A lot of people, especially in the early days, did a great deal more than we did in PRU'. Frank was immediately and obviously a chap of thoughtful, observant, pacific nature with a sound family basis, centred

'I am sure we enjoyed our beer more when we were drinking from jam jars than when we had normal beer glasses. These evenings relaxed the tension and for a while we could forget the war and our flying missions.' (Dennis Cooper via Theo Boiten)

completely around his splendid wife Joyce and a steadily growing family. Decidedly not the type to lead a riot in the mess, or 'High Cockalorum' or the singing of 'Eskimo Nell'. He would mingle, join in the fun and melt quietly into the background. He would always enjoy a chuckle, as the time when we were harried by some flak somewhere. The Form Green issued as a summary of the trip, sent over the stuttering Teleprinter made a slight error. It should have said: 'on returning base, hole found in starboard wing'. What appeared was: 'On returning, asshole found in starboard wing.' There was a great deal of animated discussion in the crew room about which member of the crew had been thus deprived by the Hun.

Eric Hill DFC DFM, Mosquito navigator, 544 Squadron PRU, talking about Flight Lieutenant (later Group Captain) F.L. Dodd DSO DFC AFC

Our mess parties had a habit of accelerating as the evening advanced. On one occasion an officer rode into the mess on horseback, much to the delight of the inebriated occupants. Not to be outdone, another officer jumped on his motorcycle and rode that into the mess. Then there was the night of the duel. A RAF officer who, unbeknown at the time, was suffering from appendicitis, was throwing beer mugs up in the air, breaking the chandeliers. At the same time he was telling the Canadians present that he didn't want any damn Canadians over here to fight his battles and why didn't we get the hell home? I figured that kind of talk called for a duel and we took down the two crossed sabres hanging on the mess wall and started fencing. When I nicked him between the eyes, over his nose, our medical officer, who was black as the ace of spades (fondly referred to as old 23:59 – one minute to midnight), decided it was time to end the duel.

Pilot Officer J. Ralph Wood DFC CD RCAF, 692 Squadron Mosquito navigator

'Swing the hot numbers! Swing and lilt and laughter/And let there be no crowding at the bar,/Before another night has drooped from sunset,/Some of our comrades will have travelled far!/Start up a song now! Let it be a good one −/"There's no promotion, this side..." Oh! we know/That's just an old one... "Hi-jigger-jigger mush-mush"./Raise up your voices, chaps and let it go!' (RAF)

One boozy night in the mess, there was a sudden decision by everybody there to plant somebody's footprints around the semi-circular ceiling of the Nissen hut − merely to convince gullible visitors that somebody had taken a running jump to do it. Well, it was decided that I was Joe, being fairly light in weight. A sort of scaffolding of tables and chairs was constructed, gradually rising in height towards the centre. I took off my shoes and socks. Somebody else blacked the soles with shoe polish and I was carefully lifted up and had my feet planted on the ceiling one at a time. All was going well until we reached the highest point in the centre. The scaffolding began to falter; the structure collapsed. I fell from a great height and my right palm came down, unfortunately, on to a piece of broken glass on the floor. I don't remember much of what followed but the Doc (Vyse) was on hand and took charge. I was losing blood at a fairly fearsome rate to start with apparently until he staunched it. I was carried by ambulance to the Norfolk and Norwich Hospital and was wrapped in a plaster cast for some time. The end result was the cutting of a tendon, a messy right palm and a permanently bent first finger. At home on leave in Southend, I'd be showing my messy right palm to relations and friends and explaining frankly how it had happened. Somebody whispered to my mother that I was almost certainly concealing the real facts and that it was a war wound.

Flight Lieutenant (later Air Vice Marshal CBE DFC AFC) Jack Furner, 214 Squadron, Oulton

Dining-in nights in sergeants' and officers' messes have always been occasions for high jinks! When the formality of dinner is finished all manner of games are played. After a dinner in the sergeants' mess at Foulsham mid-1944 and following the usual capers, there was a 250cc DR motorcycle race around the anteroom! Another bit of nonsense was the challenge to hang upside-down by the crook of one's legs from a high open rafter of the mess anteroom and drink a pint of bitter.

The officers' mess at RAF Marham is an imposing three-storied building built during the 1936 RAF expansion programme. Those cars that were sprinkled around the car park were mainly pre-war vehicles such as 'E'-Type Morrises, early Fords, Hillmans and Standards. One chap had a nice little Austin 7, which was his pride and joy. A dozen of his fellow officers went outside and managed to lift the little car up the steps and into the entrance hall. When the officer blew his top, the culprits carried the little car back down the steps again!

Having formed up, the parade was brought to attention and 'open order' by the adjutant and handed over to the new, nervous, station commander for inspection. His first task was to prepare the parade for an address by the padre. Unfortunately he issued the never-to-be-forgotten command: 'Fall out Romans, Catholics, Jews and other denominations!'

Group Captain Jack A. V. Short

When ops were scrubbed too late for going to the 'flesh-pots', which was not unusual, homemade entertainment in the mess was the order of the day. High Cockalorum was a favourite sport, especially on two squadron stations, as most were, and usually when sufficient anaesthetic had been consumed in the bar to deaden the pain! There were several versions but it was usually one squadron against the other. There were various formats but that which I remember best was where one team formed a pyramid in the corner of the anteroom with the trophy on top – sometimes a body and at others, something considered to be of value to the opposition. The object was for the attackers to capture the trophy and of course, it resolved itself into a heaving mass of injured bodies! There were also numerous stories of motorcycles and horses being ridden around messes, which I have heard, told at various stations but never actually witnessed. At Syerston, it was said that a motorcycle was ridden up the left-hand stairs, round the upper floor, down the right-hand stairs and out of the front door. It was also reported that the padre's horse did a similar circuit, but this time in the officer's mess. I have not the slightest doubt that these incidents happened but when, where and how many times, I cannot be sure. What is certain, however, is that some lucky aircrew, like me, were in somewhat more danger of injury in the mess than we ever were out of it!

Derek Smith, Lancaster and Mosquito navigator

What started off as a civilised party developed into a real 'thrash'. Ossie, the Scots tea planter from Ceylon, climbed on to the bar counter.

'Right!' he bellowed, 'I think we all need a bit of practice at landing on FIDO [fog investigation and dispersal operation]. I'll be the controller.'

Newspapers and magazines were confiscated from the lounge, rolled up and placed in almost parallel lines on the highly polished mess bar floor. Tins of Ronseal were sprayed on the papers.

'Let's make it realistic', said someone. 'Get the feather cushions from the lounge and we'll have 10/10ths feather visibility.' The idea was to slide down the polished line between the burning papers and have the air full of feathers at the same time. Ossie bellowed out the time-honoured phrase:

'Come in number one, your time is up!'

Whereupon the CO whipped down the burning line of newspapers on his bottom and crashed into the stove at the other end. The atmosphere of the burning papers plus the clouds of feathers made the bar almost untenable.

It could have been worse. They could have burned the place down. At one party a bunch of aircrew from another squadron had found a pile of bricks, sand and cement. Contractors were building an extension to the mess. The chaps used the lot and bricked up the CO's car, which was parked outside. The contractors had been reported as saying that he hoped these officers were better flyers than they were bricklayers.

Pilot Officer Johnnie Clark, navigator, 162 Squadron Mosquito, in One Man's War

THIRTY-SIX
PATHFINDERS

He led that crucial raid without which our war was lost
Or, even if won, then at far more fearful a cost.
His flying days were o'er when he and I first met,
I calling at the old pre-fab: where, with typewriter set,
He planned, unassuming man: no flash 'war-hero' looks,
Retired Air Commodore, yet nought of rank would show
As on equal terms we chatted, I but an ex-NCO.
Once he complimented me on some verse I had composed
And confided in me regarding a book that he proposed.
Several times I was to call, natter a while and leave him at his door,
But then he passed, precluding my calling any more.
I have wondered. In his hours of writing and remembering alone
Did he once more hear that four-fold 'Merlin' drone?
Recall intercom talk? 'Some poor sod's bought it out to port!'
'That bloody gauge's still reading nought!' 'Cup of coffee, sport?'
Then: 'Half an hour to run! Turn on to O-four-O!'
And, did he in retrospect look down on Peenemünde's awful glow,
Seeing each bomb-load pulverising his target there below?
(Five and a half hundred 'planes on this, his greatest show)
And, as he wrote of it, did ghosts of they with whom he flew
Whisper odd, half-forgotten details which only they knew?
And did old Bomber-boys, having pre-knowledge of his impending fate
Gather and escort the Master Bomber up to Valhalla's gate?

'The Master Bomber', An appreciation of Air Commodore John Searby DSO DFC, by G.R.J. Miles

'Facing into the wind, the captain would call for 'full boost' and then, releasing the brakes, the aircraft would gather increasing speed nose-down to lift off its massive load just before the end of the runway.' (Author)

Duty: Operations Peenemünde (Baltic)

'Master of Ceremonies'. Night-fighters accounted for many of our aircraft in bright moonlight. A good attack and resulted in the destruction of the Experimental Establishment.

Attacked by fighter and we claimed it as damaged.

John Searby, CO, 83 Squadron, the first of the Pathfinder Force Master Bombers, log book entry for the night of 17/18 August 1943 when 596 heavies of Bomber Command raided the V-2 rocket site at Peenemünde. In the daylight reconnaissance twelve hours after the attack, photographs revealed twenty-seven buildings in the northern manufacturing area destroyed and forty huts in the living and sleeping quarters completely flattened. 500–600 foreign workers, mostly Polish, were killed. The whole target area was covered in craters. The raid is adjudged to have set back the V-2 experimental programme by at least two months and to have reduced the scale of the eventual rocket attack on Britain. Searby ended the war with a DSO and a DFC and retired as an air commodore in 1961. He died in 1986 and is buried near RAF Honington

The Pathfinder crews were said to be the cream, the elite of Bomber Command. High skill, accurate navigation and complete reliability were the hallmarks of these flyers, but needless to say events did not always proceed exactly as planned. One such operation that comes to mind was on 29 February 1944. The target was Augsburg and I remember it as six hours of sheer black comedy.

We took off about 10 p.m. and proceeded to the turning point. In fifteen minutes or so we should have crossed the coast had we been flying in the right direction, but red on black does tend to make navigation difficult. When it was realised which way we were going the navigator's language was picturesque to say the least. We were due over the target in the first few minutes of the raid and the navigator reckoned that if we put on a few extra knots we might just get there before it was all over, so off we went.

Well we arrived just in time and it was probably the only time in our forty-five ops that we were pleased to see the flak and activity over a target. Our pilot expressed our feelings admirably – 'Let's get rid of this bloody lot and get the hell out of here' – so in we went bombs gone and homeward bound. We now all felt rather more cheerful and were settling down for what we hoped would be an uneventful run back to base when our calm was shattered by the engineer reporting that we still had all our bombs on. The bomb aimer had forgotten to put the fuse in and after the bad language had died down we came to the conclusion that it was just not our night.

So that our efforts were not completely wasted, a small German town en route was selected to receive our payload. We made a nice diving run and dropped the bombs; one moment later it seemed all hell was let loose. Flares made it as bright as day, 'Monica' began pipping away like mad and it seemed as though our time had come. We corkscrewed all over the sky and relief only came when coloured stars began to come out of the 'fighter flares'. We had completely forgotten our markers and losing height to bomb this poor town meant that they burst almost as soon as they left the bomb bay.

It was a very jaded crew that arrived over base about 4 a.m. and whilst taxiing back to our dispersal we made sure we were going to tell the same tale. It did occur to one of us that we might well have an excellent picture of some obscure town in Germany so a torch was duly shone into the camera.

When we went into debriefing it seemed rather quiet but they let us sit down and tell our story, which needless to say left out the majority of the night's events. When we had finished there was a long silent pause and then followed the punch line of the evening from the intelligence officer: 'I've only one thing to say to you lot, next time you cook up a story don't leave your R/T on.'

A Night to Remember, R.G.

Our load for the trip to Leopoldsburg was four times seven hooded flares, six target indicators yellow, five TI yellow, one 4000lb 'cookie'. The weather over the target was no cloud and the vertical visibility good. The target was identified visually, aided by a red target indicator and flares. On approach to the target, at 0159hrs, two red target indicators seen on aiming point. I broadcast from 0201hrs to 0213hrs. Our own yellow target indicator was dropped on the north-west end of the red target indicator. I instructed the Main Force to bomb on the yellow target indicators. White target indicators were well backing up yellows. I instructed the Main Force during the last three minutes to bomb on whites to port and this with one-second overshoot. The Main Force bombing was good. One large explosion from the centre of target, rising well above ground with minor explosions in the air and this at 0207hrs.

Wing Commander S.P. Daniels of 35 Squadron, Master Bomber, Bomber Command raid on 27/28 May 1944 on Bourg-Leopold where 10,000 SS Panzer troops and their vehicles were quartered in the former Belgian Gendarmerie barracks. The purpose of the operation was to eliminate the threat posed by these troops to those of the Allied invasion forces, Five 'Oboe' Mosquitoes dropped TIs and the third and most accurate salvo fell within 320 yards of the aiming point. 331 aircraft – 267 Halifaxes, fifty-six Lancasters, eight Mosquitoes – attacked the camp. Nine Halifaxes and one Lancaster were lost

On the night of 21/22 June 1944 Lancasters of 83 (Pathfinder) Squadron took off from Coningsby, Lincs, to mark and attack Wesseling, a town 9 miles south of Cologne. At 2318hrs Flight Lieutenant Ron Walker DFC and his very experienced crew on their forty-fifth operational flight lifted off from Coningsby's long runway and set course across the North Sea and enemy held Holland. The flight proved relatively uneventful until reaching Eindhoven, when without pre-warning the Lancaster was attacked by a German night-fighter. Accurate cannon shells ripped into the Lancaster and the aircraft exploded in the air while loaded with bombs. Walker was blown from the plane by the explosion and miraculously came down to earth while unconscious and suffered only bruised leg and back. The remainder of the crew died in the aircraft. Walker was quickly helped by Dutch Resistance workers and after a series of adventures and hair-raising escapes from searching German troops, he reached, on 8 July, the home of a very brave lady, Jacoba Pulskens, in the town of Tilburg. Here, with two shot-down navigators, Roy Carter RCAF and Jack Knott RAAF, they waited their next move across the Belgian border to safety. Six members of the Gestapo burst into the house and, in a flurry of shots, the three aircrew were killed. Jacoba Pulskens was arrested and, after much suffering at the hands of the Germans, was put to death in the gas chamber in February 1945. In June 1946 the Germans responsible for the shooting were put on trial in Essen and four sentenced to death.

Frank Harper, 83 Squadron

Chop Rate: Killed In Action, one-sixth of all Bomber Command fatal casualties (55,000men) were Pathfinders. This represents the equivalent aircrew strength of some twenty squadrons.

THIRTY-SEVEN
LANCS

Where are the bombers, the Lancs on the runways,
Snub-nosed and roaring and black-faced and dour,
Full up with aircrew and window and ammo
And dirty great cookies to drop on the Ruhr?

Where are the pilots, the navs and air gunners,
WOPs and bomb-aimers and flight engineers,
Lads who were bank clerks and milkmen and teachers,
Carpenters, lawyers and grocers and peers?

Geordies and Cockneys and Wiltshire moon-rakers,
Little dark men from the valleys of Wales,
Manxmen, Devonians, Midlanders, Scouses,
Jocks from the Highlands and Tykes from the Dales?

Where are the Aussies, the sports and the cobbers,
Talking of cricket and sheilas and grog,
Flying their Lancs over Hamburg and Stettin
And back to the Lincolnshire winter-time bog?

Where are the fliers from Canada's prairies,
From cities and forests, determined to win,
Thumbing their noses at Goering's Luftwaffe
And busily dropping their bombs on Berlin?

Where are the Poles with their gaiety and sadness,
All with the most unpronounceable names,

The arrival of the Avro Lancaster in squadron service with 44 Squadron, which finished converting from the Hampden to the new four-engined heavy early in 1942, ushered in a new era in RAF Bomber Command. (BAe Manchester via Harry Holmes)

Silently, ruthlessly flying in vengeance
Remembering their homes and their country in flames?

Where are the Kiwis who left all the sunshine
For bleak windy airfields and fenland and dyke,
Playing wild Mess games like high cockalorum,
And knocking the hell out of Hitler's Third Reich?

Where are they now, those young men of all nations,
Who flew though they knew not what might lie ahead,
And those who returned with their mission accomplished
And next night would beat up the Saracen's Head?

The Lancs are no more, they are part of the Legend,
But memory stays bright in the hearts of the men
Who loved them and flew them through flak and through hellfire
And managed to land them in England again.

The men who were lucky to live to see victory,
The men who went home to their jobs and their wives,
The men who can tell their grandchildren with pride
Of the bomber which helped to save millions of lives.

'Lancasters', Audrey Grealy

I can remember going into the target which was a very hot target. There was a hell of a lot of flak and searchlights and night-fighters and I saw a big piece of flak heading towards where I was sitting. Next thing I knew, I'm in a forest, covered with blood and with a cracked hip. I was in a very bad state. In fact my whole face was ripped off. I didn't have a clue where I was. The last thing I know was that we were bombing the Krupps Works. It was pouring with rain so I remembered the edict we had been given to walk by night and hide by day. So I hid under trees, smoked cigarettes with my hand over and chewed gum and didn't know what the hell to do. I could hardly walk. I thought that if this is somewhere near Essen, I'll head out that way and perhaps I can get somewhere near the Allied front lines. I crawled along the ground. I don't know how far I went. I think I just kept going round in circles. On the second morning, I heard an aircraft coming in low and I looked up and saw that it was a British Beaufighter. I saw the direction it was heading and I started crawling that way. I picked up a stick and tried limping along with the stick. Through the mist I saw an enormous Germanic-looking castle. At the side of it was an old man raking and hoeing what appeared to be early onions. I thought I would crawl up to this old bloke. He didn't hear or see me, probably because he was concentrating so much on the onions. I pulled a big knife from out of my flying boot and put it in his ear. I said to him, reading off a language card, which had four different languages on it, in German – 'Wo bin ich?' ('Where am I?') – in French – 'Comment s'appelle ce place ici?' – in Dutch and in Flemish. In the end, I said, 'You stupid old bastard, where am I?'.

He said, 'Ye be in Norfolk lad. Over thar be King's Lynn!'.

I was probably the only bloke in the war who did an escape and evasion around England.

We had been hit over Essen and I was hit underneath the turret and knocked unconscious. Apparently, we had an engine shot out and another one was burning. Having dropped our bombs, the pilot headed back over the North Sea. The plane had iced up and we couldn't make height. We just got over the sea and crashed into an enormous oak tree on the huge Houghton Park estate near King's Lynn, which was owned by Lord Cholmondeley, the British High Chancellor. We had a stray bomb on board and it went off when we hit the oak tree. My turret was blown as a unit to something like a mile away from the rest of the plane, which burned immediately. My six friends were burnt to death. Later, my unopened parachute and harness was found in the top of a tree. I had fallen out of the tree and that's where I woke up in the forest.

Nineteen-year-old Flight Sergeant J. G. 'Jack' Cannon RAAF, mid-upper gunner, Lancaster III H-Harry Two of 460 Squadron, flown by twenty-two-year-old Pilot Officer D. R. G. Richins RAAF, which was carrying one 4,000lb HC HE, five 1,000lb HE, six 500lb HE and 1,000 4lb incendiaries in SBCs. One of twenty-six aircraft that took off from RAF Binbrook bound for the Krupps Works at Essen on 23 October 1944, H-Harry Two had been hit by flak shortly after bomb release had and been damaged. Severely iced-up and unable to climb above cloud, an SOS message was received from the aircraft and the Lanc was diverted to Bircham Newton, Norfolk, on return. It is believed that while the Lancaster was making a very low circuit over Bircham Newton prior to landing, it struck a tree near Houghton Hall and blew up on impact at 9.15 p.m. when an HE bomb which had hung-up, exploded. The main portion of wreckage crashed against a large beech tree in a wood in the grounds of the Hall and exploded in flames, killing six of the crew. The five RAAF who died – Richins (twenty-two), Flight Sergeant Ken T. Frankish (twenty), navigator; Flight Sergeant W. Stobo (twenty-eight), air bomber; Warrant Officer J.R. Treloar (twenty-one), WOP; and Flight Sergeant R.W. Bergelin (twenty) rear gunner – are buried in Cambridge City Cemetery. Ken Frankish's headstone records: 'Farewell Ken.

Houghton Hall, Norfolk. (Author)

A good innings. Well Played'. Stobo's says: 'Loved Husband of Flo and Daddy of Frances'. Treloar has the Latin inscription Tradidit Lampada Vitai. *Sergeant E.A. Sutherland RAF (twenty) is buried at Shipley (Nab Wood) Cemetery, Yorks. The old man was Fred Dye, Houghton's estate gardener, who took Cannon to the Hall and an ambulance then took him to the SSQ at Bircham Newton where he was under sedation for two days*

We were briefed to fly operations to Munich on 24 April along with fifteen other crews. The bomb bay was filled with incendiaries: 136 36lb and six 500lb 'J' Type clusters. Taking off at 2050hrs, we headed south, crossing the Sussex coast near Selsey Bill. The Dutch coast was identified on the radar (*H2S*), then we headed deep into southern Germany before turning on a north-easterly direction towards Munich. There was a long wait as the target was identified and the markers, bright coloured flares, were dropped. Those carrying out this work were Wing Commander Leonard Cheshire, Squadron Leader Dave Shannon and Flight Lieutenant R.S. Kearns, all from 617 Squadron and flying the Mosquito. Looking down at them from our higher altitude, I wondered at the time who on earth I was watching fly so close to the ground, as just about every gun available to the defence force was firing at them… Later in the year Wing Commander Leonard Cheshire (then group captain) was awarded the VC and the Munich raid featured largely in the citation.

Sergeant Roland A. Hammersley DFM, 57 Squadron Lancaster WOP/AG

My crew and I arrived at 61 Squadron, Skellingthorpe, on the morning of 27 September 1944. During the next ten days or so we carried out our first two operations. We were then allocated a permanent aircraft, QR-M, with the nose art of *Mickey the Moocher* [a name derived from Cab Calloway's popular slow blues song, 'Minnie the Moocher'], a real veteran, with 119 trips on the nose. It was quite something to have our own plane, another milestone in our air force career. The ground crew was very proud of their plane and the number of trips completed. This showed good maintenance and a lot of luck. We hoped that the luck had not all been used up as it was usually considered that to survive a tour required about 70 per cent luck and 30 per cent skill. By this time *Mickey* was nearly worn out. The four engines were close to the hours for a complete change, the controls were sloppy and she had dozens of patches on wings and fuselage. She took a lot of runway to get off the ground with a full load of fuel and bombs. We were the new crew given the oldest Lanc on the squadron, but we were proud of her.

She took us on our first trip on 11 October, a daylight one to the Dutch coast, with a fighter escort to bomb sea walls (dykes) in an attempt to flood German artillery batteries that were holing up the advance of the British ground forces. The raid was not successful although we bombed from low level. At this stage I could sense through *Mickey* the feelings of all the crews that had survived over 100 trips in this special aircraft, passing on their experience and good luck for a successful tour, a sort of feeling of comradeship and well-being which is hard to describe. *Mickey* was something to look up to, a guiding star. I get a similar feeling now, when, as a bushwalking guide, I lead a group of walkers through our magnificent Karri forests.

Our next trip was a seven-and-a-half-hour night flight to Brunswick with 233 Lancs and seven Mosquitoes. This was an area attack with cookies and incendiaries. A large amount of damage was inflicted. This was also a milestone as it was my twenty-first birthday 15 October, and we had our first fighter combat. Nearing the target area the mid-upper gunner spotted a fighter approaching from the port quarter above. It then appeared to side-slip into position behind them, he ordered the pilot to corkscrew as he opened fire, while also giving the rear-gunner the fighter's position and who, upon seeing it too, also opened fire. The fighter dived quickly away; the mid-upper gunner giving it a final burst as it disappeared out of range.

The next trip was another night one, seven hours to Nuremberg with 263 Lancs and seven Mosquitoes, again area bombing, with a large amount of casualties and damage inflicted. We were beginning to get a little confident now, with our navigator keeping us on time and track and hence in the middle of the stream and our bomb aimer directing the bombing run with precision and we were obtaining good target photos. Our next trip was another daylight one to the Dutch coast to attack the same batteries as before, also unsuccessful.

Mickey took us for her last operation on 6/7 November to bomb the Mittelland Canal at Gravenhorst. The marking force had difficulty in finding the target due to low cloud. We were called down to bomb at low level and I recall selecting full flap and wheels down to enable us to lose height in time. We were one of the few Lancs that bombed before the Master Bomber abandoned the raid due to low cloud.

On 9 November we flew *Mickey* to Netheravon, one-and-a-half-hours' flight from Skellingthorpe. Along with a Halifax and a Stirling she was loaded with Red Cross parcels to ascertain the number that could be carried to relieve Allied POWs as they were released by the advancing British troops in Europe. *Mickey* remained there till 30 November, when we flew her back to Skellingthorpe. Some other crew must have flown her away to 1653 CU after this, as possibly we were on leave. We were allocated our new QR-M on 18 December. What a difference to fly. When doing our first air test with no bombs and limited fuel, I opened the throttle on take off and we were flung back in our seats. She behaved like a sports car. We had now completed twelve trips and flew the new *Mickey* (although no art was ever painted on the nose) to the end of our tour except for a few weeks in January and February when she was being repaired after getting shot up and having a dicey landing.

Flying Officer Frank Mouritz RAAF, pilot, Lancaster Mickey The Moocher, *61 Squadron*

(Jack Hamilton 463 Squadron RAAF Collection via Theo Boiten)

Spitfire and Lancaster passing Attlebridge airfield, Norfolk. (Author)

The morning of 7 January 1945 started much the same as many others – the last-minute scramble to complete ones ablutions, into battledress, a quick dash to the sergeants' mess for the last of the breakfast, a few minutes in the anteroom looking at the previous day's papers. Then with crew complete a gentle walk to the hangar and 'B' Flight office. Our skipper, Art Whitmarsh, followed us in. Amid the smoke haze and noise a telephone rang, an Aussie voice yelled 'Quiet!'. The chatter stopped. Bob Henderson, our flight commander, replaced the phone: 'OK it's on.'

We all know what he meant, so the crew dispersed with the exception of the pilots and reported to our individual sections. Ken De La Mare, the mid-upper gunner, and I disappeared into the Gunnery Section, set about checking our Brownings, cleaning – four in the tail and two on top. Pull throughs, check the return springs take them out to our dispersal and to our Lancaster, O-Oboe. Sergeant Spud Murphy with his team of fitters and armourers met us. Spud with his black curly hair, wide grin was more like an Irish gypsy than a real digger.

The turret covers had already been removed and the guns fitted. All the systems were checked. Spare sight bulbs. What little Perspex we had was given a quick polish. Most of it we had removed – a bit more draughty and a lot colder but it did improve vision: less frightening and made less work. Last job – fit the celluloid caps over the flash eliminator, put the turret covers back on, meet up with the other crewmembers and hot-foot it back to the mess.

As we entered the foyer there for all to see was the Battle Order – a list of names, aircraft, main briefing time etc. A call at 1500, flying sweaters on, a walk to the mess, into the servery with its large trays of fried eggs, streaky bacon, baked beans and fried bread, plenty of bread and margarine, all to be washed down with hot tea or coffee. Somebody dropped his plate. A mighty roar went up. Then quiet for a few seconds before the low murmurings return, but not for long, time to leave. Greatcoats on and join the growing crowd on its way to the briefing room.

In a few minutes we saw the corporal SP outside the double door and we passed through and there, past the rows of tables and chairs, the low stage with black curtains closed. We took our seats in line with the skipper and navigator with pilots sitting in the aisle seats. The room was thick with cigarette smoke and noise: eighteen crews operating tonight, 126 men. The intelligence officer, flight commanders and specialist officers took their place on the platform either side of the curtains. Loud and clear came the call: 'Atten-shun'. Everybody stood; it was quiet and down the aisle walked the station commander, Group Captain Keith Parsons, and Squadron Commander Mike Cowan. A curt 'Good-evening gentlemen. Be seated'. The intelligence officer drew the curtains apart and the target was revealed – MUNICH. A large groan went up. For all to see the thin red tape stretched from Binbrook, southwards to Reading, then altering course to Beachy Head, over the Channel, south-east towards a point north of Mulhouse, where the track turned north-east and headed toward Stuttgart. A right turn on to a south-easterly heading, passing Ulm on our port side and on to Memmingen and then a left turn heading direct for Munich.

This was to be the second attack on Munich this night; 5 Group squadrons were to attack, with an H-Hour of 2030; we in 1 Group at H-Hour 2230. The briefing went on, we could expect moderate to heavy flak with fighter activity, the target and plan would be Paramatta with emergency sky marking. Finally the Met.-man. A small cheer went up as he told us 10/10ths cumulus from France to the target area with tops to 85,000ft with a frontal belt lying SE of Paris with winds at 18,000ft of 270/30 knots and tops 8–10,000ft near the target. No moon during the operation and the likelihood of snow on return with possible diversions.

The briefing came to an end. Everybody stood. The hierarchy left and the crews dispersed to the changing rooms to empty pockets change into flying overalls, long socks,

Left and above: *'Mickey was something to look up to, a guiding star.'* (Author)

flying boots, gloves and helmet. Check the oxygen mask, collect parachute and harness, put Mae West and harness on, collect escape kit, place in inner battle-dress pocket, and then out into the cold night. The crew bus soon arrived and, with other crews with aircraft in adjacent dispersals, we were soon there and again met by Spud Murphy. He told us all was well and the aircraft serviceable. We climbed aboard, stowed our 'chutes and carried out the necessary pre-flight checks. Whitmarsh signed the Form 700. Most of us went for a quick 'leak' then, with harness fastened, into the aeroplane. While the others went forward I clambered over the Elsan, turned on to my back, slid over the tail spar legs down and I was there. Check 'chute was secure, remove cotton reel from the oxygen economiser, close the doors, plug in the intercom and connect oxygen tube to mask tube, fasten seat belt, open the breach covers and arm the four Brownings. Make sure they are all cocked and fire/safe to safe, a call to the skipper, 'Rear Gunner ready, turret serviceable'.

'OK', came the reply and I heard the others reporting. At last it was time to start the engines.

Now, time to check the turret; full rotation, guns elevate and depress, gun sight switch to dim, check radar systems and report all systems serviceable. One could hear the power increased to the engines. We moved forward then almost stopped as the brakes were checked; a quick thumbs up to the ground crew as we taxied out of the dispersal and on to the perimeter to join the queue of Lancasters. Slowly past the hangar and control tower, down the hill past the bomb dump, then on to the end of Runway 22. Then, in turn we moved on to the runway, final checks, a steady green from the runway controller, the engines roared, the brakes released and the take-off run started, the mighty Merlins giving full power, the tail came up. I was airborne. I heard the engineer call, 'Full power, temperature and pressures normal'. We were airborne at 1847. Flaps and undercarriage

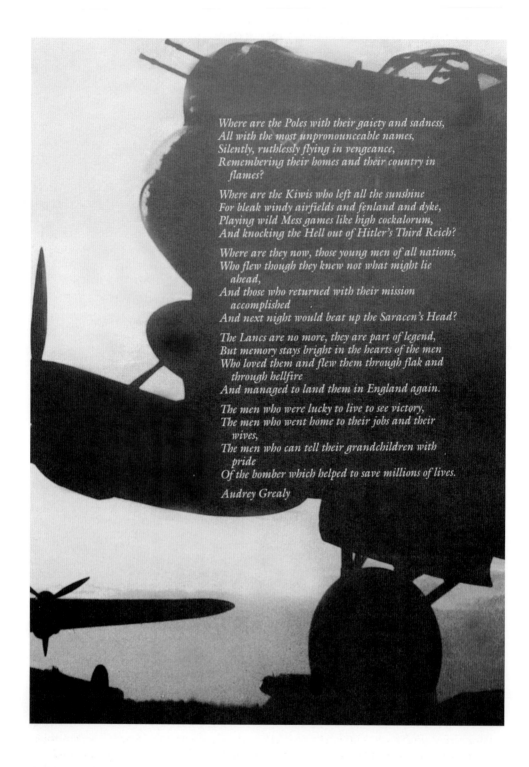

Where are the Poles with their gaiety and sadness,
All with the most unpronounceable names,
Silently, ruthlessly flying in vengeance,
Remembering their homes and their country in
*   flames?*

Where are the Kiwis who left all the sunshine
For bleak windy airfields and fenland and dyke,
Playing wild Mess games like high cockalorum,
And knocking the Hell out of Hitler's Third Reich?

Where are they now, those young men of all nations,
Who flew though they knew not what might lie
*   ahead,*
And those who returned with their mission
*   accomplished*
And next night would beat up the Saracen's Head?

The Lancs are no more, they are part of legend,
But memory stays bright in the hearts of the men
Who loved them and flew them through flak and
*   through hellfire*
And managed to land them in England again.

The men who were lucky to live to see victory,
The men who went home to their jobs and their
*   wives,*
The men who can tell their grandchildren with
*   pride*
Of the bomber which helped to save millions of lives.

Audrey Grealy

came in and the skipper called for 2,650+9 and *Oboe* climbed away with a 4,000lb cookie and incendiaries. We turned on to course for the rendezvous at Reading and we climbed to our first height, the guns were set to 'fire' and the methodical search pattern of the gunners' started, reporting any other aircraft that might put us at risk.

Occasionally, the whole aeroplane shuddered due to turbulence from other Lancasters joining the bomber stream. Eventually the flight level was reached and the navigator gave the skipper a new course to steer. At the appointed time we turned into the new course and started to climb to our next flight level, carrying on to the next turning point, Beachy Head. So far so good and soon we altered course again, crossing the Channel, on to the French coast and the long leg towards Mulhouse. Paris was passed well to the south of us. A shower of red sparks flew past the turret but it was no cause for alarm: the engineer was clearing the engines. So on we droned soon to run into the front with its associated cloud as forecast by the Met.-man. The thought of flying in cloud in daytime was bad enough but at night in a bomber stream it was not at all pleasant. We kept going; sticking to the briefing we flew on toward the high ground of the Voseges that rises up to more than 4,600ft, close to the German border.

The weather worsened with more frequent turbulence. A voice on the intercom suggested that we should climb above the weather. There was unanimous agreement and after a second or two the skipper called for climbing power and one felt the mighty bomber climb through the murky skies. In a few minutes we were in and out of the tops, seeing the stars in the sky and the dim shapes of other Lancasters, who had climbed earlier. 'Christ!' came a shout over the headphones, together with a crash and the tearing of metal. *Oboe* rocked. 'We've been hit', said another voice.

'Did you see that other Lancaster, it's falling away?'

Our port wing dropped and *Oboe* fell back into the clouds in a spin. Art Whitmarsh fought with all his strength to regain control. After what seemed an eternity we were straight and level. Skipper called for the bomb doors to open and Jock jettisoned the bombs: 'safe'. The clouds lightened with a flash. Our bombs or the other Lancaster? Who knew?

Our four engines were still running, the skipper still struggling to maintain control, as he told us that the ailerons were jammed. He called for a head count and serviceability check. The skipper decided that we must return if possible. The wireless operator was instructed to advise Binbrook on W/T, the IFF was switched to 'on', and a gentle turn started for a course to the emergency airfield at Manston. The engine power was increased and slowly we started to climb to clear the cloud and the front, also to reduce the risk of icing. Eventually we reached 20,000ft and were able to see and estimate the extent of the damage. The trailing edge of the starboard wing was well chewed up, the aileron and wing tip missing. Ken in his mid-upper turret reported that the floor and starboard side of the fuselage was missing, as was the *H2S* assembly for about 10ft. Ken was assisted out of his turret by using the escape rope and the help of the warrant officer to the relative comfort and safety of the flight deck.

The tail end of the aircraft was swinging with lots of vibration. It was impossible for me in the tail to come forward. I was given the option of bailing out but I preferred to stay and stick with each other. Besides, the risk of the enemy was still present. The skipper reduced the power and this helped reduce the vibrations but with a lower speed. We flew on. Not a lot was said. The skipper had his hands full maintaining our crippled machine. Eventually the Channel came up, with a descent to Manston, which could be seen. Whitmarsh decided to make a flapless landing. The undercarriage was lowered (thank goodness they both extended) – two green lights. And with a long flat approach a safe landing was made at 0049hrs. We taxied slowly behind a 'FOLLOW ME' ATC truck and parked the aeroplane. The engines were closed down. It was so quiet but slowly we emerged from the exits, me from the door, the rest of the crew via the front escape hatch down the ladder. We looked at the damage. I suppose we said a silent 'thank you' then into the transport for a debriefing in the air traffic. The night's events were recalled, then a 'phone call to Binbrook to confirm that we were safe, a meal was soon provided and then a long sleep.

Next morning we went to inspect the aeroplane. It was not a pretty sight. The way she held together was a tribute to Avro. The starboard side of the fuselage from trailing edge almost to the entrance door was missing, as was the floor from the bomb bay; 3ft of wing tip and trailing edge all mangled and chewed up by the other Lancaster's propellers, with little left of the aileron. Our crew had survived a mid-air collision, we considered ourselves lucky. After a short training flight we were back on operations to finish our tour of operations. Little thought was given to the unknown aircraft with which we had collided or that of the crew.

D.G. Fellowes, rear gunner, Lancaster AR-O, 460 Squadron RAAF, Binbrook, flown by Flying Officer A. Whitmarsh. The Lancaster of 103 Squadron crash-dived into a hill, killing all in the all-Canadian crew

This flight was our most remembered. About an hour from the target my mid-upper gunner suddenly shouted, 'Down skip!'. I pushed the stick forward hard and saw another Lanc sliding over the top of us on a slightly different heading, same height. My gunner saw the exhaust flame just in time as it was closing in on us. The searchlight activity over Berlin was intense and we were just sliding past one that was fixed when it suddenly locked straight on to us and I was completely blinded. I started to change height, speed and direction as taught and went into a diving corkscrew, pulling out the bottom

Lancaster and Spitfire passing Ely Cathedral. (Author)

dive quite hard and throwing the old Lanc around by feel as I was still blinded by the searchlight. Then suddenly we were clear before the night-fighters spotted us and we dropped our load on the target and came home OK.

The next day down at dispersal the ground engineer said, 'What were you up to last night?'

I said, 'Why?'.

He said, 'Look at this', and he took me up the steps and showed me the upper wing between the fuselage and the starboard inner. The skin had a wrinkle in it. We must have pulled out of the dive with our full bomb load on board and the old Lanc had taken it under protest.

Maurice Bishop, pilot, Lancaster III Winsome Winnie, *218 'Gold Coast' Squadron, Chedburgh, operation to Potsdam, Berlin, 14 April 1945*

THIRTY-EIGHT
AIR VICTORIA CROSS AWARDS,1939–1945

Any operation that deserves the VC is in the nature of things unfit to be repeated at frequent intervals.

Air Chief Marshal Sir Arthur T. Harris

Recipient	Sqdn	A/c	Action	Award
Gray, Sergeant Thomas, observer	12	Battle	12.05.40	11.06.40★
Garland, Flying Officer Donald Edward, pilot	12	Battle	12.05.40	11.06.40★
Learoyd, Acting Flight Lieutenant Roderick Alastair Brook, pilot	49	Hampden	12.08.40	20.08.40
Nicolson, Flight Lieutenant Eric James Brindley, pilot	249	Hurricane	16.08.40	
Hannah, Flight Sergeant John, WOP/AG	83	Hampden	15/16.09.40	01.10.40
Campbell, Flying Officer Kenneth, pilot	22	Beaufort	06.04.41	
Edwards, Acting Wing Commander Hughie Idwal DFC, pilot	105	Blenheim	04.07.41	22.07.41
Ward, Sergeant James Allen RNZAF, second pilot	75	Wellington	07.07.41	05.08.41
Nettleton, Acting Squadron Leader John Deering, pilot	44	Lancaster	17.04.42	28.04.42
Manser, Flying Officer Leslie Thomas RAFVR, pilot	50	Manchester	30/31.05.42	20.10.42★
Middleton, Flight Sergeant Rawdon Hume RAAF, pilot	149	Stirling	28/29.11.42	15.01.43★
Malcolm, Acting Wing Commander Hugh, Gordon, pilot	18	Blenheim	04.12.42	27.04.43★
Newton, Flight Lieutenant William Ellis RAAF				16.03.43
Gibson, Acting Wing Commander Guy Penrose DSO DFC, pilot	617	Lancaster	16/17.05.43	28.05.43
Trigg, Flying Officer Lloyd Alan DFC RNZAF, pilot	200	Liberator	11.08.43★	
Aaron, Flight Sergeant				
Arthur Louis DFM, pilot	218	Stirling	12/13.08.43	05.1143★
Reid, Acting Flight Lieutenant William RAFVR, pilot	61	Lancaster	03/04.11.43	14.12.43
Barton, Pilot Officer Cyril Joe RAFVR, pilot	578	Halifax	30/31.05.44	27.06.44★

Wing Commander Guy Gibson VC DSO DFC. (IWM)

Hornell, Flight Lieutenant David Ernest RCAF	162	Catalina	24.06.44★	
Cruickshank, Flying Officer John Alexander, pilot	210	Catalina	17.07.44	
Cheshire, Wing Commander Geoffrey Leonard DSO DFC RAFVR, pilot	617	Lancaster	08.09.44	
Lord, Flight Lieutenant David Samuel Anthony DFC, pilot	271	Dakota	19.09.44★	
Thompson, Flight Sergeant George RAFVR, WOP	9	Lancaster	01.01.45	20.2.45★
Palmer, Acting Squadron Leader Robert Anthony Maurice DFC RAFVR, pilot	109	Lancaster	23.12.44	23.04.45★
Swales, Captain Edwin DFC SAAF 'Master Bomber'	582	Lancaster	23/24.02.45	24.04.45★
Bazalgette, Acting Squadron Leader Ian Willoughby DFC RAFVR 'Master Bomber'	635	Lancaster	04.08.44	17.08.45★
Jackson, Sergeant (later Warrant Officer) Norman Cyril RAFVR, flight engineer	106	Lancaster	26/27.04.44	26.10.45
Trent, Squadron Leader Leonard Henry DFC RNAZF, pilot	487	Ventura	03.05.43	01.03.46
Scarf, Squadron Leader Arthur Stewart King, pilot	62	Blenheim	09.12.41	21.06.46★
Mynarski, Pilot Officer Andrew Charles RCAF, mid-upper gunner	419	Lancaster	12/13.06.44	11.10.46★

★Posthumous award

THIRTY-NINE

THUNDERCLAP

The destruction of Dresden remains a serious query against the conduct of Allied bombing.
  Winston Churchill

My three years as a POW started in June 1942 at a place called 'Knightsbridge' in the Western Desert where we were surrounded by the Afrika Korps. After my time in two camps in Tripoli and Italy I was sent to Stalag IVB near Dresden. It was a small working camp of about forty men in an area, which we thought safe and peaceful. Our work on the Eisenbahn (railway) took us to many places in the Dresden area. The rail network in the centre was very busy so we rarely went into the main station. I remember being taken to the dentist in Dresden by a guard old enough to be my grandfather. That visit impressed me very much. There were streets of beautiful buildings of old architectural design. Later, after the RAF and US Air Force had done their duty, I felt sad that such a grand place had been reduced to rubble.

The two days 13 and 14 February 1945 gave us all in the camp an experience which is almost impossible to describe. On the night of 13 February we were all in our bunks after lights out (our days started at 5 a.m. so early to bed was the order) when the sound of 'planes approaching and flying over became so loud it was as if the planes were just above the roof tops. There had been no warning, but these planes were not moving on to another target. They were too close. The noise of the aircraft and the thump of the bombs was frightening and I am sure we all expected our camp to be struck at any moment. How long it was before the noise faded away I have no idea, but the relief was immense when all was quiet again.

The following morning 14 February, instead of small gangs being sent under guard to various work locations, we, the whole camp were marched into Dresden. The situation was chaotic. Civilians who had survived were fleeing the city and every street we could see was just a smouldering ruin. The intention was that we would assist the SS and civilian railway men to repair damage sustained to the tracks outside the main station. We refused and stood around doing nothing, whilst the Germans were trying to do the impossible.

(Evening Standard)

The whole situation was unbelievable. Germans were frantically removing rails with sleepers still attached pointing vertically from gaping holes. The total area was cratered and littered with burnt out rolling stock including steam engines in the skeleton of workshops. We stood in the centre of this carnage and confusion like bewildered schoolboys doing nothing. Thinking back I suppose we were fortunate that no one reacted against us or attempted to force us to take part in the clear up operation.

Just before the alarm sounded, and the US Air Force arrived in formation I remember it was a clear blue sky and those enormous Flying Fortresses looked very menacing. We did not wait to welcome them, just ran for shelter which we found in the boltholes built into the walls of a brick railway cutting. This saved us. A bomb dropped on our side of the cutting about twenty yards away. The blast ripped past and two of our lads were cut with shrapnel.

Following this we were moved to an army barracks about 10 miles from Dresden. Here we suffered more machine gun assaults from the US Air Force and two of our party were killed. Enough is enough I thought, the Russians were getting ever closer from the east, so I took off with a friend who could converse in German. We eventually met the Americans who flew us from Leipzig to Reims and the greatest honour for me was flying home in the rear gunner's seat of a Lancaster bomber.

Bill Gough, English POW, Dresden, 13/14 February 1945. Dresden was targeted as part of a series of particularly heavy raids on German cities in Operation Thunderclap, with a view to causing as much destruction, confusion and mayhem as possible. The other cities were Berlin, Chemnitz and Leipzig which, like Dresden, were vital communications and supply centres for the Eastern Front. Thunderclap had been under consideration for several months and was to be implemented only when the military situation in Germany was critical

A biting wind, a searing frost,

A dome of cloud, a misty moon,

Below, a flaming holocaust…

Audrey Grealy

'The destruction of Dresden remains a serious query against the conduct of Allied bombing.' (Via Geoff Liles)

As far as Bomber Command was concerned, the plan of attack on Dresden was as follows: 5 Group was to attack at 2215hrs on February 13th, using its own Pathfinder technique to mark the target. This was a combination of two Lancaster Squadrons, 83 and 97, to illuminate the target and one Mosquito Squadron, 527, to visually mark the aiming point with Target Indicators from low level. The aiming point was to be a sports stadium in the centre of the city situated near the lines of railway and river which would serve as a pointer to the stadium for the Marker Force, especially since it was anticipated that visibility might not be too good. The bombing technique to be carried out by the main 5 Group Lancaster Force was known as the 'sector' type, which had been developed by 5 Group in area attacks. This meant that each aircraft headed up to the aiming point on a different heading – in the case of the Dresden attack from about due south to about due east, each with differing delays for bomb release after picking up the aiming point on the bombsight. This meant that the bombing covered a wedge-shaped sector, resulting in a great number of fires being started over the whole sector, since a great proportion of the bomb load consisted of incendiaries.

Cloud cover over Dresden when the illuminator force of the Pathfinders arrived was 9–10/10ths up to about 9,500ft. The Marker Force of Mosquitoes found the cloud base was at about 2,500ft. The cloud was not too thick and the flares illuminated the city for the markers who placed their red Target Indicators very accurately on the aiming point. 244 Lancasters commenced the attack at 2213hrs and it was completed by 2231hrs, being controlled throughout by the Master Bomber.

For the second part of the plan Bomber Command had calculated that by allowing a delay of three hours for the fires to get a grip on the sector (provided the first attack was successful) and allowing the fire brigades from other cities to concentrate in fighting the fires, a second attack was timed for 0130hrs on the 14th by 500 aircraft of the remainder of the Main Force of Bomber Command. In this second attack target marking was to be

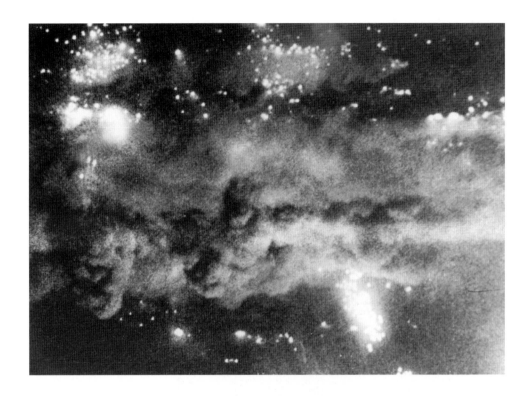

Above: *The raid on Dresden in progress on the night of 13/14 February 1945. (IWM)*

Right: *'Suddenly, the whole 'plane exploded…' (George Kercher via Theo Boiten)*

'We cannot send a thousand bombers a time over Germany every time as yet, but the time will come when we can do so. Let the Nazis take good note...' (Via Theo Boiten)

carried out by 8 Pathfinder Group. By the time of this attack cloud cover had cleared to 3–7/10ths but, despite this, the Master Bomber for this plan could not identify the aiming point due to the huge conflagrations and smoke and a decision was made to concentrate bombing on areas not already affected. An area was marked by the Pathfinders both to the left and to the right to assist in concentrating the bombing and good concentration was achieved. So great were the conflagrations caused by the firestorms created in the great heat generated in the first attack that crews in the second attack reported the glow was visible 200 miles from the target.

In addition to these attacks the 1st Air Division of the US 8th Air Force dispatched 450 B-17s, of which 316 attacked Dresden shortly after 12 noon on 14 February. To assist the night operations of Bomber Command, various 'spoof' attacks were made by Mosquitoes on Dortmund, Magdeburg and Hanover and 344 Halifaxes attacked an oil plant at Bohlen near Leipzig at the same time as the first attack. In addition to the above the routing and. feints carried out by the Main Forces involved caused night-fighter reaction to be minimal. In the case of the 5 Group attack our outward route consisted of no less than eight legs with feints towards the Ruhr, Kassel, Magdeburg and Berlin using 'Window' at the same time. An indication of the effectiveness of these operations was that out of over 1,000 aircraft taking part only six were lost.

Much has been written about the tragedy of Dresden. Probably the primary factor (and here I may be prejudiced!) was the highly successful first attack by 5 Group which resulted in an almost perfect 'sector' attack. Also the great strength of the wind helped create the firestorm conditions and spread the conflagrations. At my own bombing height of 13,000ft the wind speed was seventy to 75 knots.

An interesting point here is that on the very next night Chemnitz was to be the target of a similar attack, 330 aircraft to make the first and 390 the second attack three hours later. In this case Harris at Bomber Command (probably under pressure from Bennett of the Pathfinder Group) decided that 8 Group's Pathfinders would carry out the marking for both attacks

'There are many kinds of fear but our training had been designed to make us aware of these – like the fear of injury, of burning in a crash or even death itself.' (IWM)

and we in 5 Group would carry out a separate attack on an oil plant at Rositz near Leipzig. However, with cloud cover and with 5 Group low-level marking, 8 Group had to rely on sky marking and no concentration of bombing was achieved. I saw personal evidence of this as our (5 Group) withdrawal route linked up with the force returning from Chemnitz and I well remember the fires were scattered over 20 miles. Would Chemnitz have been a second Dresden had the same procedure as in that attack have been carried out?

Personal recollections of the Dresden raid are few since, at that time, we were operating at considerable pressure, with deep penetration operations – in fact three in six days, of nine hours forty minutes, nine hours five minutes, and nine hours twenty minutes duration. Points that do stand out are:

1. The long duration of the operation (nine hours five minutes).
2. The use we were able to make of Loran, one of our navigation aids, despite jamming.
3. The wind speed set on the bombsight computer box was the highest I recall (about 75 knots).
4. The clarity of the red Target Indicators despite almost 10/10ths cloud.
5. As the target was relatively close to the advancing Russian lines, our being issued with Union Jacks to put across our chests – if we were shot down behind their lines – with the words 'I am an Englishman' (in Russian, of course) printed on it. We thought they were not much of an asset – rather they would present a better target!

Afterwards, when I read criticism of the bombing, I did wonder what I'd been a part of. But at the time it was just a job we had to do. We knew the time on target was between 10 and 10.30 p.m. and joked that we'd catch the Germans just as they were coming out of the pubs. In hindsight I don't feel good about that. But for the most part, we didn't think in terms of people being killed, but of areas we had to hit.

But then that was how things were in 1945.

Flight Sergeant John Aldridge, 49 Squadron Lancaster bomb aimer, 13/14 February 1945, when Dresden was bombed in two assaults, the first by 244 Lancasters, the second by 529. In total, 2,659 tons of bombs and incendiaries fell on the town. Next day, 311 bombers of the 8th Air Force followed with a raid. Over 32,000 people were killed. John Aldridge flew thirty-three operations as a bomb aimer in 49 Squadron from September 1944–April 1945

*Don Bennett (centre)
planning another
8 Group operation. (Via
Tom Cushing)*

Moving out heading east lifting off the track
Who goes home is still tomorrow's riddle
It's scary up the front and it's hairy at the back
And it's not exactly Butlins in the middle
But its loud talk, cold feet, muscles knotting tight
Head and eyes a'moving as they said
Throbbing through the cavern of an inky velvet night
Peering for the Jerry coast ahead.

Cream of the mob
On with the job
Muster the skipper and crew
If you don't want to fly
Get out of the sky
There's plenty of others who do.

Hingeing on a bombers moon, wheeling on a cloud
Oboe's fingers nudging us on course
Living for the fight, living with the fright
Flying to the pulsing goads of Morse
But its dog-leg, half-turn, weaving through the fray
Every gunner wants to bring us down
Off to mark a target with a firework display
The Pathfinders are out to paint a town.

Pick of the ranks
Mossies and Lancs
Kin of the wandering goose
Sing as we go
Look out below
Bennett's Brigade's on the loose.

How to turn a bomber stream, heading for the Bight
Spread for miles across the starry dome
So we bombed the sea, tight and constantly
Whilst the hunters sickled on the foam
But its eyes left, eyes right, where's the eagles brood?
Some poor beggar burning out to port
If you crave excitement for a pessimistic mood
Join the club, we never sell it short.

Huntingdon Hounds
Going the rounds
Scenting the prey in the nest
If you jib at the odds
Don't bother your gods
Percentages baffle the best.

Cunning games of cat and mouse, nights of mortal chess
Blind mans buff with bullets for a lark
We drop window strips, foil the radar blips
They build decoy towns for us to mark
But its high cloud, ground mist, vision minus nil
Mute defences hoping we'll go by
We've not the need to guess now we've mastered *H2S*
And our Wanganui candles ring the sky.

Yellow and green
Calling the stream
Fling it out onto the glow
You don't have to care
When you're up in the air
For those in the cauldron below.

Single star-shells blossoming, flak-flowers in the pyre
Twinning trails of burning buzzing bees
Cones of funnelled fire from the ground suspire
And 'keep the blighter steady' if you please
But its left trim, right trim, hold it, hold it, Now!
Down the green and yellow markers go
Back and join the queue, still a job to do
Still a bombing run before we blow.

Flying elite
Cock o' the fleet
Out for a tryst with the pack
Timing is tight
Must get it right
Or Gawd 'elp us when we get back.

Some will live to wear the badge, some to shoot the line
Some to curse the bits that came adrift
If your comrades pass, turn over a glass

> Throw the stayers back into the sift
> But its minds blown, brief ease, laughter over high
> Ops are scrubbed; the fleets are standing down
> Swagger in the walk, singing in the talk
> The Pathfinders are out to paint the town.
>
> Off into town
> Can't settle down
> Last at the bar is a hound
> If you don't want to fly
> Get out of the sky
> They're queuing four deep on the ground.
>
> *'Bennett's Brigade', Geoffrey R. Reeves*

Never before has an Allied air raid produced a reaction such as we see now. The familiar epithets – *terrorflieger*, *Luftgangster* and *kindermorder* – are spread lavishly across the front pages of the German dailies in condemnation of the Allied bomber crews.

Oddly enough, there is no great hostile reaction towards us on the part of the German guards, many of whom lost families in the Dresden *terrorangriff*.

Most of them, particularly those who experienced the holocaust, seem too shocked and dazed to be capable of normal emotions like hatred and a desire for revenge.

One guard who was on duty in the stalag when Dresden was bombed applied for leave to see if his family were still alive. On arrival in Dresden he not only failed to locate his family or his house; it was also impossible to identify the street and the suburb. When he left Dresden, eastbound German troops stranded in the burning city were turning their flame-throwers on the ruins to cremate the thousands of trapped bodies and prevent outbreaks of disease.

Geoff Taylor RAAF, POW, Stalag IVb, Mulhlberg-on-Elbe, Saxony, 25 miles from Dresden

The most successful of our night-time operational flights and the ones that I remember so well, were those on Dresden and Chemnitz. Since the Second World War some Germans have complained about those raids having taken place. Have they conveniently forgotten, how for the first *two years* of the war, the Luftwaffe was bombing London (where I lived) and elsewhere in the UK day and night! Have they also forgotten the V-1 flying bombs and V-2 rockets they were still indiscriminately sending to kill innocent women and children in England? Surely they haven't also forgotten about the gas chambers they used!

Sergeant Frank W. Tasker, Lancaster mid-upper gunner, 622 Squadron. The second in a series of terrifying area-bombing raids on German cities which had thus far escaped the bombing, went ahead on February 23/24 1945. Over 360 Lancasters and thirteen Mosquitoes of 1, 6 and 8 Groups carried out the first and only area-bombing raid on Pforzheim, a city of 80,000 people, from only 8,000ft and 1,825 tons of bombs were dropped in just over twenty minutes. More than 17,000 people were killed and 83 per cent of the town's built-up area was destroyed in 'a hurricane of fire and explosions'

We witnessed the bombing of Dresden. We were supposed to sleep in a barn on the outskirts but the sirens went. The RAF came in and bombed all night, the Yanks came in and bombed all the next day… The German guards told us that more than 100,000 civilians had been evacuated from the Russian front at Breslau. They never did get an accurate count of their dead from that raid on Dresden.

Boston Patterson RCAF, POW

FORTY

VARSITY

Inspire, O Lord, our men who fly
Their winged chariots on high,
A cross the dark and tortured sky.
Take them whereso'er they fare
From all the dangers of the air.

'Hymn to Airmen', Group Captain E.B.C. Betts, July 1940

In the Horsa glider, the two pilots sat side-by-side in a cockpit not unlike a conservatory, with almost 360 degree view. There were two control columns of the spade-grip type and the only instruments were an altimeter, airspeed indicator, a compass and another colloquially called the 'angle of the dangle'. It was a Heath Robinson device in which thin cord only a few feet long was connected to the towrope and this indicated, in an illuminated panel, where the glider was situated in relation to the tug aircraft. This was essential when flying in cloud or at night. The Horsa could carry twenty-eight fully armed troops and the idea was to land them at some strategic point, such as a bridge or enemy gun emplacement, possibly at night.

In the summer of 1944 over 200 graduates from 4 BFTS [British Flying Training School], Falcon Field, helped the Army as glider pilots. The newly trained RAF glider pilots were split into two groups. Roughly half of them were allocated to UK airfields for the Rhine crossing and were attached to No.1 and 2 Wings of the Glider Pilot Regiment; making up the crews with survivors from Arnhem. The remainder were allocated to man the six squadrons of RAF glider pilots, 668–673, which made up 343 and 344 Wings, founded in India for airborne assault in South East Asia. Each of these squadrons had an establishment of eighty Hadrian gliders – known to the Americans as Wacos [the name of the manufacturer].

Back in the UK, the time was drawing near for the Rhine Crossing and between 20 and 22 March 1945, RAF Bomber Command and the US 8th and 9th Air Forces

made 16,000 sorties over the area and dropped 49,500 tons of bombs. At 1700hrs on 23 March the entire artillery of the British 2nd Army opened fire on enemy positions and maintained the barrage of shells until 0945 on 24 March. The total airborne force consisted of 1,795 paratroop carriers and 1,350 towing gliders, escorted by 889 fighters – a total of 3,989 aircraft.

With this massive formation, the Allies were able to land all 21,680 glidermen and paratroopers of the British 6th Airborne Division and the American 17th Airborne Division in two hours thirty-six minutes. The Varsity drop was to be the largest single airborne attack made by either side during the war – even larger than the one made in Holland.

Herbert Buckle, glider pilot and 4 BFTS cadet

'Wakey-wakey!'

I half-opened my eyes and looked towards the door of the hut. The light had been switched on and two WAAFs, accompanied by a mess corporal, had entered. They were carrying an urn of tea and a tray of mugs. A few minutes later the sixteen of us were sitting up in our beds sipping hot, sweet tea. It was still dark outside, but a clear sky promised a fine day. In a few hours we would be landing our gliders in German-held territory on the far side of the Rhine. It was Saturday 24 March 1945.

Tea in bed was followed by a most exceptional breakfast in the mess: eggs, bacon, fried bread, sausages and tomatoes. This was certainly no ordinary day. The meal had produced a noise of excited conversation and a feeling of being appreciated as special people on a special occasion. Back in the hut we gathered our equipment together and waited for the lorries to take us out to the aircraft. It was getting light on the way out and everyone was now quiet. Ron and I were dropped off near our glider and we put our gear on board. About sixty Stirling tugs were lined up on the runway on alternate sides, already roped up to the gliders, which were parked at an angle on the grass. Ron did an external check of our Horsa and I checked the inside, including the fastening of the load. We then sat in the cockpit and waited for the arrival of our passengers.

Sitting in a glider, armed with a rifle and 100 rounds of ammunition and waiting to fly into battle in Germany, was not how I had visualised my career as an RAF pilot. It was brought about by the disastrous attempt in September 1944 to take and hold the bridge across the Rhine at Arnhem to enable Montgomery's army to advance into Germany. So many Army glider pilots had been lost that the only way to replace them in time for another operation was to transfer hundreds of RAF pilots not currently on operational duties. Volunteers were asked for, but few offered and many were chosen. Of the latter, I, with a number of my friends, was taken away from a Tiger Moth refresher course, given a week's leave and we started our training. Thirty of us were formed into a flight and we stayed together throughout our training and on to our operational station. The training period lasted from the beginning of November 1944 until the middle of January 1945, at five different stations. Infantry training was given by the Glider Pilot Regiment; flying training by the RAF.

From our seats in our glider we heard lorry loads of troops arriving and left the aircraft to watch. A major came up to us and introduced himself as being in charge of the party to join us. There was a sergeant and some half a dozen other ranks. They settled down on the seats ahead of the jeep and trailer, close to the left-hand door, through which they would leave. One at least had not flown before. The major told us that a soldier had refused to get into the Horsa behind us and had been taken away by Military Police.

Dozens of Stirlings had started their engines and were doing power checks. The noise was very impressive. It was about 07.30 and now daylight. After a short while the noise died down as the pilots throttled back to idling speed. The first aircraft moved slowly along the runway until its glider had lined up behind it, then the pilot increased power and accelerated along the runway. The Horsa lifted off and then both were airborne and clearing the perimeter of the airfield. With the second pair already lifting off as aircraft after aircraft pulled their gliders from alternate sides of the runway I could see the stream of them forming ahead, all still climbing and bobbing gently up and down in relative movement.

'Rolling now' came over the intercom. Our tug's engine opened up and it moved forward. The towrope lifted, there was a gentle surge forward and Ron guided us across the grass and turned into line. The tug gathered speed and we lifted off, settling down a few feet up, waiting for the tug to get airborne. As usual it seemed a long time before it left the runway and then Ron gradually increased height to keep above the tug. The Stirling's undercarriage came up and speed increased. We could relax a little.

The aircraft ahead were turning now and still climbing. Our cruising altitude was to be 3,000ft, but before we could set course our squadron, currently manoeuvering into formation as a squadron, had to manoeuvre into a large stream with aircraft from other glider squadrons throughout East Anglia. This took up some fifteen to twenty minutes, during which time I took over control of the aircraft. Eventually we appeared to have settled down on a south-easterly heading. I was lost as to our position, but soon saw the Thames ahead. London was away to the right and the Thames Estuary to the left. We must have crossed near Gravesend and I wondered if we could be seen from Wilmington. We were now in level flight at 3,500ft and on heading for the Rhine. Time now to settle back and enjoy the view.

It was a beautiful day, clear blue sky and good visibility. The Kent coast came into view and then the line of the coast of France. The Channel looked quite narrow as we left the land and it seemed almost crowded with boats. Up ahead a Horsa separated from its tug and descended quite steeply towards the sea. I watched it all the way down, until it levelled off and hit the water with a great white splash. It remained afloat and then it was out of my vision. Three launches were converging on it well before it ditched.

I had finished my first stint of piloting by now and was studying the map as we came up to the French coast. A year earlier this would have been 'Enemy Coast Ahead' and the rest of the route would have been extremely dangerous, but there was no danger today until we reached the Rhine. To our right was Cap Gris Nez, the land above its cliffs pitted with bomb and shell craters. There was still over two hours' flying time to go; I decided it was a good time for refreshment. The mess had given us a large flask of tea, which I took back into the main fuselage and offered some to the major, who properly answered: 'Serve the lads first.' I unscrewed the bowl-shaped covers from the row of lights in the ceiling of the fuselage and served the tea in these. It didn't get a round of applause, but it caused some smiles and remarks.

Our armada continued over the flat countryside until I could see, in our 10 o'clock, the smoke haze of a very large town. My map reading told me it was Brussels; we were passing over the Field of Waterloo.

While flying along, I had in my sight dozens of aircraft ahead and to our left. There was no view behind, but I knew there were hundreds of us. I pictured being near the front and at the right-hand side of possibly miles of aircraft. Now, to my right, I could see another stream of hundreds of Dakotas towing Hadrian gliders. They were converging on us and then turning on to a parallel course close to us. The Americans had joined us from their bases in France. It must have been an awe-inspiring sight from the ground.

After another hundred miles or so, alternately piloting and relaxing, we saw far ahead the unmistakable line of the Rhine meandering across our course, showing clearly by its reflection of the bright sunshine. 'Point Alpha' came from the tug and I turned and indicated '10 minutes' to the major. By 'Point Bravo' it became obvious that the battle area on the far side of the river was much obscured by smoke haze: finding our target might be difficult. Ron was flying now and was to do the landing. I had the photographs in my hands and would give him directions for landing.

As we came up to the Rhine we flew into anti-aircraft fire. Just ahead of us, then all around, small black clouds materialised with a large yellow spark in the middle of each one. We could not hear them and they just floated in the still air as we passed them by, some quite close. The gunners had obviously got the altitude just right. I saw a Dakota diving steeply with smoke and flames streaming behind it. We passed over it before it hit the ground.

The Rhine was behind us now, the visibility straight down was all right, but slant distance was poor. The anti-aircraft fire had stopped. 'Point Charlie coming up. Release Point NOW', came over the intercom. Ron released the tow rope. The Horsa slowed down and started a gradual descent. We were at about 3,500ft and had several minutes before landing. I had to pick out the corner of a small wood, in an area of farmland and other small woods. I had decided to concentrate on the one outstanding feature in the area: what appeared to be a quarry with bare sand hills showing a lighter colour against the generally dark earth. Ron was doing S-turns, losing height without going too far from Release Point, while I was looking ahead and around in the somewhat limited field of view one had from the glider. I was trying to get the photos and the land features to agree somehow, while concentrating on a sighting of the quarry. As our speed dropped off, our rate of descent increased. I was getting a bit worried, but then I spotted the quarry, tapped Ron's shoulder and pointed to it, indicating where I thought we should land.

Ron made a slow turn to get onto a good approach path. The smoke below showed us there was no wind, which gave us a choice of landing direction, but also meant no wind to slow our landing speed. As the flaps were lowered, our rate of descent increased greatly and we could judge where we would land. We were heading for what appeared to be an area of small saplings, but our descent and a closer view revealed them as trees big enough to damage the glider. 'They're too big. Go left!' I shouted. We were quite low by now. Ron went into a sharp left turn, straightened up and levelled the wings and we smacked down into the bare soft earth, clear of the trees, going quite fast. There was a harsh grinding noise as the floor beneath our feet scraped along the ground; the nose wheel had obviously broken off. Our aircraft stopped in a very short distance.

The drill was to leap from our seats and get out of the aircraft immediately, but for a few seconds we sat still, waiting for our insides to settle back into position. There was the feeling as well that we had accomplished the essential part of our mission. Then we left. Releasing my harness I got up and found myself standing on bare earth; the floor of the cockpit had gone. I picked up my rifle and ammunition and went out through the left-hand door. All our passengers were already lying on the ground under the left-hand wing. I lay down next to the major. We were all soldiers now and had joined the battle.

L.A. Kemp

We crossed the Rhine enveloped by the now-famous 'Monty's smoke-screen'. We couldn't see the river but we overflew Hamminkeln and I could see the river Issel and our bridge. By this time the AA fire was heavy. Tracer bullets crept up towards us and then flashed past and the sky was filled with exploding shells. I saw the leading glider, flown by Capt. Carr, break up in the air and the men falling out. Other gliders in the North Bridge Group were hit. Then it was our turn.

Our tug took us right over the Dropping Zone and they shouted 'Good Luck' over the intercom as we cast off. The glider with our jeep on our starboard disappeared and then a shell exploded under us. I pinpointed our spot in a field as per the photograph we had been given and Pete Ince dived for it.

We left the flaps until the last moment, but when I pulled the flap lever nothing happened – our air supply had been cut. We gained speed and the airspeed indicator went off the clock! It took both of us all our strength to pull out of that dive. We hit the ground hard, raced along at practically zero feet and I remember the German machine-gunners ducking for cover as we almost decapitated them. Our excess speed made us climb away and, as we tried to turn back into our field, we hit the top of a belt of trees. These helped to save us and as the port wingtip touched the ground we came to a sudden stop and I was thrown out through the nose and made a dent in the ground.

Those of us who survived were pinned down under the wreckage by machine-gun fire. Soon the glider began to burn and as the flames drew near our cargo of explosives we had little option but to race across the field to a trench we could see in the distance. It was only then that I realised the two soldiers lying on either side of me had both been killed since we landed. We all made the trench without further casualties, but discovered that the said trench was an open sewer. We sank in up to our waists. For once in our lives we were glad to land in the...

Jock Davies and I looked for arms and picked up a PIAT gun. We were then told to fire it toward a gun emplacement. After a large group of the enemy, consisting of German Home Guard and an SS officer, had surrendered, I found myself with one paratrooper in charge of them. As we marched them off I could not resist ordering them to give an 'eyes right' to an airborne colonel, who, seeing my RAF pilot's brevet, was kind enough to congratulate the RAF pilots on their showing.

Hamminkeeln was still receiving the occasional shell as we began to pull out. When we drew near the pontoon bridge across the Rhine, the Commandos who had crossed the river in boats lined up to cheer us on our way out. We were taken to Helmond, where the Dutch people looked after us very well. Then to Eindhoven and flown back to RAF Down Ampney on 30 March. There we were met by HM Customs, who wanted to know where we had spent the past few nights! The answers they received were varied to say the least. Tempers were short and they soon diplomatically ran out of forms. Maybe the threat to burn their hut down helped.

Sergeant Pilot F.W. Ayliffe

The British Glider Force consisted of 440 Airspeed Horsas and General Aircraft Hamilcars. Anti-aircraft fire was murderous and only eighty British gliders landed unscathed. The assault resulted in an outstanding victory. It was not, however, achieved without cost, for the Glider Pilot Regiment had suffered 101 pilots killed, of whom sixty-one were RAF glider pilots. Of the 440 British gliders, ten were shot down and 284 were damaged by anti-aircraft fire. Only eighty-eight came through undamaged. Fire destroyed thirty-seven that landed. They brought in 3,303 troops, 271 Jeeps, 275 trailers and sixty-six guns and other equipment, including trucks and bulldozers. Of 880 British glider pilots, seventy-seven were wounded and 175 were killed or missing.

"*I'm afraid we shall have to leave building the new wing until after the war.*"

[1943]

Below: '*In the Horsa glider, the two pilots sat side-by-side in a cockpit not unlike a conservatory, with almost 360 degree view. There were two control columns of the spade-grip type and the only instruments were an altimeter, airspeed indicator, a compass and another colloquially called the "angle of the dangle". It was a Heath Robinson device in which thin cord only a few feet long was connected to the towrope and this indicated, in an illuminated panel, where the glider was situated in relation to the tug aircraft. This was essential when flying in cloud or at night…*'
(IWM)

FORTY-ONE
DEATH MARCH

Most POW camps were put on a 'death march' by March 1945 at the latest, although I think this a bit overplayed. It was rough, but I doubt if it compares with Bataan or that rotten railway in Burma.

Geoff Parnell, POW, 1945

It was just after midnight on 6 February 1945 that we were awakened somewhat noisily by our own camp leaders with the news that we had to be ready to leave camp by midday and on foot. We were soon wide awake and making sure that a hot brew was being prepared… Our wanderings seemed to have little purpose and we were not progressing in any sort of a straight line. I got the impression that we were being moved around, still at the rate of about 15 miles a day, to the next convenient place to stop overnight. We had seen a fair amount of aerial activity and on several occasions we had to dive into roadside ditches to avoid the attention of our own strafing fighters, mostly Typhoons. Before the pilots became aware of our existence we did sustain several fatalities and other lesser casualties, but it was soon realised who and where we were and thereafter the aircraft often flew alongside the column at low level, the pilots giving us a wave. The large formations of USAAF bombers were awesome and we saw some of them shot down by defending fighters and cheered when the white canopies emerged to float downwards. One sunny day we had only just passed through a smallish town and had reached the outskirts when the Yanks came over and flattened the area we had traversed some ten minutes earlier.

Quite unexpectedly one day we were told we were to be transported by train to a camp and, true enough, after about 2 miles we arrived at the railway station of Ebsdorf, where the usual cattletrucks awaited us. Other columns were converging upon this railhead. We were packed into the trucks at least eighty men to a truck for the 50-mile journey and consequently it was a case of standing room only. The doors remained closed throughout the night. It is not difficult to appreciate what a disgusting mess we were in when we were finally let out after about twenty hours, for there were no toilet

" Don't bother to unpack, we're moving to-morrow."

facilities and many of us were suffering from diarrhoea. I know of at least one Kriegie who did not emerge alive.

Basil Craske, POW, on the march from Gross Tychow in February–March 1945

The war was now in Germany and we were in an area of constant alert. There would be no warning siren. When it sounded, it meant bombers overhead. One day, a flight of six Mustangs spotted us and mistook us for a column of German reinforcements. They came in low, with rockets and guns blazing and wiped out more than 150 of us, not counting the wounded. On 15 March we arrived at Ziegenheim, about 20 miles from the Rhine. The deep rumble of war was now to the west of us. Our original column of 3,000 men was down to 1,000. Most of us were desperately ill with dysentery and starvation. When we stood up we moved very slowly, or we would fall. When the pangs of starvation set in, you first feel the straight gnawing of hunger; then the craving for something sweet; then the craving for fat; then the craving for salt and this is when you get dizzy.

We slept under canvas and didn't march again. We couldn't have marched, even at gunpoint. The Yanks surrounded our position and recaptured us on 31 March – Good Friday. The RAF flew us to England early in April. We had not shaved, had a bath or even had our boots off in more than ten weeks. Those of us who could spare it lost about 60lb. Those who couldn't spare it – just didn't.

Boston Patterson, RCAF, POW on the march in 1945

I had heard from captured 101st 'Screaming Eagle' paratroopers about the German breakthrough in the Ardennes and Bodenplatte. They were totally demoralised and believed the Germans could go through all the way. The Russians, meanwhile, were coming like the Scotch Express. So, in March 1945, during the march westwards away from the advancing Russians, Nick Green, a prisoner since being shot down in a Whitley in 1941 and I, made our

"... and I wouldn't swop my **HERCULES** for your old kite!"

Hercules
CYCLES

THE HERCULES CYCLE & MOTOR CO·LTD·Aston·Birmingham

'She and I sneaked out through a hole in the hedge at night, Norah pushing me on her Hercules bicycle to the Marquis of Granby pub. Later, we cycled around Chessington to help strengthen my legs.'

getaway from the column. We would hide and wait for the advancing Russian Army. We hid for three days and nights in bitterly cold conditions in swede clamps, 30ft long by 10ft wide, pulling straw over our bodies for warmth. It was no good. We both got badly frostbitten limbs and gangrene set in. On the third day I gave myself up. Nick was in very bad shape.

We were taken to Neubrandenburg Kriegsgefangenen Lazarett (hospital) where a Polish naval surgeon, Captain Mickoski, who had been captured at Gydnia in 1939, operated on us. He was assisted by a Serb of the Royal Yugoslav Army. Communication was rather difficult and the two of them argued nineteen to the dozen. Our operations were carried out with spinal anaesthetic, so we were conscious all through the operations. Nick and I had a double Chopart's [operation] to remove our toes and front part of our feet. Nick was in worse condition, the gangrene having spread up his legs. His next operation was a double below the knee and then a double above the knee. After the third operation he died of shock. I had been down for only twenty months and was twenty-three years old, so I could perhaps better stand the amputations than Nick, who was in bad shape, having been down since 1941.

When the Russians overran the hospital I received treatment from one of their nurses. She had been fighting for three years and carried a sniper's rifle. Apart from her nursing duties she would direct traffic with biff-bats when 'off duty'! I spent three weeks with the Russians. The nurse gave me blood transfusions Russian style with a syringe to pump blood into my arm! It was the same needle used by everyone else in the ward!

Back in England I was sent to EMS at King's College Hospital in Epsom, where they sorted out my gangrene. I was nursed by Norah Hudson of the Physiotherapy Service who was attached to the RAF. It was against the rules, but she and I sneaked out through a hole in the hedge at night, Norah pushing me on her Hercules bicycle to the Marquis of Granby pub. Later, we cycled around Chessington to help strengthen my legs. We agreed to marry three weeks after meeting, but because of service delays we married in 1946.

Len Bradfield, 49 Squadron

FORTY-TWO
THE CAPTAINS AND THE KINGS DEPART

The tumult and the shouting dies;
The captains and the kings depart;
Still stands Thine ancient sacrifice,
A humble and a contrite heart
Lord God of Hosts, be with us yet,
Lest we forget – lest we forget.

Kipling's 'Recessional'

Our operational career came to a sad end. On Sunday 8 April 1945 we were briefed just after lunch for a raid on Lutzkendorf. At the conclusion of the briefing Wing Commander Botting, with a piece of paper in his hand, told us that we were tour-expired since the signal he had received during briefing had reduced the number of operations required from thirty-six to thirty-three. We were scrubbed from the operation and the reserve crew (Flying Officer Roger Cluer's) would take our place. Our rear gunner, Roy Wilkins, had completed about three trips less than the rest of the crew (because of illness) and since Sergeant Pollington, the rear gunner in the reserve crew, had contracted ear trouble, Roy volunteered to take his place. We all went out to the runway to see the lads take off and Sergeant Pollington came with us. Sitting on the grass on this pleasant early spring evening, awaiting Cluer to swing *N-Nuts* on to the main runway, we idly picked clover. Pollington actually picked three four-leafed clovers in succession! Laughingly, we all remarked, 'You lucky bastard... it looks like your crew will get the chop tonight'. Many a true word spoken in jest! Roy gave us a thumbs up from his rear turret as *N-Nuts* roared down the runway. We went to the Hare and

'The RAF flew us to England early in April. We had not shaved, had a bath or even had our boots off in more than ten weeks. Those of us who could spare it lost about 60lb. Those who couldn't spare it – just didn't.' (IWM)

Hounds in Fulbeck village for a drink before rolling back into our hut Although we never had the pleasure of knowingly flying our last op, the feeling of having finished was nevertheless fantastic. Next morning, Roy's bed was still empty and we thought he might have landed elsewhere but nothing more was ever heard of him or the crew with which he was flying. Roy's loss was a very tragic experience coming right at the end of a long and distinguished tour.

After the war was over we weren't treated as heroes like the boys from Fighter Command – in fact Harris was vilified. People said that bombing German cities had been wrong. But that was unfair – we simply carried out our instructions to the best of our ability. Nothing was said about all our friends that lost their lives.

Flight Sergeant John Aldridge, Lancaster bomb aimer, 49 Squadron

In 1945 the RAF's personnel strength consisted of a total 190,256 officers and 1,006,267 airmen… After nearly six years of war the RAF had developed out of all recognition from its pre-war existence. By 1945 the RAF had become the third-largest air force in the world behind those of the USA and the Soviet Union. The RAF had been involved in virtually every campaign throughout the war and had amassed a wealth of experience in a wide variety of roles and missions.

Victory had not been achieved without a high price. A total of 70,253 RAF aircrew were lost on operations between 3 September 1939 and 14 August 1945, with no fewer than 47,293 being lost from Bomber Command alone. The Air Forces Memorial at Runnymede commemorates the names of 20,435 airmen of the RAF who were lost during the Second World War and who have no known grave.

Chris Hobson, senior librarian, RAF Staff College, Bracknell, writing in 1995

In memory of Flight Sergeant Ken —— lost in action, April 1945.
We never forget – wife —— and son Peter.
Dad, the grand-daughter you never knew gets married next week.
For all those who failed to return – especially for the 'Prosper' Network – and most of all for Noor Inayat Khan – inexplicably abandoned. Not forgotten – For Lilian Rolfe.

> *Inscriptions on cards attached to wreaths, Runnymede, 1994. Noor Jnayat Khan ('Madeleine') and Lilian Rolfe were WAAFs, trained as special agents and dropped behind enemy lines. Both were executed at Dachau concentration camp*

We saw the Spitfires more in the last years of the war. They were really very daring. If you saw them coming down it was so very exciting. The Dutch of course were very much in favour of the Tommies and were so happy that they got rid of the Germans for us. I have never seen anything more exciting. They would come DOWN and then they were UP again! It was fun, even if we were feeling miserable about the whole trouble. It gave us a lift. They were our liberators. We waved, but they had no time to look at us. It was little things like this that made it bearable to be occupied. It was fun to do this. It scared the Germans. We were just so thrilled they were coming. We would never have known when the Germans might leave. If it wasn't for them they may have stayed another five or ten years. Liberation was so fantastic. Free again!

> *Twenty-six-year-old Christina van den Born, Holland, 1945. In late April 1945 the RAF and USAAF began Operation Manna to airdrop food and medical supplies to the starving Dutch population. From 29 April to 7 May Lancasters with PFF Mosquitoes 'marking' the dropping zones, took part. 2,835 Lancaster and 124 Mosquito flights were made before the Germans surrendered at the end of the war and allowed ships and road transport to enter the area. All told, Bomber Command delivered 6,672 tons of food*

22.04.45. With the war in Europe fast coming to a close, I think the number of raids before its end will be very limited – for us anyway. We have started practicing supply dropping by flying low-level across the drome and lobbing sandbags on to a white cross (I landed one on a runway!) Now that we are right across Germany, some pretty horrible things are coming to light. We are finding concentration camps complete with enormous cremation ovens and torture devices, filled with men, women and children looking like skeletons – hundreds of whom die every day in spite of all we can do. The numbers killed in these places is colossal. In one camp alone over a million died and were cremated. In another (Belsen) a laboratory was found where German doctors practiced on live prisoners and lampshades were made out of tanned human skins. Russians, political prisoners and European civilians seem to have suffered most. Ours are mostly under nourished – thousands have already been freed. I wonder if poor old Cliff is among them? Germany is beaten all right but she has left Europe in a terrible state. There can hardly be one family on this side of the globe, which has not a personal cause for hating the Germans.

1st May '45. Holland, from Rotterdam to the North is still occupied. To stop our advance the Jerries have flooded half the country, with a result that large towns are packed full of homeless, hungry Dutch. By arrangement we are dropping food on the towns, without any opposition. We set out about 11 this morning with 6,000-odd pounds of food, for a place just outside The Hague. Crossed the Dutch coast at low level just north of Overflakee. The whole coastline and the edges of the rivers are all pitted with defence posts and gun positions, though I never saw a German the whole time. I daresay they had orders to keep under cover in case we shot at them. With the Germans all under cover the population turned out in strength and waved at us. It was a heartening sight! Some of them were madly waving flags (mostly Dutch, but all red, white and blue). One little man I saw had one enormous flag in each hand and a terrific grin on his face; when

Manna.

he caught sight of the kite, he leaped off the ground in his excitement! A woman was perched perilously on the roof of a house waving like mad and shouting something. I should think every person in The Hague turned out to cheer us. Our dropping ground was in a sports field north of the town complete with a grandstand. With remarkable confidence in our aim, the grandstand was packed with the good people. I wouldn't swear to it but somebody looking remarkably like the mayor was there in his robes of office. The grandstand was only a stone's throw from our dropping point, which was marked by a white cross. Came back at nought feet above the sea very pleased with ourselves.

07/05/45. Went to a village E of The Hague this time, over a lot of flooded country, only the rooftops showing. We took a ground-staff bod with us, who was hopping up and down with excitement.

08/05. VE day! The war has lasted so long I can hardly believe it is over. I can't remember very clearly now what it was like to live without a war; it seems so long ago. Stayed in the flat this evening as the West End was pretty crowded and got through two bottles of wine. Went upstairs afterwards and watched people lighting fires and firing Verey lights (I wish I'd brought some). Singing and shouting went on to the early hours, but we were in bed by then.

Warrant Officer Arthur 'Spud' Taylor, Lancaster observer, 149 Squadron, Methwold, diary entries 18 April–8 May 1945. 'Spud' received the award of the DFC on 20 July 1945

On April 30th we did our first food drop on Operation Manna to Rotterdam and May 2nd to The Hague, both marvellous low flying 250ft. The 'Thanks' messages on the roofs with towels and sheets I will always remember.

Maurice Bishop, pilot, Lancaster III Winsome Winnie, *218 'Gold Coast' Squadron, Chedburgh, April–May 1945*

The pub was full, there was considerable excitement and the beer was being consumed in great quantities. As the evening progressed it became obvious that the celebration of the ending of hostilities was to go on well into the night. Then there was a call – 'Let's have a bonfire!'. The crowded bar emptied, the drinkers taking the bar furniture out with them into the road, dad and I stood some few yards away and watched the furniture being piled up in the centre of the road.

The next thing was that it was going up in flames, accompanied by a loud cheer from those gathered around it. We watched for a few minutes, then dad turned away and headed towards home. I followed and caught up with him. We walked in silence for a while and then dad said, 'I didn't like that.'

I told him that it was not what I wanted to see either.

Sergeant Roland A. Hammersley DFM, VE Day 1945

With the war almost over Eff and me fixed our wedding date for 11 August 1945 but before that I was sent to take the newly established Flight Engineers Leaders Course. This was a combination of an Instructors Course and Qualification on the Lancaster and Stirling aircraft so that he could act as a flight engineer on any bomber aircraft. This was in June 1945. On return to headquarters I managed to join a crew on a cross-country training flight which took about ten ground crew and was called a Cooks Tour. We flew over Arnhem to have a look at the bridge, then over what was left of Kassel, Cologne, Düusseldorf and Duisburg. Just miles and miles of utter destruction. UK cities suffered damage in the Blitz but nothing to the obliteration of the German cities. There were just skeletons of houses and factories with rubble bulldozed into long lanes to clear a way through for the roads. On the way home Walcheren Island completely flooded when Bomber Command breached the dykes to open the approaches to Antwerp.

And so to the preparation of what was really still a wartime wedding. Although the war in Europe was over and a new Labour Government ruled, there was still strict rationing of everything. Yet, somehow, a bride and six bridesmaids were dressed in Nottingham lace and [there was] a reception for fifty or sixty people in the Gimcrack Hotel in York. My parents organised enough petrol to drive half the family up from West Sussex. Half the crew of *V-Victor* and other service mates made me very drunk on my stag night. Paddy, the wireless operator, was to be best man. But by the next morning I had sobered up and made the start line on time. Everything went well to plan until it came to the photographs outside the church. The camera broke, causing problems and even film was rationed. The result was that the camera man had to go back to his studio and get another camera and everyone was hauled out half way through the reception to parade for photographs. The next hiatus occurred at the 'Going Away'. The plan was to take the train from York to my home where my car had been prepared for honeymoon in Cornwall. The train was crowded, so Uncle Billy (who was some sort of railway official) suggested that we catch the next train and he would book seats from Newcastle. This meant an hour-and-a-half wait on the main platform of York station with a very merry wedding party, getting up to all sorts of mischief. When the train came in the reserved seats had a large notice in the window. Someone found a bucket of whitewash and the outside of the train was suitably adorned, much to the annoyance of the railway staff. When the train stopped at Peterborough a crew had been laid on to clean the coach. Eventually we got to London, got the baggage to Waterloo and home via Hazlemere and a taxi, very late, very tired, but very happy.

Next day we set off for Cornwall Old George. The local garage owner had obtained two new front tyres for our car, a four-wheeled, four-seat BSA 4/4 front-wheel-drive open sports car. Don't ask where the petrol coupons had come from. Half way across Salisbury Plain there was a loud bang and both the two new front tyres had burst. I put on the spare wheel and managed to patch one of the bust ones, which got us to Blandford where a friendly garage owner found the cause of the trouble, a bent track rod causing the wheels to run out of line. This was straightened and a second hand tyre was found and

Flight Lieutenant Jim Sprackling and Eff marry on 11 August 1945. (Sprackling)

away we went again. On Bodmin Moor the petrol pump started playing up. This meant siphoning petrol into a small tank behind the dashboard to gravity-feed the carburettor but more delay, so by 10 o'clock we had only reached Launceston, so we went to the police station for help. The local Bobby knocked up a hotel for us so we did not have to spend the night in a cell.

The next day, August 13th, we made our hotel in Newquay, parked our car and prepared to unwind. That evening it was announced that Japan had surrendered and that the next day would be a Bank Holiday (the atom bombs had been dropped while Eff and I were otherwise engaged). THE WAR WAS OVER. But not the end of the story. Newquay was full of Australians rehabilitating. They went mad, no sleep that night. Next day we found someone had left the lights on on the car so the battery was flat and all the garages were shut so no recharge available. But who wanted a car? The weather was good and the sea warm and we had no care in the world.

Flight Lieutenant Jim Sprackling

For some months after the war I used to wake up in a cold sweat on the floor next to my side of the bed. The dream was always much the same – my clothes were on fire and I was baling out of a burning aircraft. My wife Marguerite would say, 'You OK Spud?'

I would reply, 'Yes thanks' and she would say: 'Well get back into bed then and stop mucking about'.

And that is all the counselling I ever received. But it worked and I soon forgot about those dreams. I have never, however, forgotten my time in the RAF, or the comrades I flew with.

Arthur 'Spud' Taylor DFC

Our generation caught a packet and the Air Crew Europe medal fetches fourteen quid or so in the junk shops. Other campaign medals make 30s apiece.

Geoff Parnell, air gunner, 1977

*'That's Henderson, our
rear gunner.'*

I was a survivor of three years and two completed operational tours with Bomber
Command and as one of Arthur 'Butch' Harris's 'Old Lags' I feel I must commit my
feelings to paper before it is too late as we are becoming rather thin on the ground.
First, I must kill the conception that he was 'Bomber' Harris, a popular press misnomer
as he was only Butch to his 'boys'. Another latter day incorrect belief was that the name
'Butch' was an abbreviation of Butcher for a belief of killing. In truth, it was the effect
of American films of the day where the tough uncompromising leader of the gang was
frequently Butch and often members of the gang were the 'old lags', as he knew us. Both
were terms of endearment as we would have followed him to the bitter end (as over
50% did) and nothing was too good for us in his eyes.

Aircrew were a reasonably well educated bunch, very young, compassionate and not
cruel in any way. We were all volunteers, fighting a war for the survival of the free world
with knowledge of what had happened to Guernica, Warsaw, Rotterdam and then the
cities nearer home. We attacked the targets we were allocated as parts of the total war we
were fighting, fortunately without thought of the civilian population below until after
the war had ended. We were fighting a battle for survival in the skies over Germany, often
two nights out of every three in the hope of returning to our quite comfortable messes
and living quarters.

Killing was not a word in our vocabularies - we never said 'Old Bill was killed last
night', he had either 'bought it', 'Gone for a Burton', 'Got the chop' or just 'had it' last
night. Nearly every day on an operational squadron there were gaps not there the day
before but it was not a thing to be dwelt on. For ourselves the powers that be and Lord
Nuffield acknowledged our position in particular. We had leave every seven or eight
weeks, comfortable living conditions, no parades or such that others suffered, bacon and
eggs on return from every operation (a luxury in wartime) and sweets, chocolate and
orange juice as flying rations, as we were often airborne for up to nine hours. I mention
Lord Nuffield as he financed a scheme under which aircrew and wives could spend
leaves in first class hotels entirely free of charge. For example, Eileen and I had a week
in The Ship Hotel at Brighton living in comparative luxury and with all fares paid and
of course, the scheme was great boon for aircrew from the Commonwealth. All this as
it was essential to keep up morale in the face of vast losses. For example, more aircrew
were killed in one night to Nuremberg than pilots were lost in the whole of the Battle
of Britain!

'Butch' was ever conscious of sending so many young men out to their deaths night
after night. But like the very great majority of the British public, he saw for so long as

the only way to carry the war to Germany and later as the way to wreck their industrial base and so shorten the war. The invasion and the battle for Normandy was only possible because the enemy transport network had been virtually destroyed, his fuel was in increasingly short supply, as was replacement armour, which unit for unit was vastly superior to that of the Allies.

In all my years of service I never heard a word of criticism of the bombing of Germany – in fact it was usually 'Give 'em hell lads' especially in London and the larger cities which had suffered so much. With alcoholic drink in increasingly short supply, it was always available for aircrew with whisky under the bar available on request.

There was no commander in WWII whose force sustained losses of over 50% killed and still retained the respect and affection of those he led nor was there one so ill treated by the politicians when the war ended. They were all so anxious to distance themselves from the bombing of Dresden which was never a target of Harris's choosing as he considered it and Leipzig and Chemnitz to be too distant and dangerous for his beloved and respected aircrew. However, the Air Ministry had agreed Operation *Thunderclap*, which was the attack on these three cities when it became necessary to support the Russian advance. Winston Churchill took a direct hand in the planning when called for by the Joint Chiefs of Staff and the Russians.

The attack on Dresden was to be a joint operation by the US 8th Air Force and RAF Bomber Command with the American attacking first on 13 February 1945 to be followed by the RAF that night. However, bad weather prevented the American operation so the first attack was by the now highly organized and efficient Bomber Command, which aided by high winds, had the inevitable result. What does not get much publicity is that the 8th Air Force carried out their attack the next day with a force of 311 B-17s which dropped a further 771 tons of bombs and escorting Mustangs strafed traffic on the roads around the city. In addition, they bombed again on the 15th and the 2nd March. Personally, I was not involved being part of the 8 (Pathfinder) Group Light Night Striking Force Mosquitoes who were mainly occupied with attacks on Berlin and looking forward to completion of our tour on 22 February 1945.

Finally it must be pointed out that Arthur Harris was the only top commander to retain his command throughout the period 1942 to the end of the war and he was probably the most respected by the Supreme Allied Commander, general Dwight d. Eisenhower. In fact, he seems to have got on better with the American high command than with the Brutish. After the wartime adulation of him and his aircrew it came as some considerable shock to be criticized by those wise after the event but it added considerable strength to, our organizations such as the Bomber Command Association and the Mosquito Aircrew Association. In this we were ever grateful for the unfailing support given by the late Queen Mother to the Bomber Command Association and for the record being put straight in well-researched books by highly qualified authors.

Lancaster and Mosquito navigator, Pilot Officer Derek Smith DFC★

How can we praise the brave young men
Who flexed their new and untried wings
And flew, like eaglets, free and bold,
No fettered slaves or underlings?

How can we tell of loyal men
Who worked long hours upon the ground
In drizzling cold or tropic heat,
To serve their crews in honour bound?

How can we laud the gentle girls
Who nursed them, fed them, mastered arts
Of radar, plotting, ground control
And tender care of engine parts?
How can we honour those who came,
Through hardship, danger, fear and pain,
From Europe's crushed and bleeding lands
To spread their wings and fight again?

How can we show our gratitude
To those who, of their own accord,
Came from our far-flung Commonwealth
To help us wield our shining sword?
How can we thank the men who crossed
The great Atlantic, deep and wide,
And left their New World far behind
To fight for freedom at our side?

A generation, selflessly,
Gave up the flower of its youth,
A sacrifice so quietly made
That we might live in peace and truth.

All tears now shed long years ago,
But memories last for all our days,
And so, with pride, we make our vow
To keep faith with them always.

'The Allied Forces: A Dedication', Audrey Grealy
This was written to mark the occasion of the unveiling of the monument to the RAF and Allied Air Forces on
Plymouth Hoe, 3 September 1989, the fiftieth anniversary of the outbreak of the Second World War

Oulton airfield, Norfolk, wartime home of 2 Group and 100 Group Squadrons. (Author)

Deserted, abandoned, an airfield spans the lonely heath,
Unkempt broken runways sprout their share of grass and weeds
Bare dispersal pans of circular concrete sit, now empty,
Lacking the black silhouettes of the bombers,
Which used to squat, etched against the darkening sky.

Empty pre-fab huts, with broken glassless windows,
Gaze sightlessly out at overgrown hedgerows,
And seem to echo back the voices and laughter of youths,
Who, in blue, once rode the skies to destruction and death.

The wind sighs in lonely desolation as if recalling
The vibrant roar of countless Merlins, coughing
Puffs of blue smoke to be whirled away
In the swirling propwash of many Lancs,
Ponderously thundering into the clouds and, when massing,
Made the very earth tremble with their passing.
Where groundcrew kept tally of every departure,
And muttered a prayer for each aerial charger;
Throughout the long nights their vigils maintained,
'Til in the grey dawn, their visages strained,
They counted the losses.

A strange way of life, to protect a way of living!
Sacrifice demanded and the ultimate too often given.
A lonely figure walked to where a runway ended,
Thoughts deep in the past as his spirit blended.
Seeing this airfield as he once knew it.
Remembering well! He'd flown and lived through
Exorcising ghosts, he roamed o'er the acres,
Recalling faces, nicknames, of givers and takers.
Pilots, navs and flight engineers too
Wireless ops, gunners, from each motley crew.
But the visions all vanished. The noises all dimmed,
'Til all that remained was the sigh of the wind;
A creaking window, the rustle of grass.
Returned to the present. bade adieu to the past.

'Old Bomber Base Revisited: A Pilot's Pilgrimage to the Past', Jim McCorkle, ex-RAF pilot

Life was a fleeting moment when
We lived from day to day,
A morning dawned, the sun broke through,
We savoured every ray,
For well we knew that, with the dusk,
There was a price to pay,
When we were young.

The dangers that we faced became
A common bond to share,

The friendships forged upon such fire
Were rich beyond compare,
So many of them all too short,
Their loss so hard to bear,
When we were young.

We lived our lives up to the hilt,
We laughed and loved and prayed,
We learned to crack the flippant joke
If we should feel afraid,
These things were all accepted
As by us the rules were made,
When we were young.

So many years have passed since then,
The flames of war have died,
The individual paths we chose
Are scattered far and wide,
But we remember proudly those
Whose lives to ours were tied,
When we were young.

'Bomber Aircrew – Times Past', Audrey Grealy

In 1943, future plans to bring the Pacific War to a successful conclusion rested on an Allied onslaught against the Japanese mainland by long-range bombers. Britain's contribution would be 'Tiger Force'. However, following the dropping of atomic bombs on Hiroshima and Nagasaki by US B-29s on 3 and 6 August 1945, Japan surrendered on 15 August and there was no need to proceed with 'Tiger Force'.

In war, resolution; in defeat, defiance; in victory, magnanimity; in peace, goodwill.
Winston Churchill

What do they know of the siren's wail
In the pitch-dark gloom of a blacked-out town,
The droning waves of the enemy planes
And the crump as a bomb comes whistling down,
The angry bark of the Ack Ack guns
And the shrapnel tinkling round one's fret,
The acrid smell and the orange glare
As the flames consume a burning street,
And the blackened shells of a city's homes,
Still smouldering in the dawn's cold light,
While the citizens calmly carry on
And brace themselves for another night?

What do they know of the waiting hours
On the grass outside the dispersal huts,
The race to the 'planes when the scramble starts
And the dried-up mouths and the twisting guts?
A Hurricane swoops and fires its guns,

A short sharp burst of chattering sound,
The sickening dive and the screaming power
As a Messerschmitt spirals to the ground,
The sky a melee of wings and guns
As the aircraft weave in the furious fray,
And the pilot's thought when the fight is done –
How many friends has he lost today?

What do they know of the briefing room
And the questioning eyes of the bomber crews
As they learn of the target for tonight
And scorn to flinch as they hear the news
That they have to go though the murderous flak
Of a well-defended German town,
And they know they must fly to Hell and back
To drop their dreadful cargo down,
The quickening pulse as the engines roar
And their journey starts in the fading light,
And the courage of men who know the odds
Against surviving this lethal flight.

What do they know of the pain of loss
As the Grim Reaper takes his pay,
The lives so young that were his reward
As the price of the freedom we have today.
We who are left have memories bright
Of those who shone in our darkest hours,
But we pray, dear lord, that our little ones
Will never have memories such as ours.

'The Grand-children', Audrey Grealy

'Loved Husband of Flo and Daddy of Frances'. Flight Sergeant W. Stobo (twenty-eight), air bomber, one of five Australians in Pilot Officer D.R.G. Richins's crew who were killed on the raid on Essen on 23/24 October 1944 and who are buried in Cambridge City cemetery. 73,741 casualties were sustained by Bomber Command, of which 55,500 aircrew were KIA or flying accidents, or died on the ground or while prisoners of war. Operational bomber losses were 8,655 aircraft and another 1,600 were lost in accidents and write-offs. Approximately 125,000 aircrew served in the front-line, OTU and OCUs of the Command and nearly 60 per cent of them became casualties. Almost 9,900 more were shot down and made POWs. Over 8,000 more were wounded aboard aircraft on operational sorties. (Author)

FORTY-THREE
LINGUA FRANCA
(LORE OF THE SERVICE)

ATS	Air Training Squadron	Bogey	Unidentified aircraft
Bang-on	Something very good or very accurate	Boomerang	Abort, turn back
		Bought it	Killed, failed to return
Batman	From the French *bat*, meaning pack saddle. A male or female mess steward responsible for an officer's wellbeing on base	Brassed off	Fed up
		Brevet	Flying badge
		BSDU	Bomber Support Development Unit
Battle Bloomers	WAAF Issue Knickers – name originally given to them by the WAAFs themselves	Cab Rank	Small formations of fighter-bombers on immediate standby for close tactical support
BBC	British Broadcasting Corporation	CH	Chain Home (early warning radar station)
Best Blue	Best uniform	Cheese Cutter	Peaked cap
BFTS	British Flying Training School	Cheesed/Cheesed off	Fed up, bored
Big City	Berlin		
Bind	A tiresome nuisance	CHEL	Chain Home Extra Low radar
Binding	Moaning, complaining	Chiefy	Head of Aircraft Ground Crew – generally well respected
Bird Sanctuary	WAAF quarters – usually well away from the rough airmen!		
		CHL	Chain Home Low
Blanket stackers	Non-flying personnel	Chop, Get the	Be shot down/killed
Blip	Radar echo or response	Clapped out	Worn out, well past its best
Blitz	A large formation of enemy bombers	CO	Commanding Officer
		CoG	Centre of Gravity
Blood Wagon	Ambulance	Cookie	4,000lb bomb
Bods	People, bodies	Crate	Aircraft

Crossbow	Offensive and defensive measures against the V-1 flying bomb	Flap	Panic
		Flight Offices	Usually occupied by the CO, flight commanders and their slaves
CRT	Cathode Ray Tube		
C-scope	CRT showing frontal elevation of target	Flight	A flight sergeant
		Flights	Where aircrew collected particularly on operational squadrons while waiting for the 'gen'. Cards and other games of chance were played here. More generally, any place around hangars where matters connected with flying took place.
Cushy trip	Easy mission		
Day Ranger	Operation to engage air and ground targets within a wide but specified area, by day		
DCM	Distinguished Conduct Medal		
DFC	Distinguished Flying Cross		
DFM	Distinguished Flying Medal		
Dicey	Dangerous	Flying orifice	Observer's brevet – the polite versions
Dicey do	An op when there was heavy opposition		
		Flying Tadpole or	Handley Page Hampden,
Dicing (Dicing with death)	Mainly operational flying, but sometimes just flying. 'Are we dicing tonight?', 'Are we on the Battle Order?'	Flying Suitcase	so called because its fuselage was only 3ft wide at its widest point and its tail surfaces were carried on long, thin boom
Ditch	To put down on water (in the 'drink')	FNSF	Fast Night Striking Force
Diver	Codename for V-1 flying bomb operation	Freelance	Patrol with the object of picking up a chance contact or visual of the enemy
Drem lighting	System of outer markers and runway approach lights	Fruit Salad	Lots of medal ribbons, particularly on Americans
Drink, the	The sea		
DSC	Distinguished Service Cross	Gardening	Minelaying
DSO	Distinguished Service Order	GCI	Ground Control Interception (radar)
Duff gen	Bad information		
e/a	Enemy aircraft	Gee	British medium-range navigational aid using ground transmitters and an airborne receiver
Eggs	Bombs		
Erks	Aircraftsmen – usually reserved for the lowest		
ETA	Estimated Time of Arrival	Get weaving	Get a move on – from aircraft taking avoiding action from fighters
Extracting the digit	Originally RAF slang term, now in common use. In RAF it implied sitting on one's hands, politely		
		Getting finger out	Ditto
		Going like the Clappers	Moving very fast indeed
Fans	Propeller on aircraft (No fans – no engines)	Gone for a Burton	Killed, failed to return
		Gong	Medal
Few, The	All the RAF pilots in the Battle of Britain	Good Show	Done well
		Goolie chit	Piece of paper bearing HM Government promise to pay the bearer a sum of money providing the airman is returned unharmed, with his 'goolies' or testicles, still attached. Dates from
FIDO	Fog investigation and dispersal operation		
Fire bash	100 Group Mosquito sorties using incendiaries/napalm against German airfields		
Flak	German term for anti-aircraft fire		

	when the RAF policed the Empire and Middle East between the wars
Got the chop	Killed, failed to return
Got the gen	Have got the true information
GP	General Purpose bomb
Gremlin	A mythical mischievous creature invented by the RAF, to whom is attributed the blame or anything that goes wrong in the air or on the ground
H2S	British 10cm experimental airborne radar navigational and target location aid
Had it	Something coming to its end. For a person, 'He's had it' means he has died or is likely to
Hairy	Dangerous or very exciting
Hallybag	Handley Page Halifax four-engined bomber
Happy Valley	The Ruhr
HE	High Explosive (bomb)
Heath Robinson, W.	Artist and illustrator (1872–1944) famous for his comical drawings of ingenious makeshift mechanical contrivances or structures. His name is used as an adjective to describe weird or imaginary devices
Heavies	RAF and USAAF four-engined bombers
HEI	High Explosive Incendiary
Hit the silk	Bail out using a parachute
HRH	His Royal Highness
IAS	Indicated Air Speed
IFF	Identification Friend or Foe
Intruder	Offensive night operation to fixed point or specified target
IO	Intelligence Officer
Kite	Aeroplane
Kite, Flying Officer	Archetypal flamboyant flying type
LAC	Leading aircraftman woman
LMF	Lack of Moral Fibre
LNSF	Light Night Striking Force

LORAN	Long-Range Navigation
M/T	Motor Transport
Mae West	Lifejacket, named after the well-endowed American actress
Mandrel	100 Group airborne radar jamming device
Manna	Air supply mission to Holland, April/May 1945
Market Garden	Ground/airborne operations, Arnhem, September 1944
MC	Medium Capacity bomb
MCU	Mosquito Conversion Unit
Meat Wagon	Ambulance
Mess	Possibly from the Latin *mensa* (table) or Old French *mes* (dish of food)
Met gen	Meteorological information
Met.	Meteorological
Mickey Mouse	Bomb-aiming equipment
Milk run	Regular run of operations to a particular target (US – easy mission)
Millennium	One of three thousand-bomber raids on German cities, May–June 1942
Monica	British tail warning radar device
MTU	Mosquito Training Unit
Mufti	Civilian clothes (Indian word)
NCO	Non-Commissioned Officer
Newhaven	Flares dropped by PFF
Nickels	Propaganda leaflets
Night Ranger	Operation to engage air and ground targets within a wide but specified area, by night
No ball	V-2 rocket and V-1 flying bomb sites
OBE	Order of the British Empire
Oboe	Ground-controlled radar system of blind bombing in which one station indicated track to be followed and another the bomb release point
On a Fizzer	On a charge in front of senior

Ops	Operations
OT	Operational Training
Other ranks	Ranks other than commissioned officers
OTU	Operational Training Unit
Paramatta	Flares dropped by PFF
Passion Bafflers	WAAF Issue Knickers – name originally given to them by the WAAFs themselves
Penguin	Non-aircrew – often used for someone not popular
PFF	Pathfinder Force
Plumbers	Armourers
POW	Prisoner of war
PR	Photographic Reconnaissance
Prang	A crash, usually of aircraft. To prang – to crash. To prang a target – to hit it well. A wizard prang – a good raid
Press the tit	Press the bomb release (bomber) or button (fighter)
PRU	Photographic Reconnaissance Unit
Prune, Pilot Officer	Everything a pilot should not be
Queen Bee	WAAF commanding officer
R/T	Radio telephony
RAAF	Royal Australian Air Force
RAE	Royal Aircraft Establishment
RAFVR	Royal Air Force Volunteer Reserve
RCAF	Royal Canadian Air Force
RCM	Radio countermeasures
RNZAF	Royal New Zealand Air Force
RP	Rocket projectile
SASO	Senior air staff officer
Scramble	Take off at once
Scrambled Egg	Gold on caps of senior officers
SD	Special Duties
SEAC	South-East Asia Command

Second Dickie	Second pilot
Serrate	British equipment designed to home in on Lichtenstein AI radar
Shaky Do	Near miss or lucky escape
Shoot a line	To brag, enlarge, blow one's own trumpet
Sky Pilot	Padre
Snappers	Enemy fighters
Snowdrop	RAF military policeman
Sortie	Operational flight by a single aircraft
Sprog crew	A new crew
Sprog	Inexperienced person, new recruit
Stooge	A boring flight
Stooge around	Loiter. Hang around; fly around waiting for something to happen.
Stores Basher	Someone who worked in Stores
Suffering from the Twitch	(Particularly pilots) – to be avoided at all costs
TI	Target Indicator
TNT	Trinitrotoluene
Torbeau	Torpedo-carrying Beaufighter
Twitch	Nervy. 'Bags of twitch' – suffered when in danger, particularly from fighters.
U/S	Unserviceable
UHF	Ultra-High Frequency
VC	Victoria Cross
VHF	Very High Frequency
W/T	Wireless telephony
WAAF	Women's Auxiliary Air Force (member of)
Waafery	WAAF quarters – usually well away from the rough airmen!
Wanganui	Skymarking a target using flares dropped blindly using H2S
Wimpy	Vickers Armstrongs Wellington twin-engined bomber (from J. Wellington Wimpy character in 'Popeye')
Window	Thin metallic strips dropped by Bomber

	Command to disrupt enemy radar screens	Wizard prang	Big crash
		Wizard	First class
		WOP/AG	Wireless operator/air
Wingco	Wing Commander, usually squadron commanding officer		gunner
		Y-Service	British organisation monitoring German
Wingless Wonder	Usually very unpopular non-aircrew		radio transmissions to and from aircraft

BIBLIOGRAPHY

BOOKS

Anderson, R.; Westmacott D., *Handle with Care* (1946)

Beede, John, *'They Hosed Them Out'* (Australasian Book Society, 1965)

Bennett CB CBE DSO, AVM D.C.T., *Pathfinder* (Panther, 1960)

Bowman, Martin W., *The Royal Air Force at War* (PSL, 1997)

Congdon, Philip, *Behind the Hangar Doors* (Sonik Books, 1985)

Craske RAFVR, Basil S., *Kites & Kriegies* (privately published)

Escott, Squadron Leader Beryl E., *Women in RAF Blue* (Patrick Stephens, 1989)

Hammersley DFM, Roland A., *Into Battle with 57 Sqn* (privately published, 1992)

Montemurro (*née* Coppard), Annette June, *Any danger of Getting a Cup of Tea?* (Stoney Creek Publishing, BC Canada, 2002)

Olson RCAF, George 'Ole', *No Place To Hide*

Pape, Richard, *Boldness Be My Friend*

Pile, Stephen, *The Book of Heroic Failures*

Raymond, Robert S., *A Yank in Bomber Command* (Pacifica Press, 1998)

Read, Ron, *If You Can't Take a Joke* (privately published, 1995)

Solberg Clark, Anne, *One Man's War* (privately published)

Taylor, Geoff, *Piece of Cake* (George Mann, 1956)

Ward-Jackson, C.H.; Lucas, Leighton, ed., *Airmen's Song Book* (Blackwood & Sons, 1967)

Wheeler DFC, Edwin, *Just to Get a Bed* (privately published, 1990)

Wood, J. Ralph, *My Lucky Number was 77: WWII Memoirs of J. Ralph Wood DFC CD RCAF* (privately published)

MAGAZINES

The Falcon, the magazine of No.4 BFTS, compiled by Captain Bill McCash

Marker, the Pathfinder Association magazine

Punch